RUNNING DOWN A DREAM

The making of a film

Paul Gorman

Rain City Cinema LLC

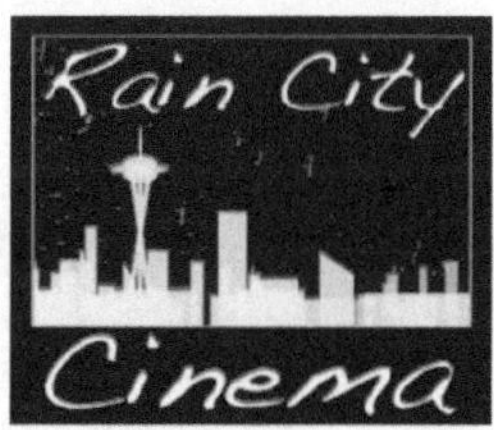

This is a true story. Some of the characters in this book have had their names changed.

ISBN-13: 978-0-578-69337-8

Cover design by: Paul Gorman
Printed in the United States of America
First Edition

To my wife Susan. Without her help I could not have written this book or made the film, "Ride The Sky"

There is only one basic human right,
The right to do as you damn well please.
And with it comes the basic human duty,
The duty to take the consequences.

P.J. O'ROURKE

CONTENTS

PROLOGUE

On a sunny Memorial Day Weekend in 1981 an attractive brunette, named Joan Carson, donned her signature white jumpsuit, harnessed on a parachute in the ground floor of the recently constructed Osprey Skydiving Club's hangar, boarded a two seat Cessna 152 single-engine airplane and jumped out over Lost Prairie, Montana.

Although a veteran of over 700 jumps, both of her parachutes failed to inflate and she impacted the ground at 120 miles per hour dying minutes later. She was thirty years old.

The events surrounding that day have remained a mystery for almost 40 years. Likewise, the reason she was a skydiver is perplexing. Raised in suburbia, and later living in San Francisco, she was sophisticated. With her death, she left few clues as to why she moved to the wilderness and jumped out of airplanes in spite of suffering two serious injuries. Carson was friendly and outgoing in person, but kept details of her private life tucked away.

In 1981, Lost Prairie, which lies 30 miles west of Kalispell, was a remote valley. Little has changed since then, other than Lost Prairie Skydive Center. An oasis in the wilderness, it resembles an ancient Kootenai Indian village, where it is flanked by pine tree covered hills and guarded by Meadow Peak Butte rising directly behind it.

The valley is an enigma. Surrounded by remoteness and pristine beauty, it is the last place you would expect to find skydivers, and see a person jump out of an airplane 10,000 feet above the valley and plummet to their death in the tall prairie grass waving hypnotically in the breeze. But that is what happened to Joan Carson in 1981. It was a date I will never forget.

The experiences I had with Joan left an indelible mark on my soul, and in 2011 inspired me to make a documentary film about her, called "Ride The Sky", which screened in Lost Prairie on the 30th anniversary of her death.

This story is about my personal experiences with Joan, the formative years that shaped me into the person and filmmaker I am today, and the making of the film. My story would be incomplete without hers.

As a side note: The world is presently experiencing a pandemic known as COVID-19. To date, the virus has infected more than 842,000 people world-wide and caused at least 41,000 deaths. For the past two weeks, here in California, we have been instructed to 'Shelter in Place' in our homes, where it is recommended if we venture out to buy food and supplies or walk for exercise that we maintain social separation of at least six feet.

Paul Gorman
April 1, 2020
Palm Springs, CA

STUNNED

Seattle: May 26, 1981

Two days after Joan Carson died I got a phone call from Spike, an old high school friend, informing me about her death. I was stunned. I had gone to high school with Carson at Redmond High School, in Redmond, Washington, during the late sixties, and had been somewhat infatuated with her then. She was a cheerleader and I was a shy gangly, Richie Cunningham type. I wasn't a nerd or a jock, thank god, I was somewhere in between.

Luckily, I had been best friends with my neighbor Todd, who happened to be senior class president, and a certifiable genius. Because of him, I was now considered to be a member of the "in crowd". If it hadn't been for his popularity, I probably never would have become friends with Spike, who was quarterback on the football team, nor would Joan ever have noticed me. Actually, other than a few passing smiles in the hallways and a single conversation in the school's cafeteria, she never let on she was interested.

One sunny afternoon, I was cutting class and figured the cafeteria would be vacant since lunch had ended an hour earlier. Even though the overhead light fixtures were turned off, there was plenty of ambient light shining in through the floor to ceiling windows. I peeked through the small vertically oriented window in the beige metal door and sure enough it looked empty inside.

Opening the door, I didn't notice Joan who was on her hands and knees painting, "Go Mustangs, Stomp Lake Washington", on butcher paper spread out on the cream colored linoleum tile floor. Before I could stop, I stepped right in the paint leaving a footprint on the paper. Embarrassed, my feet spastically stutter-stepped leaving multiple shoe prints on her creation.

"Oh my god, I'm sorry. I said, turning bright red. “I didn't know anybody was here!" Joan laughed. "That's perfect, stomp marks! It’s just what it needed. You're a genius…Paul."

I was surprised she knew my name and stood there dumbfounded while Joan bottled up the tempera paints.

"You're Paul Gorman, aren't you?”

"Uh, yeah, how'd you know?”

"I've heard about you and seen you around. Here, help me hang this banner on the wall so nobody else stomps on it. It's a masterpiece. I like it just the way it is."

Blushing again, I retorted, "You're a cheerleader, aren't you?"

"Yeah, I do it because it gets me out of class sometimes,” she said, hesitating to put the paint jars and brush into a wooden box. “So, what brings you in here? Don't tell me, you’re cutting class.”

I shuffled guiltily, and Joan laughed then said, teasingly, "Naughty boy."

A little later she asked me to help her hang the poster with masking tape, and then, not knowing what else to say, not that I had done much talking, I said goodbye.

Smiling, Joan said. "Yeah, see you around."

Still on the phone with Spike, my hands trembled slightly. Joan was the first friend I knew that had died. My knees wobbled and I reached for the fireplace mantle near an end table to steady myself. I asked Spike if there was going to be a funeral or service.

"Yeah, it's going to be in Montana -- some place called Lost Prairie."

"Montana. Why Montana?" I asked.

"Because that's where she died," he said. "They're going to name some airport or airfield there after her."

I then asked Spike if he was going to attend the service and he replied that a few classmates were, but he wasn't sure whether he was because he had to work.

I was having difficulty processing everything he was saying as my mind drifted back to one of the last times I saw Joan.

It was eight years earlier, which would make it late 1973, at a party on Queen Ann Hill in Seattle overlooking Elliott Bay and the Space Needle. Spike had called saying Joan was in town and they were going to a party, and she wanted to see me. At that time she was living in San Francisco, or at least I thought she was.

When Joan arrived I was shocked. She had two broken wrists and her face was bruised. In spite of her wounds, she was dressed flamboyantly in a faux mink jacket, stretch jeans, and mid-calf high light-brown boots.

About an hour later, as Joan was leaving the party, she looked deeply into my eyes. They were filled with sadness and pain that I didn't understand.

Just before leaving, Joan hugged me, and then handed me a piece of paper with a phone number on it. "Call me…I'm staying at my folks place in Redmond. Looks like I'll be there a while," she whispered in my ear.

I learned later that Joan had convalesced for a year at her parents place while recovering from the broken wrists and orthopedic surgery. I never called her and was now regretting it more than ever as Spike's voice squawked on the phone.

"Paul, hey man are you okay?" Said Spike on the phone, bringing me back to the present.

"Huh, yeah…yeah I'm okay."

"She always liked you, Paul."

I was blown away and speechless by Spike's revelation. I had been married now for two years and loved my wife Susan. But there had been a time, before I met her, when I considered calling Joan. But, it had always come down to skydiving; that was the clincher for me. I just couldn't understand how anybody could jump out of an airplane over and over again. It didn't make sense. It was like playing Russian-Roulette. I came to the conclusion that Joan would never stop jumping and would choose skydiving over anything, even if it killed her. Spike was risky, but Joan was dangerous. Maybe that's why they spent time together, and perhaps the reason I was intrigued by her.

Spike said goodbye to me, and I stood there holding the phone in one hand, still steadying myself with the other on the mantel. Susan entered the sun bathed living room from the bedroom where she had just put our one year old son down for the night.

"What's going on?" She said, looking puzzled.

Turning toward her, I recanted what Spike had said.

Prior to marrying Susan, I told her stories about Joan so she had heard about her.

"Wasn't she the skydiver?" Susan inquired.

I nodded, and Susan took the phone out of my hand and hung it up.

"Oh my god, what happened?"

My eyes watered slightly as I informed her about the accident. Susan hugged me. She then asked if there was going to be a funeral service and I replied, "Yeah, in Montana."

"Do you want to go?"

"I don't know," I said, shrugging my shoulders.

"You can go if you want to," she said.

I was torn, I wanted to go, but because of my love and loyalty for Susan I said that I didn't want to.

For the next month or two I couldn't stop thinking about Joan. At night, I would lay awake reflecting on the time I'd spent with her in San Francisco.

TRANSFORMATION

Berkeley: June, 1973

It was 1973 and at that time Spike and I were managing a rock band named Mojo Hand in Seattle. The band played the tavern scene six nights a week, three sets a night. It was a grind. They didn't have jobs so it was their only means of income, but they made good money doing it – sometimes $1,200 per week. Disco was just coming in though, and more and more clubs and taverns were switching over to it, because it was cheaper to hire a DJ than pay a band.

Mojo Hand was feeling the pinch and decided to send me to San Francisco to find them some gigs. Their old manger was living there and had told the drummer there were lots of clubs that still played live music. Days later, Spike dropped me off at the Greyhound bus station in downtown Seattle in the midst of a rain shower, and I was on my way to San Francisco.

After about 18 hours the bus finally pulled into an old station just off Market Street. The terminal was dingy, dirty and didn't feel safe. Rough looking characters loitered about just outside the terminal entrance, and bone weary travelers wearing rumpled clothes got off arriving buses. I grabbed the backpack I had bought in Spain four years earlier, when I had bummed around Europe for six months, and walked to the ticket office past a queue of riders waiting for their bus to arrive.

A man with thinning, greased back, black hair, and a cigarette dangling from his lips greeted me without so much as looking up.

"Where to kid?" he said, laconically.

"Berkeley", I replied.

"Seventy-five cents. Next bus departs in 12 minutes -- lane 14," the man said exhaling a cloud of blue smoke.

I laid a dollar bill on the counter and he slid me a quarter and my ticket as an ash dropped from his cigarette, landing beside my change. I hesitated, looking at it as he brushed it away and then glanced up at me. "Get going, kid, you're holding up the line."

I grabbed the ticket and change, turned and then headed back into the cavernous terminal. The lane numbers were identified overhead with signs yellowed presumably by years of cigarette smoke and diesel exhaust that hazed the room. I spotted Lane 14, and a 1940s vintage, 'Bay Area Transit', bus loading passengers. I got in line and soon clambered up its steps handing the driver my ticket.

About 30 minutes later the bus dropped me off at the corner of Shattuck and Ambrose and after asking a stranger for directions to Raleigh's, it wasn't long before I was strutting down Telegraph Ave. My flared jeans flapped in the breeze, and I absorbed the 75 degree sunshine of where my generation had blazed a new trail. I was at ground-zero. I couldn't get over the thought that this was where the whole counter-culture, anti-war movement had begun with Joan Baez, Pete Seeger, Bob Dylan, and others. They no longer played here, but their music still resonated.

Upon entering Raleigh's Pub, I was greeted by a smiling blue-eyed blond girl with glistening white teeth and a breezy smile. *Wow,* I thought, *Here I am, a Seattle boy who has just left the rain behind and I'm in California, and it's sunny. Yes!*

I asked to be seated in Joan's section and was led to a table along the street-side windows where I watched a smorgasbord of tie-dyed hippies, students, and middle aged professors stroll down the sidewalk. It was lunchtime and everybody was on the street looking for a place to eat. It didn't matter who you were, food was all that mattered now.

My stomach growled as I glanced at the menu. I hadn't eaten since the candy bar I had bought at the stop we made in Eugene, which was 12 hours earlier. As hungry as I was, I wondered who could afford the prices. I thought hippies were broke like I was – not that I considered myself to be a hippie.

I rested the menu on the table, sipped on a glass of water the busboy had set on my table five minutes earlier and glanced around. Vines cascading from overhead planter boxes contrasted beautifully with the rustic fir flooring, booths and table tops. Everywhere you looked it was fir, brick and hanging plants -- very nice.

At first I didn't recognize Joan because her wavy brown hair was now permed into an afro. The rays of sunlight streaming in through the windows backlit it, giving it a dandelion glow. She was wearing a white muslin pullover top, flared blue jeans and sandals. Not recognizing me, she arrived at my table. It had been five years since high school, and three years since running into her at Bellevue Community College. At twenty-three my blond hair was longer than my old Richard Cunningham crew cut had been. I now sported medium length hair about half way down my ears and over the collar. Gone too were the "Happy Days" short skinny white pants, white socks and short sleeved shirts, which were replaced with a jean jacket, flared jeans, platform boots, and a form fitting burgundy shirt unbuttoned 1/4 of the way down my chest. Tied around my neck was a rolled blue bandana. I looked like a cross between a young Tom Petty and Bryan Adams -- not that they were famous then. This "look" would be my uniform for the next two or three years.

Picking up the menu again, I pretended to read it. When Joan arrived at my table, my eyes peered over the top of it. I smiled at her.

She stood there holding a pencil in one hand and receipt book in the other ready to take my order.

"Hi Joan, remember me?" I asked nervously.

Looking at me like I was pulling her leg she said, "Should I?"

"I'm a friend of Spike's," I replied, closing the menu.

"You are?"

Concerned that she had forgotten who I was, I elaborated saying that I had gone to high school with her.

"Oh really," she said, seemingly trying to place me.

"Yeah, Redmond…Remember me now?"

"Sort of," she mused.

"Paul's the name," I said smiling.

"Oh yeah, that's right," she said, returning my smile, "you put stomp marks on the banner I was painting in the cafeteria."

Blushing, I said, "I was hoping you'd forgotten that."

Chuckling briefly, Joan became silent, and stood there looking like she was absorbed in the past. An awkward moment of silence hung in the air. I broke the silence, "Spike said I was coming, didn't he?"

Reacting to my question, she was suddenly back in the present and said, "I haven't heard from Spike in months." "

He didn't call?"

"I don't have a phone anymore."

"You don't, well, Spike said he was going to see if I could stay at your place."

"Oh, he did huh," Joan said, crossing her arms. I was striking out, and wasn't sure if I would have a place to spend the night. Along with my return bus ticket, I only had seventeen dollars left and that was for meals, beer and cigarettes. Joan seemed uncomfortable about my surprise visit. I can't say I blamed her because she hadn't really known me, and by the sounds of it had pretty much forgotten who I was.

Feeling uneasy, I just wanted to leave. "Look I'm sorry, I'll find some other place," I said, setting the menu down.

Joan demurred briefly. She glanced at the closed menu, and then back at me. "How long you in town for?" she asked.

"A couple of days."

"And what brings you here?"

"Spike and I are managing a band," I said, pulling out an 8-1/2 x 11 flyer from my rucksack . "I came down here to score some gigs."

"Oh yeah," she said, looking at the flyer, "Spike mentioned something about a band a while ago."

"Yeah."

"Yeah, but nothing about you," she said with a twinkle in her eye.

Touché' for Joan. She was teasing me now and it was titillating.

At that point she pulled up a chair alongside me and invited me to stay at her place. She apologized for not remembering me right away, and wished she would have know I was coming because her place was a mess. I assured her that her place couldn't possibly be as untidy as mine.

Rising, Joan smiled warmly at me. "Well, it's a nice day and I'm off work in half an hour. Have you been in San Francisco before?"

"No, this is my first time," I said.

"Great…we'll drop your things off at my place, then I'll show you around town and we'll get something to eat."

Turning, she headed for another table and I stole a glance at her as she walked away. She was even more attractive now than she had been in high school. Gone were the freckles and teenage innocence, which were replaced with maturity, confidence, good looks, and a killer smile.

On our walk to her place we stopped at a phone booth so she could call Spike. I didn't want to listen in on their conversation, so I deliberately moved about fifteen feet away. Still, every now and then I could hear her voice rising as she chewed him out. I felt uncomfortable because I didn't know whether she was mad at him for not calling her at the restaurant so she would know I was coming, or if it was something else. She never said anything about it and neither did Spike.

A short while later, Joan opened the door to her duplex and we stepped inside. It was small and cozy, and wasn't messy at all. The only thing that looked out of place was a few dirty dishes in the kitchen, which was the first room we entered.

"Come on, you can put your things in the living room," she said, leading the way.

Curtains separated the kitchen from the living room. Joan held them open and I followed her through the entrance. The fir floors were darkened with age; the walls were pale yellow with green colored trim. Several bean bags, a coffee table, an end table with a lamp, and a floor lamp were the extent of her furniture. A Panasonic tuner, turntable and speakers rested on a shelf constructed from cinder blocks and wood planks.

Joan turned on the receiver and a Crosby, Stills, Nash and Young song played. She turned to me. "You can put your things over there," she said, pointing to the corner nearest the kitchen.

I set my bags down.

"Pull up a chair," she said, gesturing to a bean bag fairly close to me.

Wearily, I drifted over to it and plumped down. I had never been a fan of bean bags, but this one felt great after almost twenty-four hours of traveling.

"Can I get you anything…a beer, or wine?" She asked.

"A beer would be great," I smiled.

"Coming right up," said Joan as she disappeared into the kitchen through the curtains, leaving them waving in her wake. I could hear a bottle cap pop off a bottle of beer and then being poured into a glass as CSNY continued playing on the radio.

A brief time later the curtains parted and she entered the living room carrying a long necked bottle of Budweiser for me and a glass of white wine for herself. She handed me the beer. I thanked her as she settled into the other bean bag chair sitting kitty corner from me.

Joan asked me what I had been doing since high school and I told her that I had worked at Boeing for a year, spent six months traveling around Europe, co-managed several clothing stores, and was now managing the band. She seemed genuinely interested in my trip to Europe saying she hoped to go there someday and visit relatives in England.

I polished off my beer about the time Joan finished her glass of wine. She got up and reached for my empty bottle. "You want another one while I shower and change?"

"Yes, please. I said, nodding. You mind if I smoke?”

“Go ahead, but let me open a window first,” she said, sliding up a sash window next to me.

Joan retreated once again to the kitchen and I lit a cigarette. I could hear the refrigerator door open and close and then the sound of a beer bottle being popped open. *Ah, nothing like having a beer along with a cigarette.*

Joan appeared seconds later. "Here you go, it's my favorite brand," she said, handing me a beer.

I studied the label and then replied, "Anchor Steam, I’ve never heard of it."

"It's brewed in *The City*,” she said, looking proud, “and is really popular here."

Thanking her for the beer, she told me to make myself at home while she changed her clothes. Then she headed towards the bedroom, which was separated by a bead curtain. The beads rattled like a maraca and shook when she passed through them. The beer went down easily; it was smooth and caramel flavored and had more body than a Bud. I smelled incense coming from her bedroom and glanced in that direction. I took a drag from my cigarette and watched Joan's silhouette through the beads as she undressed, and then enter her bathroom. I heard the bathroom door close and shortly thereafter the sound of the shower.

About ten minutes later her bathroom door creaked open followed by the patter of bare feet on the hardwood floors. Several seconds later the sound of dresser doors sliding open and then closing shut drew my gaze, and I could see a pixelated silhouette of her through the spaces between the beads as she got dressed. It wasn't long before the beads parted and Joan nonchalantly made her entrance into the living room. My jaw dropped. She had metamorphosed from a hippie chick into a vixen dressed in stretch blue jeans, black cashmere form fitting turtleneck sweater, and mid-calf high black boots. *Oh my god,* I thought as I gulped on my beer. *Man is she hot! I don't know if I can handle her.*

"You ready for some action?" Joan said, confidently flashing her killer smile.

I was more nervous now than I had been at the restaurant and replied, "I think so, I mean, yeah sure."

"Okay, let's go then," she said, as she sashayed over to me, grabbed my empty beer bottle and strutted across the room with me following her like a lost puppy dog.

Out on the street, we walked and talked, actually Joan did most of the talking -- about what it was like living in Berkeley. She liked it because there were a lot of people her age, and always a lot of things going on, even if some of the students were gone for the summer. She also liked it because rents were cheaper and it was quieter than San Francisco.

Maple trees lining the residential streets provided shade and gave it the feel of being a small town. Actually, compared to San Francisco it was, as I was about to learn.

We arrived at a bus stop and soon afterwards a *Bay Area Transit* came along with the destination *San Francisco* at the top. We boarded the bus and Joan paid my fare before I could get any money out. In about 40 minutes we were downtown and got off at Market and Powell Streets. An arriving cable car clanged across the street and she said, "Come on, let's catch it!"

We rushed across the street, dodging cars, and climbed aboard. The conductor came around collecting fares and again Joan paid my way. As the cable car clanked its way up Powell Street, she enthusiastically pointed out iconic sights. "That's Union Square, and over there that's the Transamerica Building," she said, pointing at the landmarks; I was impressed with her knowledge of the city and a little uneasy because I felt indebted to her, and already had a girlfriend. Her name was Astrid and she was Swedish. We had met a year and a half earlier, spending six months together, before she returned to Sweden. Astrid would be arriving in a month to see me.

STRESSED

Seattle: June, 1981

In the month since I had learned about Joan's death it had been a stressful time for me. Susan and I had a 9 month old son, Kelly, and I wasn't sleeping well. I still couldn't shake what had happened to Joan. Things weren't going well at my engineering job; I was forgetting things and was snapping at coworkers. My boss noticed and called me into his office. He asked me what was going on and I said a friend had just died and I was stressed out about it.

Talking with my boss helped me sort things out a bit and I made the decision to transfer to another group where I could start off with a clean slate. I also chose to go see my doctor about my lack of sleep and stress.

My doctor recommended that I start running, which I did. Susan and I lived about two miles from Green Lake in Seattle and it had a nice jogging trail around it. All told, it was 2.8 miles long and was flat. Perfect. I found that exercising lowered my stress level and I slept better. Over time, I thought less about Joan's death and my experiences with her.

There was one time in particular that I do recall though. It was Father's Day right after Joan had died. I came into the kitchen where

Susan was fixing me Puttanesca for dinner. The smells and sounds suddenly transported me back to Joan's where we had just arrived back at her place after eating at an Italian restaurant in San Francisco's Little Italy.

INTOXICATED

Berkeley: June, 1973

Joan opened the front door and we entered the kitchen, arriving back at her place from dinner at a place called U.S. Restaurant. She said for me to make myself comfortable while she put away food she had bought at a deli along the way. Already stuffed from our meal, I wasn't sure why she had bought it, unless she thought I was too skinny.

I lit up a cigarette and Joan opened a bottle of Anchor Steam and handed it to me. After pouring herself a glass of red wine, she sat down at the other end of the small kitchenette table.

For the next two hours or so we talked a little bit about our families and growing up. Mostly though, we talked about teachers and people we had known in high school. As the evening wore on we nibbled on the snacks she had bought.

Joan was on her third glass of wine, and I had downed three or four beers and smoked about four or five cigarettes. The room was filled with smoke. She opened a window above the sink to air it out, then hoisted herself up on the kitchen counter and sat there while I continued to sit at the table sipping on my beer and snacking.

By 10:00 PM I had a moderate buzz going and Joan was definitely getting intoxicated. She wasn't slurring her words and swaying, like a classic drunk, but the sophistication she exhibited earlier in the day was gone.

Suddenly, something snapped. Joan became boisterous and licentious, boasting about her sexual exploits. I was shocked. I had never heard a female talk like this. The magic and teasing that had been there earlier was gone -- at least for the time being. She had abruptly transformed into a totally different person.

Waving a glass of wine in the air she peered down at me from her perch on the counter and proclaimed how much she enjoyed sex.

I grabbed my beer and held on to it for dear life. "That's good," I said, taking a sip.

Baiting me, she said, "How about you?"

"What about me?" I retorted.

"Do you like sex?" she asked, incredulously.

"Sure," I said, suddenly realizing that the chase was over for me.

"I'll bet you like all of the groupies too," she said disdainfully as she swirled the wine in her glass before taking another sip.

"What groupies?"

"The band's groupies."

"I don't have any groupies," I said, dismissively.

"And why not?" Joan asked, leaning toward me with a perplexed look on her face.

"Cause the manager never gets the groupies," I said, cracking a slight grin.

Getting down from the counter and sauntering towards me she said, "Well, I'll be your groupie."

"That's okay," I said, clearing my throat. "I really don't need a groupie."

"Yeah, but I need a manager."

Trying to steady my neves as Joan slid in alongside me, I took a gulp of beer.

"I've never made it with a manager before," she said placing her hand on mine. "I'll bet they're good."

"I wouldn't know," I smiled nervously, shifting uncomfortably in my chair.

Realizing that she had hit a dead end, she changed the subject. "Let's smoke some pot, okay?" she said, opening a small wooden box on the table.

"It's getting late," I replied.

Joan pulled out a joint and lighter. "I like it; it intensifies everything, and helps me sleep," she said.

Joan lit the joint, took a deep drag and handed it to me. I took a hit then passed it back to her. Over the next ten minutes or so, we shared the joint. The conversation slowed. My mind was getting foggy as a billowing cloud of smoke drifted upward dimming the overhead light.

She took one last drag, handed me the roach and with glazed eyes turned to me and said, "Well, I'm ready for bed. How about you?"

I took another hit. "Yeah, I'll probably just sleep in the living room," I said, holding in the marijuana smoke.

"On what, a beanbag?" she kidded, chuckling at her own joke. She then leaned over resting a hand on my shoulder and looked longingly into my eyes.

"Joan, I've got a girlfriend," I said, softly.

"You do?"

"Yeah, I do," I said.

"So?"

"So I like her."

"You do?" Joan said, swallowing hard.

"Yeah, I like her a lot," I said, not quite sure if I was referring to my girlfriend, Astrid, or Joan.

Conflicted, I looked deeply into her eyes, which were filled with a vulnerability that hadn't been there earlier.

Sensing my dilemma, Joan stroked my hair tenderly and said, "So, you can sleep with me anyway."

She turned and headed for the bedroom, passing through the kitchen curtains. I took one last toke, and sat there momentarily deciding what to do. Exhaling the smoke, I put the joint out in the ashtray, staggered to my feet, and headed for the bedroom.

Joan was in the bathroom getting ready for bed when I entered. I stripped down to my briefs and climbed into the bed, which was just a mattress on the floor. A few minutes later she came out attired in panties and a tee-shirt. She lit an incense stick and slid into bed, lying on her back. In a matter of minutes she was sound asleep, or at least I thought she was. I lay awake for about an hour fully expecting her to make a pass at me, and maybe even wishing she would. But she never touched me, and I never touched her.

SKYDIVER

Berkeley: June, 1973

In the morning I awoke to an empty bed; filtered sunlight shining in through the curtained bedroom window. At some point during the night, or morning, Joan had gotten up but I hadn't noticed. I could hear a lawnmower and garbage truck outside, and the clatter of dishes and smell of fresh brewed coffee coming from the kitchen. I got out of bed, put on the same clothes I had worn the day before and exited the bedroom.

Passing through the living room, I entered the kitchen, still buttoning my shirt. Joan was setting the table.

Still groggy from the beer, marijuana, and lack of sleep, I stopped at the same chair I sat in the night before. “What time is it?” I queried.

"Seven," Joan said, and then paused momentarily.

“Coffee?” she asked, picking up a pot.

"Please," I said, sitting down.

Joan was dressed in a burgundy turtleneck sweater, gray mechanics' monkey-suit, and hiking boots. Almost immediately I could tell by her demeanor she was back to being the way she had been before she got intoxicated. If she remembered the previous evening, she didn't let on and I didn’t intend to remind her.

"I didn't hear you get up," I said while Joan poured a cup of coffee for me.

"Yeah, you were snoozing pretty hard," she said placing the cup of coffee on the table next to a bowl of granola she had fixed for me.

"Sorry about that," I said, before taking a sip of coffee. "I hope I didn't wake you up."

"No, I slept just fine and needed to get up anyway. I've got something I need to do today. Joan grabbed an orange and a banana lying on the table and put them into her backpack sitting on one of the chairs.

"Oh yeah," I said, swallowing a bite of granola. "By the looks of it you've got a part time job at Firestone overhauling cars.

She grinned at my teasing. "Close, I am going skydiving today in Antioch," she said, proudly.

"Skydiving!" I blurted, almost spitting out some cereal. Joan chuckled.

"Yeah, do you want to come along?"

"You want me to jump out of an airplane?!"

"Only if you want to," she said, smiling as she slipped on a brown bomber jacket.

"Uh, I've got things to do today, I said, taking a sip of coffee, "I've got to land some gigs."

"Well, it's up to you, but I'd really like it if you came along," she said, zipping her bomber jacket and leaning down next to me. "It's the most amazing experience…even better than sex."

"Uh huh," I said, facetiously.

"Yeah…it's incredible."

"Yeah, incredibly dangerous."

"It's no more dangerous than crossing the street or driving a car," she replied.

Concerned about her safety, I stopped chewing on my cereal and looked up at her. "How many times have you done this?" I probed.

Strapping her canvas bag over a shoulder she beamed, "I made my first jump about six months ago, and have jumped about 30 times since then."

"Isn't that enough?"

"Look, I love it okay," she shot back. "You don't have to come if you don't want to, but I would really like it if you did."

I hesitated a moment and then grinned at her. "I'd love to, but I've got things to do today."

"Hey, it's not for everybody, she said, taking a sip of milk and then setting her empty glass on the table. "You do what you need to do and I'll see you around 6:00.

"How are you getting there?" I asked, calling after her.

"On my motorcycle," she said, with a wink. "Oh, I almost forgot, here's the key, put it under the mat when you leave."

I was amazed. This woman was one of a kind.

Handing me the key, Joan opened the door and went outside. I got up from the table and followed her. *Unbelievable, I've gotta see this,* I murmured to myself.

I watched as she strapped on a helmet and ski goggles, and then straddled her Yamaha 250cc. motorcycle. She put a key in the ignition and kicked it to life. She waved to me, revved the engine several times then took off down the street.

Several hours after Joan had left, I came out of her place freshly showered and shaved, and sporting my gig hunting duds, which weren't too much different than my everyday duds, with the exception of a black rhinestone western shirt, embroidered with red roses, beneath my faded Levi Jean jacket. Of course, I wore a proverbial bandana cinched around my neck, but this one was red. Properly attired in my image of what band a manager should look like, I stepped onto the porch, locked the door, leaving the key under the mat, and headed off to score some gigs.

DECISIONS

Redmond, WA: March, 2010

Twenty-eight years passed since Joan had died and I rarely thought about her. The dreams I had shortly after her death in 1981 had stopped. So it came as a surprise to me when I started dreaming about my experiences with Joan again. At that time in my life, I had just finished making my first feature film called, *Broken Frame*, and was not sure what my next project would be.

In January, 2010 I told Susan that I'd had a few dreams concerning Joan.

Susan stopped eating her dinner, at the kitchen island, and looked at me inquiringly, "What sort of dreams," she asked, with a hint of concern.

"Nothing sexual," I said. "Just dreams about my experiences with her, that's all."

"Okay, and why are you dreaming about her all of the sudden?"

I put my fork down and looked at Susan. "I wish I knew, it feels like I met Joan for a reason," I said. "I think she wants me to tell her story."

"And what's her story?" Susan asked.

"I don't know," I said, shaking my head. "I'd like to know why she was a skydiver. Something must have been driving her that made her take the risks she did, and to keep jumping after suffering two serious accidents. And I'd like to know what happened the day she died."

"Well when you find out, let's talk about it," she said, washing down a bite of food with a sip of red wine

"I've just got this feeling that there was a reason she did the things she did," I said. "I need to know."

"Look into it. Do some research, find out her story. Maybe there's a connection to the dream you had years ago, or maybe it's just coincidence. It's been troubling you ever since she died; you need to resolve it. If Joan really wants you to tell her story, she'll let you know."

In addition to being my best friend and the love of my life, Susan was the best thing that ever happened to me. She was also the most intelligent, fair-minded, and insightful person I've ever known. She was the anchor and ballast I needed.

It wasn't that we hadn't had our cat fights and disagreements from time to time, mostly about politics, but overall there had almost never been any major conflicts in our marriage. The exception would be when I was working on a film in Tacoma in 1989 called "Adventures in Spying". The film starred Bernie Coulson, Seymour Cassel, Jill Schoelen, John Billingsley, and of all people G. Gordon Liddy of Watergate fame.

I was Transportation Coordinator, and as such was working sixteen hour days including my forty-five minute commute to and from Seattle to Tacoma. At that stage, we had two adolescent children. Susan had just started a preschool, and as a fledgling business owner was there all day long and would bring work home. In addition to running the preschool, she was doing the shopping, laundry, cooking meals, and taking care of the kids all by herself. After about a month she was done with it, and gave me an ultimatum to either find another type of work, after the film was finished, where I could help out more at home, or find another person to be married too. I chose Susan over working on movies and never regretted it.

Convincing Susan that I should make a documentary film about Joan Carson wasn't going to be impossible. She was supportive of me and onboard if it was something I wanted to do, and made sense. She believed in my abilities. But I had to convince myself Joan's story was interesting enough to spend two years of my life making a film about her. The film had to be unique and compelling, and had to appeal to more people than just me. That evening I started writing a script about my experiences with Joan in Berkeley.

GIG HUNTING

Berkeley: June, 1973

While Joan was skydiving, I spent the afternoon going to bars and clubs and invariably getting the same answer: "We don't do live music anymore. We only play disco. Try the Long Branch and the Keystone, they still play live music."

I stopped at the Long Branch on San Pablo but it was closed for renovation. I saw a phone booth nearby and entered it. Thumbing through the phone book I found the address of the Keystone and wrote it down on the back of my business card.

Looking my best in my self-appropriated band manager's outfit, half an hour later I arrived at the Keystone on University Avenue. Walking under the marquee I noticed that Jerry Garcia was playing there that evening and the following night. The Keystone Berkeley was well known in music circles as Jerry Garcia's favorite place to play. Even though it was only a five hundred seat venue many other famous bands had played there as well, including Dr. John, Michael Bloomfield, Elvin Bishop Group, Cold Blood, and Tower of Power to name a few. The Keystone was also known for hiring unknown local bands as warm-up acts, and to fill gaps between renowned artists.

Holding a black and white flyer of Mojo Hand I knocked on the wooden door, it was 4:15 PM and this was the last place I had time for. I waited for about thirty seconds and knocked again, only harder. There was still no response. Glancing about, I noticed a sign on the adjacent wall in the alcove that said: "Doors Open At 8:00 PM. I wasn't going to wait until then to talk to somebody. Joan was going to be home around 6:00, and I wanted to be there when she arrived. I turned to leave and stopped when I heard the door open.

An unfriendly looking, muscular, man wearing a tight fitting white tee-shirt opened the door. He had blonde hair and appeared to be in his mid-thirties. Standing in the doorway he identified himself as the manager and growled that they didn't open until 8:00.

"Yeah I know," I said handing him my promo piece.

"I can't be here then. I'm managing a Seattle band and I've got a meeting scheduled someplace else at 8:00," I lied.

"Come back tomorrow night then," he said, taking a step backwards.

"I'm leaving town tomorrow," I said, truthfully.

The manager looked at my poster curiously. Mojo Hand looked different than most bands back then. The drummer was Filipino and the other three band members were white. They all had long hair, with the exception of the lead singer. His hair was cut short and dyed orange. He was dressed in black with a shirt that was opened all the way down to his belt buckle, which consisted of two shiny silver hands linked together. Appropriately, his name was Michael Silversmith. I never asked if it was his real name or pseudonym, and didn't care. It sounded cool at the time. In any event, I was proud of the artwork and proud of the band. My marketing material seemed to work because he rubbed his chin and said, "What kind of music do they play?"

"Original music," I stammered, having been caught off guard.

"No, I mean what type of music do they play?" he said gruffly. "Is it R&B, Funk – Blues? What's their genre?"

"They play hard rock," I said, feeling like the amateur that I was, having only co-managed the band for three months.

I could tell he was not impressed, and knew I had better come up with a hook quickly or forget it.

I remembered that Steve Miller was from the Bay Area and was a local favorite so I told him some of their songs were like his. I also named dropped that Mojo Hand's former manager was a friend of Bruce Lee. He took the bait. "You gotta tape?" he said, shaking my hand.

"Yeah," I said, reaching into my pocket, pulling out an 8mm audio tape along with my business card. “Here's my card too."

He looked at it and grinned. "Cloud Productions -- High Altitude Music. That’s catchy."

I nodded proudly taking credit for it, even though it had been Spike's creation.

"Well, I'll tell you what, I'll listen to your tape and if they're good I'll call you," he said. "But I'll be honest, odds are slim. I've got hundreds of bands who can't find work because of disco and they all want to play here. We pay them one hundred dollars a night. It seems like a long way to come for one hundred bucks, wouldn't you say?"

Deflated, I suddenly felt like a sucker for agreeing to come to San Francisco. Mojo Hand's former manager, who lived here now, said there were plenty of gigs in town. He had convinced them that I could find work here. That was probably the case several years prior when he had first moved here, but times had changed since then and I was getting an education from a professional who knew what he was talking about. I was pissed. The only good thing that had come from this trip was seeing Joan, and even that was questionable after what had happened the night before.

I thanked the manager for his time and shook his hand, knowing that I would never hear from him again.

On the way back to Joan's, I grabbed a slice of pizza at a deli on Telegraph Avenue and sat on the University of Berkeley Campus lawn munching and admiring the palm trees. As students passed by, I smelled patchouli oil, freshly mowed grass, and the skunky odor of another kind of grass.

A little later on, I stopped at a small Asian run market and bought a six pack of long-necked Budweiser and a pack of Marlboros. My little splurge left me with $12.75. It had to last until I got back to Seattle and could cash the unemployment check that should be sitting in my mailbox.

THE DREAM

Berkeley: June, 1973

The sunshine felt nice as I arrived back at Joan's place having spent four or five hours looking for gigs. I leaned over, picked up the key from under the mat and unlocked the door. Putting the key back in its spot for her, I entered the kitchen, closing the door behind me. Our dirty dishes were still in the sink so I knew she hadn't been there while I had been gone. The pad felt empty and cold. Oh well, Joan would be home soon and would warm it up.

I pulled out one of the Buds I'd bought, opened it and put the rest of the six-pack in the fridge. I then washed and dried the dishes. Afterwards, I went into the living room, turned on the stereo and plunked down on a bean bag. I took a sip of beer, sat back reflecting on the day waiting for Joan to get home. It was 5:20 so she should be home pretty soon. I was anxious to see her and hear about her day, and tell her about mine.

Every now and then I would go outside to the porch and have a cigarette. Each time I would grab a beer on the way back in and would return to my favorite bag.

I checked my watch again, it was now 7:35 and Joan still wasn't home yet. I wasn't worried. *She must be stuck in traffic,* I thought.

Two hours passed and it was dark now, and the beer was going fast. I checked the kitchen clock and it was 9:47 PM. Surely she would be home soon. *She must have stopped off for a bite to eat,* I supposed. *She'll be walking through the door any moment now.*

I had to pee so I went to the bathroom.

While washing my hands, I noticed deodorant, Kotex, and lipstick on shelves above the sink. I had four sisters, so it all looked familiar to me…I also spotted birth control pills. *Big deal*, I murmured. *Every girl I know uses them.*

On the way back to the living room I passed through the bedroom, and stopped to look at some photos on her dresser. Some were of Joan, and some were of her parents and siblings I assumed.

Also on her dresser was an ashtray with several roaches. I lit one up and toked away, holding in every inhale.

I finished off the joint and returned to my bag of beans and flopped onto it. It was getting late…Where was, she?

Surely she would be home any minute now and would want to crash…Then again, it was Saturday night and she was single so maybe she stopped off with a friend for a drink…or two…or three…or four.

It was now past midnight and the beer was gone, and so was Joan. She must be out dancing with friends and would be home when the bars closed…No sense staying up; I might as well crawl into bed, and wait for her to get home.

So, I went to bed and fell into a deep sleep. That night I had a dream.

I dreamt that Joan's bed left her bedroom and was floating in the sky and I was on it. A magic bed it was -- Joan's magic bed. It was surreal. It was magical. It was ethereal.

I wasn't scared. I wasn't worried. I was along for the ride.

Swooping low, banking right, going up, banking left, diving down, climbing again, and then gliding along, her bed and I flew.

Finally, hovering over a dance floor I looked down and saw Joan dancing. I peered into her life, into her future, and into what she was doing then.

She was spinning. She was laughing.

The music got faster. The music got louder. Lights were flashing. Round and round she went, surrounded by people. They were clapping as she spun. She was laughing. She was having fun.

The music got louder. It got faster. Red lights flashed. White lights flashed. She was spinning. Faster and faster she spun.

The crowd was stomping their feet and clapping. They were yelling.

The music got louder. It got faster. She was screaming now. They were laughing. She was screaming. She was no longer having fun.

Faster and faster she spun. Red lights flashed and white lights flashed. The music got louder and faster. Round and round she went. She was reaching for help. She was reaching for hands. She was grasping for something.

Red lights flashed and white lights flashed. The music got louder. It got faster. Round and round she went.

She was calling my name, softly at first. It echoed over and over again. She was calling my name louder now. It reverberated again and again.

The crowd was yelling. The crowd was laughing. The crowd was clapping and stamping their feet.

Joan was yelling for help, "Help me, I can't stop. Somebody, please help me!"

Her legs became wobbly. Her arms became rubbery, her voice became hoarse.

"Oh no, I'm falling, I'm falling. Help me, please. Please…"

At that instant, Joan fell, smacking the floor and crumpled into a heap.

The music stopped. She didn't move. The crowd fell silent. Nobody moved. Nobody spoke.

A white parachute settled next to her. Red lights flashed. White lights flashed. The parachute turned red. The crowd didn't move; they didn't speak. A siren wailed in the distance. It grew louder piercing the night; louder and louder it became.

Suddenly, I bolted awake and sat up. A siren blared outside. I was hyperventilating. I tried to catch my breath. I was breathing hard, gasping for air. I was sweating. My heart was beating fast. My heart was beating hard. My heart was beating loud. I could hear it. I could feel it. I was scared. My heart pounded. Thump, thump, thump! Finally, I caught my breath. Finally, my heart slowed down. Finally, I started breathing normally. Finally, I stopped perspiring, and settled down. I looked around the room. It was dark. I couldn't see anyone, I couldn't hear anyone, but I felt Joan's presence. I was sure she was somewhere in the room.

"Joan, is that you?" I called. "It's me, you know, Spike's friend. I know you're there. It's late, come to bed. Joan, are you there? Jesus, where are you? Oh my god, Joan. What's happening?"

I reached over, turned on a nightlight and looked at the alarm clock. 4:15 AM. The taverns and bars had closed more than two hours ago. She should have been home at least an hour ago…So, where was she?

The rest of the night I tossed and turned, never getting over my nightmare, and never going back to sleep. I was certain Joan had died in a skydiving accident and had been calling out to me. It felt odd to be lying in her bed. I barely knew her. She was practically a stranger, and here I was in the bed of someone who I was sure had just died. It would only be a matter of time before the police or somebody else showed up to check on things.

AFTERMATH

Berkeley: June, 1973

About 7:00 AM I finally dragged myself out of bed and got my clothes on. I went to the bathroom, and then into the kitchen and made myself a cup of instant coffee, and then another. I hadn't eaten since the slice of pizza, but the thought of food made me feel nauseous. My second cup of coffee was spent smoking a cigarette on the porch – even it didn't taste good, but it helped calm my jangled nerves.

The police would be showing up pretty soon, I was certain of that so I had better clean this place and myself up. I went inside.

I took a shower and cleaned the kitchen. I carried the trash out to the garbage can and then sat on the porch steps waiting for the cops to arrive and confirm the inevitable. "Joan is dead. We're here to collect her belongings…Who are you?"

Good question. *Who was I, and what was I doing at her place.*

Not that I had anything to do with her skydiving death, but it was strange. *I spent one day with a person that I really didn't know, had an unforgettable time with her, and now she's dead. And even more bizarre, that night I slept in her bed and she died in my dream. How weird is that?*

My head was spinning and my heart was aching.

I had a bus to catch to Seattle in the afternoon, so that further complicated the situation. I could only hope the cops would show up right away and put me out of my misery so I could go home.

About 10:30 a motorcycle cop pulled up and parked in front of Joan's place. The officer dismounted the bike and approached the steps. When the cop was about fifteen feet away a female voice spoke to me. The police officer then removed her goggles and helmet. To my astonishment, it was Joan.

"Hi, how was your day?" she asked as if nothing had happened.

"My day," I said, flabbergasted.

Joan had no idea what she had put me through or maybe she did. Perhaps it was payback for rejecting her the night before. I wasn't sure. Regardless, I was angry.

"Yeah, how was your day yesterday, she said, smiling. "Did you find any gigs for the band?"

The band was the last thing on my mind at that moment and my response was automatic, "The band? I don't know, I mean maybe."

Joan picked up on my vibe that I was irritated. "That's good," she said.

Avoiding eye contact, I looked off to the side and didn't respond.

"Well, I've got to get ready for work," she said as she climbed the porch steps past me and headed for the open kitchen door. "When's your bus?"

"My bus?" I said, calling after her.

Joan stopped and turned to me. "Yeah, your bus to Seattle. When does it leave?"

"It leaves at 2:00," I said, wondering whether she was wishing I was leaving earlier, or staying longer.

"Good, then that'll give us a little time to talk before I go to work and you have to leave," she said, smiling.

All I could muster was a nod as Joan turned and entered the kitchen. A few minutes later I went inside. I could hear water running so I knew she was showering. I packed my bags, carried them outside and sat on the porch steps waiting for her.

About a half hour later Joan opened the door and came outside onto the porch dressed for work. I turned to look at her and she looked great. She was dressed in a form-fitting short-sleeve burgundy top, light blue hip-hugger stretch jeans tucked inside tan cowboy boots. As far as my taste was concerned, she was much better attired than the day I had met her at Raleigh's Pub. Aside from being a little bleary eyed, this cowgirl was ready to ride.

"There you are," she said, standing at the top of the porch. "I was wondering where you were."

Still pissed about last night, I took a drag on my cigarette. "Yeah, and I was wondering where you were last night."

“Oh, sorry about that,” she said coming down the stairs and stopping at the landing. "After we jumped, I went to a party and everyone got stoned so I ended up spending the night there…I would've called but..."

"I know you don't have a phone."

"No," she replied.

I took the cigarette out of my mouth and turned to her. "Well, I was worried about you."

"Why were you worried about me?"

"Because I thought something had happened to you."

"Well, I'm a big girl," she said. "I know how to take care of myself."

I paused to take another drag from my cigarette, and to collect my thoughts while she looked at me impassively. I exhaled deeply. "Joan, I thought something horrible had happened to you. I couldn't sleep."

Preparing to defend herself, Joan took a deep breath. "Well, I'm sorry you were worried, but it was just a party," she said, shaking her head in disbelief.

"Joan, I thought you had died while skydiving…I had this dream…"

"Well, I'm just fine; I'm here, aren't I?" she said, folding her arms.

I rose to my feet and climbed down the stairs to the landing. "Yes," I said, turning to face her, "but it was real…You've got to quit skydiving…It's going to kill you."

Joan looked at me like I was strange, and moved away. "How do you know?" she said, turning her back to me. "You're not God, you know."

"No, I'm not," I said, pulling up behind her and placing my hands on her waist. "But you died in my dream. You probably think I'm crazy, but it's going to kill you some day"

Apparently processing what I had said, Joan hesitated momentarily. The thought of death really didn't seem to frighten her, or she just didn't care. I couldn't figure out which one it was. Unfolding her arms she turned to me and said, "It's safer than all those cigarettes you smoke."

"No it isn't," I said, shaking my head.

Joan shot back with what I would later learn was a well-rehearsed defense of skydiving by skydivers. "Yes it is. 250,000 people die from smoking in the U.S. every year. You know how many people died from skydiving last year in the U.S.?"

Caught off-guard by her scripted response, all I could do was shake my head *no*.

Having fought this battle before, Joan had the facts at her fingertips. "Forty-Two," she said, smugly.

"It's not the same. You can't compare smoking with skydiving."

"Yes, I can," she said, gesturing with her hands. "You like smoking, and I love skydiving. There's a greater chance you're going to die from lung cancer than I'm going to die from skydiving. There I just compared it."

Joan had won the battle. She stood there basking in her victory and the late morning sunlight. At that particular moment she looked sexy and confident. I felt intimidated. She had won the debate hands down. But in spite of that, I sensed a vulnerability in her. I decided to try to appeal to her emotional side. It was my only chance of changing her mind. "Joan, listen to me...you've got to stop. Do it for me, please."

"Why should I do it for you?" she said with a twinge of bitterness in voice.

"Because I care about you," I said, making eye contact with her.

She smirked slightly and then said, "You care about your girlfriend."

"Yeah, but I care about you too."

"Right," she said.

She paused momentarily, pondering what I had just said. My approach seemed to resonate with her. Time would tell if she would ever stop jumping. Joan looked at me and said, "Well thanks, but I'm never going to stop skydiving, so if you really care about me please don't bring it up again…Now let's get going, I've got to get to work and you've got to catch a bus to Seattle."

As we walked through town, I told her about my gig hunting the day before. By the time we arrived at the bus stop she was in a much better mood and I was sorry to say goodbye. I thanked her and said I was going to miss her, but said I would be in town again in about a month to pick up my girlfriend who was arriving on a charter flight from Sweden. Joan offered to let me stay at her place if I wanted to, but to call her at the restaurant to remind her first. If she wasn't there, she would leave the key under the mat.

My bus arrived and she gave me a hug and a kiss on the cheek, then walked down the street as I boarded the bus. I slid into a window seat and watched as the bus drove past her. She didn't look up. I slept a lot during the ride back to Seattle and dreamt about the tumultuous experience I'd had with Joan.

RESEARCHING

Redmond, WA: March, 2010

A day or two after I had told Susan that I had been having dreams about Joan, I started researching her online. I wondered if anybody still remembered her, considering it was now 2010, having been almost 30 years since she died and almost forty years since she started skydiving in San Francisco.

I did an Internet search for "Joan Carson" adding keywords to her name such as San Francisco, and Redmond, Washington. Nothing came up and I was getting frustrated. I finally got two hits when I added the string "skydiving fatality". The hits came from a skydiving blog called, DropZone.com.

One of the postings was from a guy named Fred Sand and was in the website's *Blue Skies - In Memory Of* section. His posting was brief; all it said was: "Joan Carson 28 years ago today -- Fly High Beagle Boogie Babe."

The other posting was from a skydiver named Rodney Holberton and his posting said, "Joan Carson was on the load when I made my first jump in 1974."

This was exciting, I was getting somewhere now, which was great news, and maybe they could lead me to other skydivers that had jumped with Joan.

I emailed both of them through the website, leaving my email address and phone number and asked them to contact me. I explained that I was making a documentary film about Joan Carson and would like to interview them since it looked like they had known her.

A day or two later Rodney Holberton called me on our home phone. Susan and I had just finished dinner. She was cleaning the kitchen so I took our cordless phone outside onto our deck overlooking Ames Lake where it was quiet.

Rodney said he had met Joan in 1974 at Beagle Sky Ranch in Medford, Oregon. She was a skydiver and his father George owned the skydive facility there. He was only fifteen and was making his first jump. Joan was on the plane, along with Linda McGinty and a guy who went by the nickname of Zimmo.

I was surprised. I had no idea Joan had moved to Medford and jumped there. The last time I saw her she was living in San Francisco. It didn't make sense that she had moved to Medford.

Growing up in Seattle's suburbs and then living in San Francisco *Joan was much too sophisticated for Medford,* I thought. Having driven through Medford five or ten times over the years, my impression was that it was a rough and tumble farming and timber town. So what was she doing there?

Rodney spoke fondly of Joan saying that she had been like a big sister to him, and that her nickname was *Beagle Boogie Babe*. The guys who jumped at Beagle Sky Ranch called themselves the *Beagle Boogie Boys.* Joan and Linda McGinty, who was in her early twenties at the time, were the first two female jumpers at Beagle Sky Ranch. Not wanting to be out done by the guys, they had called themselves the Beagle Boogie Babes. Joan coined the phrase so she became Beagle Boogie Babe #1, and Linda became #2.

My mind was buzzing with excitement and trying to process all of the information Rodney was giving me. Striving to calm my nerves, I took a sip off the glass of beer I had been working on when he called.

After my stay with Joan in San Francisco, all I had known about her whereabouts, was that she had died in Lost Prairie. What had she been doing there? Had she lived there, or had she just gone there for a weekend jump? My curiosity was consuming me. I had to know. "So tell me, why was Joan in Lost Prairie when she died?" I asked.

"Well, it's like this, in the fall of '75 a group of skydivers from Kalispell came down to Beagle Sky Ranch in their Twin Beach 18 to winter over," Rodney said. “Joan fell in love with the leader, a guy named Dave. When it came time for him to head back to Kalispell, in May I think, Joan went with them. She owned a Tioga motorhome and drove it there with him."

Rodney continued on for several more minutes telling me about some of the crazy things the group had done when they returned to Kalispell, and provided a rough sketch of how Lost Prairie was created.

About then, I heard a woman's voice in the background say something to him. "Just a second," Rodney said, “my wife is trying to talk to me."

Rodney covered the mouthpiece of his phone giving me a chance to take another sip of beer and collect my thoughts.

Oh my God, this is getting better by the minute, I reveled by pumping my fist in the air.

It wasn't long before Rodney got back on the phone. "I've got to get going soon, he said. “I'm a commercial pilot and my wife reminded me that I have an early flight tomorrow morning to Anchorage. I live in Portland now but we can talk later."

"That's good because I live in Redmond, Washington," I said. "Would you be willing to let me interview you for the film? I could come to your place.”

"I'd love to help, but I fly freight so I never know what my schedule is going to be or where I'll be."

Before the conversation ended Rodney gave me his father's phone number, and Zimmo's email address. "You should really talk to Fred Sand, he still lives in Lost Prairie and so do some of the other jumpers," he said.

I informed Rodney that I'd already emailed Fred and was still waiting to hear from him.

"Fred's the man," Rodney said, "you should also go to the annual boogie in Lost Prairie. It's in July. A lot of old timers will be there. I'm going to try to make it up there too. Well, I've got to go to now. Good talking to you and good luck with the film. Feel free to call me if you have any more questions."

I thanked Rodney and hung up the phone. I knew right then and there that I was going to make a film about Joan Carson. "Yes," I whooped as I entered the living room.

Susan was just finishing the dishes. Hearing me, she looked up from the sink. "Who were you on the phone with?" she asked.

"It was a guy named Rodney Holberton," I said, excitedly, filling her in on what Rodney had told me.

"Boogie, what does that mean?" Susan asked.

"It's an event where a bunch of skydivers get together to jump. They call it a boogie," I said.

Continuing on, I told Susan how Joan had gotten her nickname and that she had started a club for the female skydivers.

"Yeah, why not," Susan said, smiling, "I'm liking her better all the time."

"Me too," I said.

I went on to say how Joan ended up in Montana, and that eventually she and four others bought acreage in Lost Prairie and built their own skydiving center there.

"Oh my god," Susan said, "that's amazing."

"That's not all," I said. “A handful of the same skydivers that wintered over in Medford still live in Lost Prairie.”

Engrossed, Susan took a step closer to me. "You’re kidding me," she said, "sounds incestuous, and intriguing. Well, you know what your next film is going to be about."

"Yeah, I sure do," I said, "and I know what I'm going to call it."

"What's that?" Susan said.

Beagle Boogie Babe, I said, grinning.

"Perfect," Susan said, "It's catchy and makes you wonder what it means."

"Yeah," I said, "it's all coming together. Rodney even gave me names and contact info for some of the people who jumped in Medford while Joan was there."

"That's a good sign," Susan said, "I've got a good feeling about this."

"So do I," I said, "but I still need to track down more people -- including her family."

"You will, Joan is guiding you," Susan said, hugging me. "Exciting; I'm happy for you."

Susan was my biggest cheerleader and would play a vital role in the film when we got into production.

Meanwhile, I continued writing the script, which brought back memories of my return to Seattle after staying at Joan’s place.

CONFIRMATION

Seattle: June, 1973

By the time I got back to Seattle after my wild experience with Joan in San Francisco, I was pretty well rested but couldn't stop thinking about the time I had spent with her there. It was gloomy and raining in the late afternoon when I entered my old four story brick apartment building at 12th and Republican on Capitol Hill. I stopped just inside the entrance at the bank of bronze mailboxes, inserted a key into my slot and pulled out a manila envelope containing my unemployment check, and a *Par Avion* letter from Astrid. Oh, how I loved Swedish super lightweight envelopes and the way they indicated it was being sent by Air Mail – along with the subtle fragrance of her perfume. It always felt so sophisticated and exotic to open a letter from her.

Lugging my backpack, I climbed the stairs to the third floor. The floors creaked under my Rock 'n Roll boots as I shuffled down the dimly-lit hallway. Compared to the gloom outside, it seemed particularly dark and dingy indoors. Normally I wasn't home until late at night to notice the difference. Nearing my room, I ran into a local folk singer by the name of Jim Page. He regularly played Mojo Hand's breaks. He didn't live in the building and said he had been visiting a friend who did.

After a brief exchange of *so what have you been up to,* we said our goodbyes and I stopped at my room, #302. I unlocked the door and entered my apartment. It was a depressingly drab studio consisting of a Murphy bed, couch, dinky kitchen and kitchen table with two chairs, and a small bathroom with a tub. Its windows looked out over the black tar roof of another apartment building. Built in the twenties or thirties, the building was the perfect haven for junkies and struggling artist types looking for low rent. Fortunately, it was mostly populated by elderly pensioners who I rarely saw, or heard. Occasionally though, I would hear, late night domestic fights coming from some of the rooms down below, gunshots and police sirens outside.

My room was stuffy and hot so I opened the windows to cool it down and turned on my Panasonic stereo to drown out any unwanted noise from the streets below. By coincidence, it was similar to Joan's stereo. It was tuned to a local Rock Station, known as KISW.

I opened my Unemployment Check. The weekly amount was $75.00, which covered my monthly rent. The band paid me $100 dollars a week, which along with the other three unemployment checks I received monthly paid for my cigarettes, beer, gas, food, and utilities.

Next, I opened the envelope from Astrid and read her letter. She said that about ten days earlier she'd had a dream, and in her dream I had met somebody else and was going to marry her. Continuing, her letter explained that she didn't want to come to Seattle if her dream was true. She needed to know if I still loved her.

Later that day, I wrote a letter to Astrid apologizing for not having written her for more than a month, explaining that I had been busy trying to find work for the band in San Francisco. I reassured her that I loved her, and would be there to pick her up in July when her charter flight landed at San Francisco International Airport.

A month later I phoned Raleigh's Pub. A hostess answered. It had been almost five weeks since I had seen Joan. She wasn't working so I left a message reminding her I was going to be in town that weekend to pick up my girlfriend, and would love to see her and stay at her place, -- if that was still okay. The hostess said she would give my message to Joan when she came in later that day for work.

SURREAL

Berkeley: July, 1973

About a month after getting Astrid's letter, I arrived back at Joan's place in the early afternoon and rang the doorbell several times. There was no answer so I looked under the mat for the key. As promised, she had left it there and I let myself in. She had also left me a note on the kitchen table that said she had gone skydiving for the weekend to a place north of Lake Berryessa, and to make myself at home. I did, but was disappointed she wouldn't be there. The place felt eerily empty without her.

I decided to go for a walk up Telegraph Avenue, stopping to buy a slice of pizza at the little shop where I'd bought a piece the time before. The pizza wasn't great, but it was cheap and quick and I was hungry.

To my surprise, I ran into Jim Page who had just performed a gig at Sproul Hall on Berkeley Campus. We hung out briefly, with him telling me the students there thought he was the second coming of Dylan. Once a year he would come down for a week or so, make a ton of money, and then head back to Seattle.

A half hour or so later, I said goodbye to Jim and returned to Joan's place. Kicking back, I had a few beers and cigarettes and listened to music on her stereo. I missed her, and wished she were there, remembering the last time I had seen her before she moved to San Francisco.

It was 1970, and I was leaving the Cafeteria at Bellevue Community College while a student there.

Joan and Spike were talking as I walked past them heading for a class having just eaten lunch. "That's it Paul," said Spike calling out to me, "just walk on by without saying hi."

"Oh, sorry about that, I didn't see you there," I fibbed, not wanting to be late for class.

Spike glanced at Joan. "I don't know Paul. I'm not sure we can forgive you," he said, in mock anger.

"Go easy on him, Spike," Joan joked. "He's blushing."

"You remember Joan, don't you Paul," Spike said, rhetorically.

"Hi Joan," I said, grinning and nodding at her.

Joan smiled. "What class are you taking?"

"Chemistry," I said. "That's impressive," she said. "My dad's a chemist. How do you like it?"

"I hate it, but it's a science credit," I said, shrugging.

"Alright, go on, Paul," Spike said, teasingly. "Go to your stinking chemistry class, Mister Science Major."

Joan laughed.

Forcing a laugh of my own, I said goodbye and walked off, having no idea that three years later my path would cross with her in San Francisco.

Around 11:00 PM I took one last gulp of beer, and a few minutes later went into Joan's bedroom and crawled into bed. It felt surreal to once again sleep alone in her bed, considering the dream I'd had the time before. I had trouble sleeping that night, thinking about Joan and wondering if she was okay.

The next day I left Joan a note thanking her.

Thank you for letting me stay at your place and for the food and beer. I'm sorry you weren't here. I really missed you and was looking forward to seeing you again. I washed and dried my dishes, but left them on the counter because I didn't know where to put them. I hope you are doing well. I care about you, and would love to see you again sometime!

DISCONNECT

San Francisco: July, 1973

Early in the evening I came out of Joan's duplex and locked the door. Hesitating a moment, before I put the key under the mat, I turned to look down the street hoping she would show up so I could say goodbye to her.

About an hour and a half later I arrived at SFO to pick up Astrid. Wating outside the Immigration Office for her, the disembarking passengers walked through a doorway past me carrying their luggage. I waited until there was nobody else, and wondered whether she had changed her mind. At last the door opened and there she was. I hugged her and she gave me a kiss, but something was missing. The flame was an ember. I wasn't sure if it was her or me, but something had definitely changed.

We caught a 10:00 PM Greyhound bus to Seattle. It was hot and unventilated inside as we drove though the San Jacinto Valley. We sat side by side and didn't talk much. After about an hour Astrid fell asleep. I couldn't sleep, and kept thinking about Joan skydiving somewhere north of San Francisco for the weekend. Was she sleeping now, or was she partying? Was she having sex with someone? Was she injured? Was she dead? It was all giving me a headache.

Astrid woke up and looking at me perplexed said, "What's wrong?"

"I can't sleep," I said, turning to her. "I've got a headache."

"Maybe you need fresh air," she said, feeling my forehead and comforting me. "You feel warm. Why don't you sit in that seat up there on the left and open the window."

Not wanting to hurt her feelings I stalled for a moment: "You don't mind?"

"No, I need space too," she said. "We've been apart for more than a year so it's okay if we take our time."

Astrid patted my hand reassuringly, and kissed me on the cheek. “Now go ahead my darling,” she said.

She had such love and warmth and made everything seem so natural and comforting in an earthy sort of way. She was the quintessential *Hard Headed Woman,* exactly the type of woman I needed at that time in my life. No wonder, Cat Steven's song, *Hard Headed Woman* was one of my favorite songs at the time. Every time I heard it, I would think of her.

The bus hit a few potholes and bounced several times snapping me to action. I grinned at Astrid sheepishly and moved to the empty seat three rows up on the other side of the bus. Tired, I slumped into the seat, and slid the window open several inches. A gush of warm air blew on my face and tousled my blond hair. The breeze felt refreshing. Gradually my headache dissipated and I fell asleep. The next morning I was awakened by the sun shining in my eyes and a bloody nose as the bus came to a stop. "Klamath Falls," the driver’s voice crackled over the PA system. "Fifteen minutes."

I turned and looked back at Astrid. She noticed blood streaming out of my nose and looked concerned as she was getting up. I waited for her to arrive alongside my seat where she handed me tissue paper and then followed her off the bus. After I stopped the bleeding, we hugged each other and then went to the restrooms. On the way back to the bus, I stopped at the terminal's small snack bar and bought some snacks for us. Astrid sauntered up and we got on the bus sitting together, eating the snacks and sipping on our Styrofoam cups of coffee. She was into organic health foods, introducing me to granola with fresh fruits, nuts and yogurt. Alas, the two oatmeal cookies and trail nuts I bought were the healthiest food they had to offer. She was appreciative, but didn't want her cookie and gave it to me.

As the bus traveled further northward, desert scrub, tumbleweeds, and pine trees gave way to evergreen trees and green hills. During the journey, we hadn't talked much at all, but that wasn't unusual. In 1972 we spent a lot of time together and Astrid tended to be quiet, often occupying her time by writing letters, knitting, and sewing. In the meantime I watched Johnny Carson, listened to music, read magazines that dealt with the music business such as Rolling Stone, and Seattle's Rocket magazine, and watched her being productive. She was so absorbed in what she was doing that it was entertaining watching her. But this was different; we had hardly spoken at all on the trip -- other than perfunctory talk. You would have thought after being away from each other for such a long time that our conversation would be overflowing. But it wasn't. Maybe things would open up when we got to my place. At least that's what I hoped would happen.

We made several more stops before pulling into the Greyhound Bus terminal in Seattle on 7th and Stewart Street and then got off the bus. It was early evening, and was sunny and warm. Yes, Seattle was gorgeous in the summertime. As far as I was concerned, there was no place that compared to it.

When I met Astrid, in 1972, I was twenty-two and so was she. At the time I had been living at my folks place in Bellevue, Washington overlooking Lake Sammamish, and she had been a nanny several miles away for Dr. Green and his wife Ann, taking care of their two kids.

At that stage in my life, Astrid was much more sexually advanced than I was and I learned a lot from her. Unfortunately, she had had an abortion when she was fourteen and another one when she was eighteen. They left emotional scars on her that I can only imagine. I think the emotional baggage she carried had something to do with her coming to nanny for the Greens. She needed a break and to get away from her past. She never really talked about it all that much, and would only say that she would never have another abortion.

Before departing Seattle, three days earlier to pick up Astrid in San Francisco, I had parked my '62 Plymouth Valiant in a pay parking lot a block away from the bus terminal. Carrying our bags, we arrived at my dented white workhorse and tossed our bags into the trunk. I drove her to my apartment and she didn't like it; she wanted to stay at the Green's.

An hour later I parked my car outside the Green's and we talked about our relationship. It wasn't working and we both knew it. After about half an hour she informed me that she had met somebody else in Sweden. She felt so sorry for not telling me, but had felt obligated to come because she didn't want to hurt me. I wiped away her tears and said that it was okay because I had met somebody too. It was a lie but it made her feel better. She stopped crying and hugged me. I felt glad that she had a new boyfriend, sad that I didn't have a girlfriend, and conflicted about Joan.

Feeling horrible about the way things had turned out, I wished her well and said goodbye. Before she got out of the car, we agreed there probably wasn't any point in us getting together again before she returned to Sweden.

REUNION

Bellevue, WA: August, 1974

A year after Astrid left, I got a call from Spike telling me that Joan had broken her ankle skydiving and that she was staying at her folks place in Kirkland while her foot healed. I couldn't believe it; a year earlier in 1973 she had broken both her wrists and now this. My dream seemed to be manifesting itself. It was unnerving.

By this time Spike and another high school friend thought Joan was crazy. Spike nicknamed her Popeye (after *Popeye the Sailor*) when she had broken both her wrists and the other friend referred to her as Peg Leg when she broke her ankle. I think they were just as surprised and concerned as I was that she continued skydiving, and made jokes about her as a means of dealing with their worries. Whatever the case may be, I doubt they ever actually expressed their concerns directly to her.

During Spike's call, he said that he and Joan were going to an unofficial five year high school reunion party for their class. Even though I had graduated a year earlier, she wanted me to see me and meet them there. I accepted the invitation and was excited to see her. It had been almost two years and at this time I still didn't have a steady girlfriend, other than my off and on relationship with Rochelle, who I'd met while managing Mojo Hand. Maybe she was candy for others, but she was poison for me. For the next couple of years I wasted my time pursuing her with a more off than on relationship.

The party was being held in Bellevue, Washington. At the time I was living a few miles away in a house in Kirkland with several roommates, and going to school there at Lake Washington College studying Electro-Mechanical Design. When I finally graduated, I would be designing Printed Circuit Boards and plastic injection molded cases for electronic products.

I showed up at the party before Joan and Spike arrived. When they made their grand entrance she was on crutches. She spotted me and hobbled over to where I was standing leaving Spike on his own with adoring classmates. She kissed me on the cheek. "I got the note you left," she said, looking into my eyes. "I'm sorry I wasn't there. As it turned out a jumper got killed so they cancelled jumping for the rest of the weekend. It would have been nice to spend time with you…So, Spike tells me you're going to school, and that you're going to be an engineer. How's it going?

I shuffled my feet nervously and looking into her eyes lied.

"It's going good," I said.

Things weren't going well for me. Astrid had been gone for a year, and I had broken up with Rochelle again, and was wondering whether I'd ever get married. In a month I would be twenty-five. I wasn't getting any younger and age was starting to wear on me. Wanting to deflect the conversation off me, I asked, "So, how's your ankle?"

Joan paused a moment and shifted weight on her crutches. "It's doing great," she said, avoiding the subject of skydiving altogether, knowing how I felt about it.

"That's good," I said, glancing down at the cast protruding from her split pant leg. Several signed messages were scrawled on it.

She shifted painfully and looked at me. Before she could respond, a female classmate of hers, who I didn't know, came along and the next thing I knew Joan was saying she'd talk to me later before the two had moved away to talk with other classmates of theirs.

As the evening wore on, the party became more boisterous and the Bee Gees Saturday Night Fever album blasted from a high quality Sansui Stereo. I was stoned now from all the joints being passed around, and for the first time ever I appreciated their music.

Joan became the center of attention in the kitchen with guys writing on her cast. She was intoxicated and basking in all the attention. As far as I could tell, I was the only guy that hadn't signed it. I felt uncomfortable seeing her surrounded by a room full of guys whooping it up every time another one left a raunchy remark on her cast.

Disappointed, I left the party saying goodbye only to Spike. I had gone to the party to see Joan, hoping that her broken ankle had been a wakeup call for her to quit skydiving. It had not been. She was still just as wild as ever.

ENGINEERING

Seattle area: 1975 – 2008

A year and a half after seeing Joan at the "reunion party", I graduated from Lake Washington College and was hired by an audio company called TAPCO (Technical Audio Products Corporation) that made power amps and PA mixers for rock bands. It was December 1975, and I would have no girlfriends for two years until I met Susan. I can honestly say that several times I contemplated trying to contact Joan, but never did. Once again, I didn't want to have anything to do with skydiving.

For the next thirty-three years I worked in the Electronics industry for various high tech companies, as a Designer, Senior Designer, and Supervisor. Initially I enjoyed the work and found it creative and challenging, but after ten years I was tired of engineering and spending seventy-five percent of my time doing documentation, which was tedious.

I wanted to do something creative. Since 1971, I had explored filmmaking on the side. It wasn't until 1985 that I decided to get serious about it.

FILMMAKING

Seattle area: 1971 - 2019

I suppose you could say my filmmaking journey began in 1971. I was in my early twenties and two of my friends that where film students at the University of Washington asked me to act in their student films. I enjoyed being involved in their projects and thought about pursuing filmmaking too. However, I knew that in order to make a living at it. I would need to move to L.A. I didn't want to live there so I didn't see it as a viable career path and abandoned the idea.

By the mid 1985 I was tired of engineering and looking for a change. To my surprise, more and more films were being filmed in the Seattle area. After taking several filmmaking classes at a community college I wrote a feature length screenplay called "Offsides". It was about a fictional Russian football team that challenges the Super Bowl Champs to a football game.

Luckily, "Offsides" landed me an agent in L.A., and inspired me to write another script, called "The Last Mirage".

A Canadian production company optioned “The Last Mirage" and took it to the Cannes Film Festival where they claimed to have a deal in the works with New Line Cinema. Unfortunately, the deal fell through when it was announced, at the festival, that New Line Cinema had been acquired by Disney. The result was that the Canadians had lost their "in".

Needless to say, I was disappointed. "The Last Mirage" had come close, and so had "Offsides", which became passé' with the tearing down of the Berlin Wall and the dismantling of the Soviet Union. With that in mind, I decided that if I was ever going to see my films on the "big screen", I'd better start making my own films, which I did.

In 1987 I wrote and produced two short films. Both of those films were shown on local TV in Seattle and caught the eye of two Seattle Times film critics giving them positive reviews.

Encouraged by their positive reviews, I decided to write and produce a feature length cop on cop film noir film entitled "Broken Frame". With a volunteer cast and crew, and a budget of only $500, we finished principal photography in 10 days. Several months later we shot some additional scenes and it was then time to do the editing. Little did I know that a series of mishaps and life's curves would relegate "Broken Frame" to the "can" for the next 22 years.

Meanwhile, in 1988 I enrolled in the film program at the University of Washington's Extension College. It was a two year program, but I got the first year waived because of the short films I had made and the screenplays I had written.

After graduation, I worked in the Seattle area on movies, commercials and training films, finally returning to my engineering job due to sporadic work, and time away from my family. For the next fifteen years, I continued making short films, and writing screenplays, several of which were produced as stage plays in Seattle.

In 2008, I had just been laid off my engineering job. I was fifty-eight then and had planned on retiring when I turned sixty-two. For the next two years I looked for a job. The economy had just tanked. Hardly anybody was hiring, and those that were didn't want to hire someone my age.

Unemployed, I spent my spare time editing the film I had shot 22 years earlier, "Broken Frame". It took about a year to finish. Sure it was faded and grainy and some of the sound had deteriorated, but I was surprised at what we had accomplished, and how good the acting and story were. As captivating as “Broken Frame” was, I felt it was part of a larger story about the reason it had taken so long to finish it and what had happened to everyone since then.

With that in mind, I turned “Broken Frame” into a trilogy, providing background on the reason it took so long to finish the film, what had happened to the cast and crew since then, and the actual film itself sandwiched in between. I then retitled the film as, “Broken Frame – The movie that took 22 years to finish.”

Acclaimed by Seattle's Scarecrow Video, and U.K. film critic Brett Gerry, who had this to say about "Broken Frame". "This is an inspirational story from Paul Gorman and Rain City Cinema, and I suggest anyone who's ever struggled to make it in the film industry watches the entire film."

With their reviews, I finally felt validated as a filmmaker, and proud to have finished "Broken Frame." But I didn't want to stop there. I wanted to make more films. By that time I was 60, and had decided to retire since the job market was still horrible. I had plenty of time on my hands. In fact I had too much time on my hands. I needed another project because Susan was still working and so were my friends. Timing wise, making a documentary about Joan Carson couldn’t have come along at a better stage.

PROGRESS

Redmond, WA: March -May, 2010

A day or two after my phone conversation with Beagle Sky Ranch skydiver Rodney Holberton, Fred Sand returned my phone calls. Living in Lost Prairie he ran the annual boogie. He also had a skydiving business there too. He gave me names and contact info for former Beagle Boogie Babe Linda McGinty (now Linda Groarke) and her husband Mike Groarke, Dick Steinke, Bill Paulin and Joan's boyfriend Dave. With the exception of Paulin, they all still lived in Lost Prairie. Most of them had also jumped with Joan in Medford, except for Dick Steinke and Paulin.

For the rest of February, 2010 and most of March, April, and May I continued tracking down people, finally contacting skydivers that lived in the Medford area and had jumped with Joan at Beagle. I also reached Zimmo, who now lived in Lincoln, California and had jumped with Joan in Medford too.

Meanwhile, I tried locating Joan's family members but was striking out. I was getting discouraged. On Ancestry.com I came across a Joan Margaret Carson who has been born in Mendocino, California on December 28, 1950. I wasn't sure if it was the Joan Carson I had known, but couldn't rule it out either. The family tree listed the father's name as Herbert Barrie Carson, and recorded him as being deceased. His wife's name was Edna with a maiden name of King. The information indicated that she was still alive and lived in Sammamish, Washington. Sammamish borders Redmond's city limits, so I was pretty sure that I had found Joan's parents, and the right Joan Carson.

I did an Internet search for Edna Carson in Sammamish and came up with the name and address of an assisted care facility. I called their number and explained why I was trying to contact her. The woman I spoke with said, "I'm sorry but I can't let you speak with her without her guardian's permission. I can take a message and pass it along to her custodian if you'd like."

Days went by with no response from Edna or her guardian. I was striking out and contemplated hiring a Private Investigator, but that would be expensive. I had an idea. Maybe Joan had siblings who had also gone to the Redmond High School. Even though I wasn't aware of any other Carsons in my class, it didn't mean there weren't any that had graduated before or after me. There couldn't be that many classmates with the same last name, so I started looking through old yearbooks on Classmates.com.

I came across a few fellow students with the same last name and called them. Invariably, I got the same response that they weren't related to Joan.

As luck would have it, I ran across a classmate named Barrie Carson who had graduated four years after me. I remembered that the Joan Margaret Carson's father I had found on Ancestory.com was named Herbert Barrie Carson. His middle name was an unusual spelling of *Barry*. I felt that either it was a coincidence or the Barrie Carson who had gone to my old high school was Joan's younger brother. There was only one way to find out and that was to contact him. It just so happened, he had a profile on Classmates.com so I emailed him through their server.

Ten days later I hadn't heard anything from Barrie Carson. I was about ready to give up hope when on May 16, 2010 I got an email from him informing me that he'd gotten my email, was Joan's younger brother, and that Joan's older sister lives in Sammamish, Washington – a mere stone's throw from where Susan and I lived. Overall, Barrie sounded genuinely interested in helping with the film and providing information about Joan.

It was a major breakthrough. I had established contact with Joan's family. I felt like I had been lost at sea and had just been reunited with a long lost family member. It was a very strange feeling, particularly since we had never met.

A day later I replied to Barrie's email thanking him for getting back to me and for his willingness to help:

Joan and I were casual friends and saw one another only a handful of times after high school, but I was struck by her passion for skydiving, fearlessness and outgoing personality. There truly wasn't a room she couldn't light up.

My quest is to understand who Joan was and what drove her to take the risks she did...and why she continued skydiving even after several serious injuries. I would also like to know what events led up to that fateful day. It is my hope that this film will be a tribute to Joan and through her we might all better understand why people skydive. I can't think of a better spokesperson than Joan.

At this point, your interest and support is about all I need. However, eventually, I would like to interview you (if you're interested) and get some footage of some of Joan's old stomping grounds in San Francisco and Berkeley.

In the meantime, it would be helpful if you could provide me with names of any of Joan's friends, co-workers, bosses and landlords that you know of. I would also appreciate it if you would scan any photos of her that you have, however, I won't need those until later.

Presently, I am still in the planning phase, but have made quite a bit of progress. The project seems to have a synergy and life of its own. In addition to your willingness, I have also made contact with several skydivers in Medford and Kalispell who knew Joan and jumped with her. They have been very helpful and excited about the project and have agreed to be interviewed. Their interviews will be part of the film. I plan to start those interviews in late June or July in Kalispell and then move onto Medford. These interviews will determine the direction of the story and ultimately whether or not there is sufficient story to continue on to the next phase.

I have also been organizing a crew and investigating some technical issues such as sound and what type of camera we will use. There is a chance we will shoot the film in 3-D, which will make it a first among skydiving films.

I will keep you posted as things more fully develop.

Later that same day I got a return email from Barrie saying he'd like to see a film that pays tribute to Joan's love for skydiving. He went on to say he had been close to her and how much it saddened him that she never got to know his and his sister Janet's children. If anything consoled him though, it was the realization she had found something she loved and was surrounded by people who adored her and that she adored.

Barrie offered his guarded support, wanting to know more about the film, my intentions, and how I intended to depict Joan. His support, he made clear was limited to the extent that the film was a tribute to her spirit and love of skydiving.

In closing, Barrie said he would go through his mementos and photos of Joan and send them to me, and suggested I contact Joan's old boyfriend, Dave, claiming he was "an amazing character."

I was buoyed by my communication with Barrie and all of the other contacts I had made so far.

I told Susan about my progress. "You've got to do it," she responded. "You've been wondering about what that dream meant all these years. It's haunted you. Here's your chance to maybe find out. So do it."

Susan was the friendliest person I have ever met, and had great interpersonal communication skills, an area in which I was I lacking. Aware of my limitations, I asked her if she would do the interviewing. I don't think she was excited about doing it. But she did it. I am forever thankful for the amazing job she did. I couldn't have made the film without her.

I'd never been the most talented guy in the world, nor the smartest, nor the best looking, yet somehow life had dealt me a great hand. Call it whatever you want, but with a few exceptions, I have always believed that I could accomplish anything I wanted if I set my mind to it.

And now my mind was set on making "Beagle Boogie Babe". I was on an adventure of the past, present and future, to learn all I could about Joan, and interpret the meaning of the dream I'd had so many years ago. Was it just a coincidence, or was it a premonition? I had to know. It's funny because I always felt that I had met Joan for a reason. Maybe it was destiny, or perhaps it was spiritual. Whatever the case may be, I wanted to find out, and didn't want to bias my telling of her story.

I had decided in advance that I was only going to initially ask Rodney and Barrie superficial questions, and did just that. I wasn't going to pre-interview anybody else. I already had a rough sketch of Joan's whereabouts and some of the milestones in her brief life to pique my interest and get me going. I didn't need more now. I wanted the story to unfold on its own, for me, my crew, and the audience as we went along. It was a gamble, but I felt like it was a risk worth taking. Time would tell if I had made the right decision.

RIDE

Bellevue, WA: January, 1974

Sometime in January, 1974 I was home studying when the phone rang. It was Spike. "Hey Paul, Joan and I are out and we need a ride can you help us?"

"Where are you?" I asked.

"We're at the Red Lion in Bellevue and need to go to Northwest Truck Leasing. My car's parked there."

I was going to school and living in Kirkland at the time, which wasn't far away so I agreed – besides, I was curious to see Joan. I hadn't seen her since the Queen Ann Hill party a month or two earlier, and from what I had heard she was still convalescing at her parents place in Redmond because of her broken wrists.

"Okay, see you there in about thirty minutes," I said.

The Red Lion Inn was a popular nightspot to dance on the Eastside on weekends. Being a Saturday night it was packed when I got there. Shortly after entering I spotted Joan and Spike on the dance floor and he motioned me to join them. I snaked my way through the crowd to the dance floor and Joan hugged me seductively; I knew she was intoxicated. She still had casts on her wrists, but the bruises on her face were gone. Dressed like Emma Peel, she looked great. She smiled at me and continued dancing with Spike. Meanwhile, I danced up a storm trying to compete with Spike, who was a showman, hoping to have Joan notice me. I'm not sure it worked though.

When we left, we hopped in my canary 1966 Chevy Malibu Coupe. It had a back seat so I was surprised when both of them slid in the front with Joan sitting next to me.

The Red Lion was located just off I-405 so it was easy to get on the freeway. From there we could take I-90 and be in Seattle at Spike's office in about 20 minutes.

Spike and Joan were much more intoxicated than I was, and neither one was making much sense. When we reached the end of I-90 and the turn for 4th Ave South, Joan said, "Let's get some booze."

There was a liquor store kitty corner from where we were. Spike knew where it was. "Pull into that parking lot over there, Paul, he commanded."

It was about 1:30 AM and I was getting tired of cavorting around with a couple of drunks and wanted to go home. I had some serious studying to do the next day for a test on Monday.

"Okay," I agreed, unenthusiastically.

Spike jumped out of the car and headed for the liquor store entrance. Joan rolled down the passenger's side window and yelled, "Get some Budweiser too."

She then slid back alongside me. "You drink Bud, right?"

"Yeah," I said.

"That's what I thought," she said, watching for Spike.

For some strange reason, neither one of us said a word as Joan continued to sit right next to me. The tension was unbearable. I felt like I was going to burst.

A few interminably long minutes later, Spike came out and got into the car and then Joan glanced at the bag. "Did you get Paul's Budweiser?" she asked.

“Was I supposed to?” Spike retorted.

“Yeah,” Joan snapped, “didn’t you hear me?”

"No, were you telling me something?" he asked.

"How could you not hear me?" Joan grumbled. "I was shouting at you."

"Alright, I'll buy Paul some goddamn Budweiser," Spike said, sarcastically.

Before Spike could get out of the car I stopped him. "No, no that's okay," I said, dismissively. "I don't want any beer. I'm going home after I drop you guys off."

I started the car and within a minute or two we pulled into the parking lot in front of Spike’s business. The place was dark other than an outdoor security light and a small light upstairs where my office had been while managing Mojo Hand. The office doubled as a studio apartment and was equipped with a bathroom, shower, small refrigerator and wet bar. Spike lived there off and on. If he was living there then, or had just had come there to pick up his car and party with Joan I didn't know.

The two tried their best to get me to come up and drink with them, but I declined and left. It wasn’t that I didn’t want to visit with Joan, it was just that I didn’t want to be with her and Spike at the same time.

Little did I know then, when I pulled away in my Malibu, is that years later I would be spending lots of time with Joan in a different way when I began filming her story.

SPELLBINDING

Redmond, WA to Lost Prairie, MT: July, 2010

At 5:30 AM on July 28th, 2010 Susan and I left our home in Redmond and headed for Lost Prairie.

About thirty minutes later, we met my Director of Photography, Mark Anderson at a Shell Station in the town of North Bend. Looking back on it, it was fitting that we met there, because it was where scenes of David Lynch's movie "Twin Peaks" were filmed, along with the TV series that Mark had worked on.

Mark and I had been friends for twenty-five years, meeting in a film class at Shoreline Community College in 1985. Afterwards we had worked together on two movies, national commercials, and collaborated on several short films.

In the nineties he moved to L.A. where he worked as a 1st AC (Assistant Cameraman) on numerous movies and commercials. That's where he met and became friends with Mickey McMullen, another Seattle transplant, who was a production sound recordist. Mark recommended him to do location audio. Based on his recommendation, I hired Mickey.

Like Mark, Mickey was a professional and veteran of countless movies and commercials in L.A.

After gassing up our cars, Mark got back in his sipping on a Grande' sized cup of coffee. Predictably, about forty minutes later we needed to stop at Snoqualmie Pass for a "pit stop".

At this rate we'll get there in about a week after the boogie has ended, I said, shaking my head in disbelief as Susan and Mark walked together into a Texaco.

And wouldn't you know it the two came out each holding a cup of coffee.

I got out of our tan colored Ford Escape. "Alright, that's it, no more coffee," I grumbled. "I want to be in Lost Prairie by 3:00, and we still have to pick up Mickey."

"Just a second," Susan said, pulling out her cell phone, "let's get a few pictures here first before we get underway."

I was becoming a little perturbed. "It's a parking lot at Snoqualmie Pass," I said, facetiously. "We've made it 40 miles, and we've got 420 more to go."

"Don't you want to document it?" retorted Susan taking a picture of Mark.

"We're making a documentary about Joan Carson, not about us," I said, as she took a photo of me.

"You never know," Susan said, snapping another picture.

"Susan's right," Mark said, "behind the scenes pictures never hurt. It might come in handy someday."

As it turned out, both of them were right, documenting the making of the film would come in handy later.

We got underway and followed Mark who was driving a black Jeep Grand Cherokee with a KZOK bumper sticker (call letters for a Seattle rock and roll station) on its rear window. We caravanned all the way to Missoula Airport, only stopping twice along the way to gas up, pee, and grab sub sandwiches at Subway. We pulled into the airport in the afternoon at 1:00 as planned, where Mark spotted Mickey waiting outside for us.

After a brief meet and greet with Mickey, Susan and I got back in our vehicle and were on the road again following Mark and Mickey.

"He seems like a nice guy," I said, to Susan as we headed towards Kalispell.

"Yeah, he seems really nice," Susan said -- and it turned out that Mickey was.

Driving northward, we passed Flathead Lake and I went over a list of questions I wanted Susan to ask all of the interviewees. From that point on she could improvise. I pretended to be a skydiver and she interviewed me. Doing this role playing helped me fine tune the questions, and her anticipate their responses when we finally got around to interviewing the skydivers.

Passing through Kalispell, I was struck by how much it reminded me of Medford, except that it was greener and had more trees.

Heading west on Highway 2, lumber trucks and jacked up four wheel drive pickup trucks, which had crawled through town, now raced down the two-lane highway. Every now and then we would see white crosses alongside the shoulders reminding us of how deadly this road was. It didn't seem to slow down the locals one bit.

Twenty-eight miles out of Kalispell, and about half a mile past Lake McGregor Resort, we turned right off Highway 2 onto Lost Prairie Road and headed north on a gravel road. Lost Prairie was only six miles away. My heart was racing with excitement and anxiety, and my mind was foggy like the dusty rooster tail kicked up from Mark and Mickey's SUV we followed.

"Man, this place is remote," I said to Susan, shaking my head. "Why would anybody come all the way out here to skydive?"

"That's a good question that we need to find out the answer to. I'll jot it down so I don't forget it," Susan said, and then wrote in her spiral bound notebook.

Fifteen minutes later, the deciduous trees lining the road gave way to a beautiful valley surrounded by tree covered hills. My question was answered. Lost Prairie was like a mirage. Hidden away from civilization this pristine valley was the Garden of Eden. You didn't have to be a skydiver to appreciate it, but it helped because there was little else to do there except skydive.

Initially, I was offended though seeing so many cars, tents, RVs, airplanes, and people when we arrived. I was irritated. It was a carnival that was out of place; much like some of the rock festivals I had gone to as a teenager. And then I was mesmerized by the sight of so many parachutes flitting across the big blue sky *like butterflies above our nation.* I was awestruck. I had never seen anything like it, and was suddenly a convert. It was a magical embrace of this prairie lost in the wilderness, where time stood still and the only thing that mattered at the moment was skydiving. I tried to imagine Joan being there 30 years ago, but couldn't. Skydiving was alien to me and so was living in the wilderness. Remote as it was now, it must have been even more isolated back then.

I was now in Joan's world and was excited by the beehive of activity and characters, and felt uneasy because of the uncertainties that go along with making a film, and knowing what had happened to her. I couldn't get the thought out of my mind that she had died right on this prairie where skydivers were currently landing, and laughing. I tried to imagine what was going through her mind as she fell. What were her last thoughts? Other than fear, I wondered whether she had thought about what I had said. That was almost eight years after the fact so probably not. More than likely, she had long forgotten what I had said then, but almost forty years later I hadn't.

The following excerpt is some of my narration from the film:

When the first boogies started at Lost Prairie, they would get about 60 skydivers who would jump out of single-engine Cessna (a small private airplane). Today they attract 300 - 500 skydivers from all over the world who jump out of de Havilland Twin Otters (a mid-size twin-engine commercial aircraft).

Unbeknownst to us, two hours before we arrived in Lost Prairie there had been a fatality. It goes without saying that nobody wanted to be interviewed by a film crew.

We finally learned of the tragedy and felt horrible for coming across so insensitively.

We explained to those to whom we had spoken that we had just arrived and had been unaware of the accident. Gradually, we won their trust due in large part to my wife Susan's warm personality and wonderful diplomatic skills.

But we couldn't get over the irony that we had come to Lost Prairie to make a film about Joan Carson, who had died on the same field almost thirty years earlier, and two hours before we arrived there was another skydiving fatality...Admittedly, it was surreal, even more so by the fact that it was only the third skydiving fatality to occur there since Joan helped found Lost Prairie.

While Mark, Mickey and I set up our equipment in a pasture at the northern end of the runway, about 100 yards beyond the Osprey's homemade hangar building and lounge, Susan went looking for Zimmo. I had emailed him and received a reply that he would be there for the boogie.

Linda and Mike Groarke, I learned after we arrived, were busy during the weekend and would not be available to be interviewed after all.

Fred Sand said he was tied up managing the boogie along with his tandem skydiving business, where novices jump strapped to an instructor, while Dick Steinke was busy cooking in The Lounge's restaurant, which he co-owned with Dave. Neither Fred nor Steinke could be interviewed until the next day. What I had thought would be a productive afternoon looked like it would nearly be a bust. I was disappointed, but at least we would be able to get our feet wet with Zimmo, who had jumped with Joan at Beagle Sky Ranch in Medford.

Now that we had finished setting up, Mark, Mickey and I spent time watching skydivers swoop through the azure sky and land on freshly cut prairie grass. A ribbon of pine trees around the perimeter fenced in the steppe of grasslands providing the perfect background for our viewing. It was spellbinding. The jumpers made it look so easy and safe.

Perhaps part of the allure of skydiving is that when done correctly it looks graceful and harmless. How could something so peaceful be so dangerous? It has been said that there's about a one in a million chance that you will die on any given jump. What many skydivers overlook, or ignore, is that the more you jump the greater the risk you will be the person to die. It's like getting older; the older you get the more likely you are going to die. The probability goes up. If you were to make a million jumps you would be dead – guaranteed. So, if you make ten thousand jumps, then your odds would be one in a hundred on every jump you do that you will be fatally injured – not the kind of odds I like. That's the reason every now and then you read about skydivers with nine or ten thousand jumps dying. *How could it happen, they had so much experience?*

Doom and gloom aside, watching the jumpers free fall and then circle overhead like hawks looking for mice in the prairie grass, I was better able to understand how Joan must have felt when she saw her first skydivers. It must have seemed enchanting, even though parachutes back then were round and clunky and not nearly as navigable as the modern ones we were watching in Lost Prairie.

It wasn't long before Susan interrupted our gawking at the skydivers by showing up with Zimmo who was smoking a cigarette, wearing a white tee-shirt and holding an opened sixteen ounce can of beer. She was laughing at something he was telling her, so I knew right away that he was going to be a great interviewee.

As it turned out, Zimmo was a character and gave a rock star performance, enthralling us with countless stories and making us laugh with his wisecracking sense of humor. Delivered with the rapidity of a machine gun, his interview lasted so long that we ran out of sufficient daylight and halted him. I asked if he could come back and finish up the following day, and he said he would.

We said goodbye to Zimmo, packed up the expensive equipment, leaving our awning, chairs, sand bags, C-Stands (a multi-purpose stand used to hold lights, reflectors etc.) and other film gear, and then headed back to Kalispell to check into the Red Lion Hotel.

That night I bought takeout pizza at Moose's Saloon across the street. The joint was totally unexpected. The exterior was done up in an old west pine facade with the word 'Saloon' painted in white western lettering on a sign hanging perpendicular to the building. Behind it was a horizontal sign on the face of the building with the same word, only in black lettering. I walked through swinging saloon-style doors and suddenly felt like I had been transported back to the 1800s. The wooden walls and booths were plastered with chiseled initials, hearts, Dick loves Jane -- and so on, and random thoughts. The chairs and bench seats were upholstered with orange seat cushions and the table tops and bar were painted bright red. It looked like a cross between an old western saloon and a cat house. As I walked to the counter to order pizza, my shoes crunched on peanut shells littering the wooden floor.

I ordered two large pizzas. While I waited, I sat at the bar, had a beer and munched on peanuts, tossing the shells on the floor like a local. Unbeknownst to me at that time, Moose's Saloon had been a favorite hangout of the Osprey Parachute Club and Joan.

I delivered one of the pizzas to Mark and Mickey's room, where they were charging batteries and copying the day's audio and video files onto a computer, and then backing them up on an external drive. I thanked them for the great job they'd done and they returned the compliment. They were just as excited as Susan and I about Zimmo's interview, and said they were looking forward to tomorrow's interviews. I said goodnight and went to my room where Susan was writing in her journal about the day's activities. I told her about Moose's Saloon and she said that we should go there for a beer the following night, which we did.

REVEALING

Lost Prairie, Montana: July, 2010

On Saturday morning we tried our best to eat the God awful complimentary breakfast at the hotel cafeteria while we had a production meeting covering the day's schedule. Nothing seemed to taste good.

Close to 9:00 AM we arrived at Lost Prairie finding the settlement coming to life. It had been a late night, featuring the *Cock Chorus* where guys take their clothes off and sing raunchy songs about women and sex. The following night women reciprocate with the *Crack Chorus* singing about men and their penises. It had been a tradition since the beginning of the Osprey Club.

While the village on the prairie was still awakening, we got shots of a few early bird skydivers practicing their maneuvers on the ground (called dirt diving), boarding planes, skydiving, packing parachutes, eating breakfast, brushing their teeth, washing their faces, and just hanging out with their buddies. In some ways it was like a high school reunion on steroids. In other ways it was like a family reunion, which is probably more appropriate because, if anything, skydivers considered themselves to be a family. It was a term we heard often.

That afternoon we continued our interview with Zimmo who was clean shaven, having showered the night before at a friend's cabin rental at McGregor Lake Resort. Living out of his camper, he hadn't bathed in the three or four days he'd been there. He cleaned up quite nicely, although I felt that his grizzled look fit better with his roguish personality. As it turned out, I edited a lot of the clean-cut Zimmo scenes out of the film, using just his voice over B-Roll footage.

B-Roll is generally non-narrative shots used to reinforce narrations, whether they be talking heads or voice overs. Often used as a means of cutting away from "talking-heads" during an interview, it can also be pieced together to create a montage under a voice over, or with just music.

Zimmo talked about meeting Joan at Beagle Sky Ranch in 1974, when he as a student at Southern Oregon University in Ashland, about fifteen miles south of Medford. The two hit it off and became great friends. Joan had finally met somebody who was as wild as she. They also shared an emotional bond that I wouldn't understand until later.

For many years, Zimmo belonged to an aerial circus where jumpers flew in formation stacked on top of each other. It was dangerous, but at the time he was fearless and was all about taking risks. On one occasion, he jumped out of an airplane more than seventeen thousand feet above sea level over Crater Lake, Oregon. He was so high he had to use oxygen and could see the Pacific Ocean one hundred miles away. His goal was to skydive 22 miles in the jet stream all the way to Medford. He almost made it, landing one mile short of the Medford Airport. In the process, he set a world's record and suffered frostbite on his fingers. It was during his years in the aerial circus that Zimmo got his nickname, his real name being, Richard Zimmerman.

When we asked Zimmo if he had ever had any parachute malfunctions, he remembered one in particular where he was on his back and pulled the ripcord. When his main parachute opened, it wrapped around him in what's called a *Horseshoe Malfunction* because it resembles a horse shoe. Half goes up one side and the rest goes up the other. You are literally lassoed in a parachute straight jacket. "It prevents you from doing a cutaway (where you discard your main parachute), and then pulling your reserve," said Zimmo, "so unless you can get if off you, you're dead."

He managed to get it untangled enough to pull his reserve. When he did this his main parachute, which was streaming above rained down on him and he gathered it up. Shaken, he was grateful to be alive and learned a lesson to never pull the ripcord again if he was on his back.

Zimmo talked about Joan's double malfunction, about his friendship with her and the impact her death had on him. When he talked about it he broke down, causing us to stop for several minutes while he composed himself. Rodney Holberton would inform me later that Zimmo had an unrequited crush on Joan and was devastated when she died.

We finished our interview with him and wished him well. He no longer skydives because of a chronic leg injury he's sustained over the years due to the jolt sustained when a parachute opens during free fall. Before he left, he invited us to visit him any time we were in the Sacramento area, an offer Susan and I would take several years later.

We broke for lunch, eating at the Lost Prairie Lounge. It was a typical pub grub and tasted great after the unsatisfying breakfast.

Susan used the time to mix with the locals, along with talking Fred and Stinky into afternoon interviews. She was definitely our ambassador of goodwill, and being good looking didn't hurt. Otherwise, I'm pretty sure it would have been next to impossible for me to get Fred and Stinky over to our set.

Stinky had to finish cooking lunch at The Lounge before he would be available. He figured that would be around 2:00 PM. As for Fred, he was much harder to pin down, and gave us the impression that he was doing us a favor, not the other way around.

As organizer of the boogie for the past 40 years, Fred was sort of a local celebrity and was accustomed to being interviewed by newspapers and television stations. There wasn't any reason he would have heard about my production company, Rain City Cinema, other than checking out the blog site printed on the business card Susan had given him. If he had checked it out, it's doubtful he would have been overly impressed. The blog was something I had created on *Blogger* for free. It wasn't that it looked shoddy, it just didn't look like a professional website. Everything considered, I don't think he felt there was much in it for him. Also, the day we had gotten there, somebody told me that several years earlier another filmmaker had attempted to make a documentary about Lost Prairie and never completed it. Fred might have felt that our production would end up with the same fate. I'd be surprised if he showed up after Stinky's interview.

A teddy bear of a man, Stinky had a fatherly presence about him and a gentle sense of humor. His sandy brown hair was graying along the temples and so was his mustache. Wearing glasses and a tan checkered cotton short-sleeve shirt with a white tee-shirt under it, Stinky looked relaxed as if he was sitting in his own yard. Actually he was. He co-owns the *community property* at Lost Prairie, and lives there too.

Many of the skydivers have nicknames so Susan wanted to find out his real name. Right off the bat she asked him for his name.

"My full name is Richard Steinke, but most people call me Stinky," he said, grinning slyly. "So I go by Dick. And I say you can call me Dick, and you can call me Stinky, but don't call me Stinky Dick."

Mark, Mickey and I laughed at Stinky's unexpected play on his name while Susan grimaced. "Okay," she said, "let's move on."

Stinky, quickly changed the subject by saying he works for the Department of Defense, as well as co-owning The Lounge with Dave. He learned to skydive in 1971 with a college student named Steve (Armo) Armitage at the City Airport in Kalispell when he was eighteen. Stinky joined the Osprey Parachute Club, where he and Dave owned the airplanes and Fred ran the Skydive business that taught beginners how to skydive.

I came away from our interview with him feeling like he was the foundation of Lost Prairie. It's safe to say that Joan trusted him like a big brother or uncle, because she came to him often for advice on how to build her house and subdivide her land.

We wrapped up our interview with Stinky and let him get back to The Lounge to fix dinner. In the meantime, we waited for Fred to show up while we charged batteries and downloaded files onto Susan's laptop and an external drive.

About half an hour later I asked Susan to check on Fred.

She took off to get Fred, while Mark, Mickey and I watched the skydivers zipping through the sky. It was exciting. As thrilling as it seemed though, I had no desire to ever do it myself. When we first arrived Susan wanted to give it a try but then she heard about the fatality, and changed her mind. As it turned out, Mark made several jumps when we got back to the Seattle area, but gave it up after he injured himself when he landed too hard. I never did hear if Mickey ever jumped, even though he said he would probably give it a try someday.

It was about 3:30 in the afternoon when Susan returned without Fred.

"Where is he?" I asked, impatiently.

"He said he'll be here in fifteen minutes. I can't do anything else."

"Hey, I'm not blaming you. I'm just wondering whether he's giving you a line. He was supposed to be here at 3:00 and it’s 3:30 now. We're running out of daylight."

"Maybe you should go talk to him then," Susan said.

"Yeah, Paul, maybe he'll listen to you," Mark said.

"He doesn't like men, he likes good looking women, "I said. "You should've seen him trying to sweet talk Susan into doing a tandem jump with him."

"So how did you get out of it?" Mickey asked Susan.

"She said, only if you jump with my husband first," Mark quipped.

"Ooh," said Mickey, chuckling. "That would be nasty."

"Especially if you're on the bottom," Mark said, laughing.

I cast Mark and Mickey stern glances and they got the message. They were practical jokers and liked to kid around at somebody else's expense, especially Susan's. She frequently got into it with them and then it would get to the point where she would tell them to knock it off. As for me, I didn't spar with them. All I had to do was give them the *evil eye* and they would knock it off. Usually though, I just ignored them and they lost interest.

There was a brief period of awkward silence and then Susan broke the ice. "Okay," she said, "if he's not here in fifteen minutes I'll go get him."

"If you flirt with him, he'll do anything you want," I said.

"Do I have to?" Susan said, scrunching her face.

"Only if you want to," I said, patting her on the shoulder, "but it'll probably work."

"Do it Susan. Do it," Mark said, jokingly.

"Yeah," Mickey chimed, "it's the way things get done in Hollywood."

"Well, this isn't Hollywood," Susan said, "and I've got my scruples. This film needs to get made, so I'm only doing it for the film."

Ten minutes passed and there was still no sight of Fred. Susan sighed, and then trudged off for Fred's office.

Mark and Mickey entertained themselves by placing bets on whether or not she would be successful. Fifteen minutes later she showed up with Fred. He was beaming at Susan who was laying on the charm.

Mark and Mickey grinned at each other and Mickey pointed at Mark and mouthed, *You owe me.*

No that makes us even, Mark pantomimed back.

I introduced Fred to Mark and Mickey, showed him where to sit, and explained that the interview should take about an hour.

"Before we get underway," I said, holding a clipboard and pen, "I need you to sign a release form."

"I'm familiar with them," Fred said, smugly. "I've done quite a few of these things."

"That's good," I said. "Then this should be easy for you."

Fred grinned impassively as he signed the release form and handed it back to me.

"Okay, let's get on with the interview," I said. "Susan will be doing the interviewing."

"We've met," said Fred, needling me, and then turning to smile at Susan. Mark and Mickey exchanged knowing glances.

"That's good," I said.

Mark adjusted the focus on his cameras. "You look really good on film, Fred," he said, flatteringly.

Fred beamed showing off a mouthful of crooked white teeth. He wore a black stocking cap, and a green 'Dale Jr.' hooded sweatshirt. His face was tan, contrasting with his grey mustache and light, copper colored, rimmed glasses. He looked relaxed and confident.

In addition to running the boogie and the skydiving center Fred informed us that he was also a certified parachute rigger, and had learned to skydive when he was 18 while his parents were out of town.

The veteran of more than 8,000 jumps Fred is in a league of his own when it comes to skydivers in Montana. Regarded as being an expert jumper, instructor, and rigger, skydivers send him their reserve chutes from all over the country to repack.

Our interview with Fred lasted about forty-five minutes. He was polished and well-rehearsed. But he came across as slightly disingenuous and overly protective of Lost Prairie and Joan. His characterization of her contradicted with what Zimmo had told us earlier.

During his interview Fred, said that Joan was not much of a partier or risk taker, and had done everything right on her fatal jump. In contrast, Zimmo asserted she was a risk taker and partier, and that she had borrowed a parachute for her last jump. I was left believing Zimmo.

A little later, Fred would give us a history lesson on skydiving saying the sport was started shortly after World War II by former paratroopers.

“After living out great adventures jumping out of airplanes as paratroopers, they came home wanting to get that same kind of adrenalin rush," Fred lectured. "They would buy a surplus parachute, find someone at the local airport, and they would take them up high enough to where they thought their parachute would open and they would jump.”

Fred continued, saying there was very little information gathering and instruction in those days, referring to it as the *barnstorming days of skydiving*. “Later on, during the 50s, it became much more standardized -- training procedures came into place, and techniques to control yourself during the freefall were developed.” Over the years the equipment improved. Gone were the round military surplus parachutes, Joan learned on, which were replaced by airfoils designed by skydivers. The new designs were much safer, and gave jumpers maximum performance to the point where they could land exactly where they wanted.

“Training techniques have changed tremendously from count to ten and pull,” Fred explained, “to now some very sophisticated programs that can take someone who’s never jumped out of an airplane and in as few as seven jumps get them to the point where they can do everything themselves without instructors and do it quite safely.”

Going on, he would say that personality wise, the sport has changed too, from the rugged guys during the ‘50s and ‘60s compared to today. “You don’t need to be rough and tough to skydive,” said Fred. “We see people from all walks of life come and join in with the sport now.”

When Fred finally left, we talked about his interview and agreed that he had only told us what he wanted us to hear. As knowledgeable and as much of an expert as he was, it had been somewhat of a frustrating, interview. Was he hiding something?

While Susan had been in the skydiving office trying to persuade Fred to come for his interview, Dave had been there too. She overhead his name and introduced herself and asked if he would like to be interviewed. He said he would and that he'd be there at 6:00.

Now that we had finished interviewing Fred we hung out waiting for Joan's old boyfriend Dave. Portrayed as an *amazing character* by Joan's brother Barrie, in one of his emails, my expectation was: *if he is half as good as Zimmo, this is going to be a great interview.*

While we waited for Dave, Mark and Mickey backed up their files and recharged batteries. 6:00 PM rolled around and there was no sign of Dave. By 6:30 there still was no sight of him. Suddenly, Susan hooted, "There he is, he just drove by and is turning around!"

We watched a pickup truck make a U-turn and then drive past us heading in the opposite direction.

"Was that him?!” I asked.

"I think so," Susan said. "He must be looking for parking and will be here any second now."

Ten minutes passed and Dave was nowhere to be seen.

"Are you sure it was him?" I said.

"Oh, I don't know now," Susan said, "I'm pretty sure it was, but I didn't get a good look at the guy in the truck."

"Maybe it was Dave and he didn't see us," said Mickey.

"Yeah, said Mark, "our tent looks like we're camping here."

"That's probably it," said Susan, “we're a really small film crew and he might have been looking for something bigger.”

"Okay," I said, "it's obvious he's not coming back, so let's call it a wrap. We'll see about interviewing him tomorrow."

We got back to the hotel, and then all of us grabbed a few beers at Moose’s Saloon. Afterwards, Susan and I went to dinner at an Italian restaurant downtown. We talked about the interviews and made adjustments to the list of questions I had come up with. Even though Susan was a natural at interviewing, I felt that there were additional questions we could ask. We had learned a lot in a short amount of time, and were improving each day.

The next morning we again ate breakfast downstairs, checked out of the hotel and drove out to Lost Prairie arriving at 9:30 AM. Today was our final day before we headed back to Seattle that afternoon. We spent much of the morning shooting more B-Roll while Susan looked for Dave and hung out with the locals, meeting Sam Scott who had jumped with Joan and owned a cabin there at Lost Prairie. He wanted to be interviewed, but we were running out of time.

Originally, I had thought we would be able to accomplish all of the filming at Lost Prairie in a single weekend, but it was now evident we wouldn't be able to do it, and would need to come back later to interview Sam Scott, Linda and Mike Groarke, and Bill Paulin -- who I had called while we were there. With the exception of Sam, all of the others hadn’t been available that weekend.

Susan continued looking for Dave and ran into him in The Lounge, confirming that he had driven past us last night, but thought we were campers. He said he wanted to be interviewed and would see us later in the day at the same spot. Hearing this, we set up our equipment again and waited for him. Again it was a waste of time. We sat there for at least an hour waiting. Mark and Mickey entertained themselves by bantering back and forth and teasing Susan. Eventually she snapped, accusing them of being less mature than the three year old kids at the preschool she directed. She would use the same admonishment from time to time to get them to back off. It worked, but invariably it would flare up again when Mark and Mickey got bored. Having worked on big budget films for years, they were used to having things well scheduled and became impatient when things weren't.

I asked Susan if she would go to the office to see if Dave was there and she snapped back at me, "Why don't you go yourself."

"Because I don't know what he looks like, and you do," I said, "Besides, you've already talked to him."

"Alright, this is the last time. Next time you go talk to people yourself if you want them to be in your film," Susan said, getting up with a sigh and then walking off towards the office.

About ten minutes later she returned. "He wasn't there so Fred called him at home and he's on his way. He'll be here in fifteen minutes."

Again we waited, and again he didn't show up. About half an hour later I got up from the chair I was sitting in. "Alright, he's not coming," I sighed. "Let's go home."

We broke down the set, packed our cars, said goodbye to a few people, and informed Fred that we would be back sometime in the near future.

About 5:00 PM we pulled out of Lost Prairie and headed for the long drive to Seattle. Along the way we dropped Mickey off at Glacier Park International Airport six miles northeast of Kalispell, exchanging hugs and wishing him well.

The night was clear during our long drive home. We followed Mark all the way to Preston, where we split up. While we drove through the high desert plateau in Eastern Washington, we watched the aurora borealis put on a psychedelic light show in the northern sky. It was quite a spectacle and felt like an appropriate homage to Joan and the filming we had done.

PLANNING

Redmond, WA: August, 2010

Being that it was August 1st, it was still warm about 1:30 AM when Susan and I pulled to a stop at the bottom of our driveway. Our first road trip to Lost Prairie had been exhilarating and exhausting. We were so tired that, other than my IMac computer we left all of the other equipment in the car, and went inside the house. It felt good to be home. Over the next month, I spent time logging footage.

Concurrently, I started planning our next road trip. On August 10, 2010, I sent Joan's brother, Barrie, an email informing him of our progress and letting him know we would be filming in San Francisco on August 24 and 25, and would like to interview him then.

Two days later, Barrie responded to my email saying August 24 was out of the question because he would be in Costa Rica, arriving late that evening and was hoping we could do the interview the following evening.

Not wanting to make a separate trip to San Francisco just to interview him, I tried again to nail down a time with him and make it fit with our interviews in Medford.

On Thursday, August 12, 2010, I responded to Barrie from our Ames Lake home in Redmond with the following email:

Our sound guy (Mickey) needs to be at SFO no later than 6:30 PM on August 25 in order to fly back to LA. Is there any chance we can interview you at your work -- preferably in the afternoon? If that isn't convenient, then we could do it at my sister's place in the Glen Park area, but we would have to wrap no later than 5:00 PM in order to get Mickey to the airport.

Later that day I received a reply from Barrie, saying that Glen Park was too far for him to go, and maybe we could do the interview at his office. He then went on to ask how long it would take.

I was getting frustrated trying to schedule Barrie's interview, and was beginning to wonder if he didn't want to be interviewed at all.

Less than twenty-four hours later I sent him another email from Redmond:

We will need you for an hour and it will take approximately 1 to 1-1/2 hours to set up and 30 minutes to wrap. If it's less of an impact, we can shoot outdoors as long as it's quiet and visually attractive.

Hope this works. If it's too much of an inconvenience I can see about changing Mickey's flight.

Barrie didn't respond. Annoyed as I was by my email exchange trying to pin him down, I gambled and decided to forge ahead anyway. I already had interviews set with skydivers Linda and Mike Groarke, Sam Scott, and Bill Paulin in Lost Prairie. In Medford, I had scheduled Beagle Sky Ranch owner George Holberton, and three other skydivers who had jumped with Joan. Satisfied that I had planned the shoots the best I could, we departed Redmond on August 20, 2010. Mickey had arrived two days earlier spending both nights at Mark's place.

Having been initiated by our first visit to Lost Prairie, it felt good to be underway. I looked forward to round two of my quest and our adventure.

SOBERING

Lost Prairie, Montana: August 20, 2010

When we arrived in Lost Prairie on our second road trip, we stopped first to check into the Lake McGregor Resort where I had rented two cabins -- one for Susan and me, the other for Mark and Mickey to share. Their cabin was called, *The Lake House* and came furnished with a full bed, bunk beds and a sofa couch. It didn't have running water or a bathroom, so if they needed to use one or get water they had to go outside and use a communal restroom, where they could also shower. Susan's and my cabin was called, *The Cottage* and came furnished with a king sized bed, and the luxury of a bathroom. Both cabins were old and musty with lots of mosquitoes outside, and a few inside. For some reason mosquitoes love Susan. Fortunately, we had brought along insect repellant and she put it on. Still she got bitten and complained. Mark and Mickey didn't complain. Their attitude seemed to be that it was all a grand adventure they'd tell their grandkids about someday.

The resort was only eight miles away from Lost Prairie. Being that close meant we could be there in about fifteen minutes, which was much better than the 45 minute drive from the Red Lion in Kalispell, where we had stayed previously.

Late that afternoon, we drove to Lost Prairie to interview Sam Scott and Bill Paulin. Mark wanted The Lounge in the background so we set up outside it in between a dirt road and the runway. It was the *Magic Hour* and the late summer sun cast a warm glow over the golden prairie grass and hand cut pine siding of the rustic structure giving it a nostalgic feel.

Just before we were ready to interview Sam Scott, Bill Paulin arrived in grand fashion. Flying in with a friend, he landed alongside us while Mickey was doing his sound check, and Mark was setting focus and exposure on his two Canon 5D cameras.

What a great way to get around, I thought to myself. I loved their freedom and independence. It was so different than the semi-rural lifestyle I was used to, and raised in.

Paulin and his friend got out of the plane and sauntered over to us. Swilling on a beer, Paulin introduced himself.

"I'm Bill Paulin and this is my designated pilot," he said patting his friend on the shoulder.

Looking at Mark, he said, "You must be Paul Gorman."

"No, that's Paul over there," Mark said, pointing at me.

"Could've fooled me," said Paulin, taking a swig from his beer.

"Don't worry about it," I said, gesturing nervously. "He's got a camera and I'm just going over questions we'll be asking you."

Paulin tensed a little. "So, you're the one I talked with on the phone," he retorted.

"Yeah, that's right," I said, extending a hand.

Paulin shook my hand. "So, why're you making this film about Joan?" he asked. "I'm really curious. People here still remember her. They loved her. You'd better be making a film that pays respect to her because we all sure did. I've got to take a leak, and will be over at The Lounge hanging out with some friends when you're ready."

"Okay, we'll let you know," I said, as Paulin headed towards The Lounge with his "designated pilot."

"Whew, he's a piece of work," said Susan shaking her head.

Mickey and Mark shot glances at each other, and tried to hold back laughter. "This here is my designated pilot," they said, in unison.

"It's a good thing he's not driving," said Susan.

"Yeah," said Mickey, "and it's a good thing he's not the pilot."

"You mean, we're better off if he's on the ground," Mark joined in.

It wasn't long before Susan seated Sam Scott and we got his interview rolling. Clad in a bright red western shirt and black Stetson hat, he grinned behind his light brown handlebar mustache. When we had met him on our first trip, he seemed relaxed and friendly, now he seemed nervous and measured. Every so often his mustache twitched involuntarily. Maybe he was camera shy, or perhaps he had been coached on what to say. But he definitely wasn't the same congenial person we had met earlier. Something had changed.

Sam told us he worked as a barber in Kalispell and owned property at Lost Prairie. He wasn't retired yet, so for the most part, he only spent weekends at his property.

When Joan was alive, Sam had jumped with her. Several years ago he broke a leg skydiving and had to hang it up. He planned to do it again after he was fully mended.

We finished our interview with Sam who seemed relieved to be done, and thanked him for coming.

"Let me know when the film is going to be showing, I'd really like to see it," Sam said, his lips barely visible behind his mustache."

"I will Sam, the plan is to screen it here at next year's boogie to commemorate the 30th anniversary of Joan's passing," I said. "There will be two screenings: one for everybody that's in the film, including her family, and one for the public. Of course, you'll be invited to the private screening."

Sam smiled appreciatively. We thanked him, and then he wandered off towards The Lounge looking like a lonely cowboy wearing his Sunday best duds.

"Poor Sam," Susan said, sympathetically, "he was so nervous. I tried everything I could to relax him."

"Yeah, what a sweet guy," I said.

"Somebody got to him and told him what to say," Mickey said, taking off his headphones.

"Yeah, he was nothing like that when we talked to him at The Lounge a month ago," I added.

"They're hiding something," said Mark changing lenses on the cameras.

"Like what?" I probed.

I already had my suspicions, but wanted opinions from the crew.

"They're protecting Dave, circling the wagons around him," Mark said, glancing at me from the lens side of the cameras.

"Yeah," Mickey said, "wagon's ho!"

They might be right, the stories we were getting from old timers didn't jive with the interviews. Off record, we were getting hints that Dave and Joan had a rocky relationship. On camera, they were the perfect couple — the royal family – the Kennedys. Then there were inconsistencies about the cause of Joan's death. Some were saying she did everything right, others said she borrowed somebody else's parachute, and a few said someone else had packed her parachute. It didn't add up. The rumors didn't mean something nefarious had happened -- and they were trying to cover it up. It was possible that all of the discrepancies could just be the result of fading memories. After all, it had been almost thirty years since her death.

"We need to interview Dave," Susan said. "He's the only one who knows what really happened that day."

"I know," I said, "but he hasn't responded to my emails."

"Call him," Susan said. "I've got his number."

"Alright, I'll call him tomorrow," I said.

About that time Bill Paulin ambled over. Holding a long necked bottle of beer in his hand, he interrupted us.

"Alright, let's get this rodeo started," Paulin said. "What do you want me to do?"

"I'd like you to sit in that chair over there," I said, pointing at a *Director's Chair.* "Susan's going to interview you."

"She's the interviewer?" Paulin said, sarcastically. "I thought she was the makeup person."

Susan bristled.

"She does that too," Mark said. "Throw him a towel Susan so he can wipe the sweat off his face. I'm getting a lot of reflection off it."

Touché' for Mark. Film crews might squabble amongst themselves occasionally, but invariably stick up for each.

"Gladly," Susan said, throwing him a towel.

"Ooh," Paulin said, "feisty filly aren't you?"

"Only when I need to be," Susan said, confidently.

"Yeah, don't cross her, right Paul?" Mark said, teasing Susan.

"Right," she's the boss," I said, diplomatically.

Feeling that the situation was escalating, I handed Paulin a copy of the release form. "I need you to sign this," I stated.

"I'll take it with me and have my attorney look at it first," Paulin said, dismissively.

"No, I need you to sign it before we get started," I said.

Groaning, Paulin set his beer on the ground, signed the document, and then handed it back to me.

I thanked him while he'd picked up his beer and guzzled the last half down. "Okay, hit me with that towel again," Paulin said, after burping.

Susan threw him another towel. "Hang on to it; you're going to need it," she said, smirking.

He wiped the sweat off his face again. "Alright, let's get on with it," he said, tossing the towel on the ground.

Tall and lean, with hawk-like facial features, Paulin wore a black sweatshirt, black "Glacier Bank" baseball cap, and bronze aviator sunglasses. His sunburned face had an unnatural tautness to it.

Paulin told us he had worked as a banker for Glacier Bank, and was now retired. He started skydiving in 1964 and jumped until 1978.

He was one of the original five owners at Lost Prairie and because of his banking expertise was instrumental in putting together the *deal* for Lost Prairie.

The day Joan died, Paulin was at Lost Prairie, and witnessed her fatal fall, providing a sobering account of the event that contrasted sharply with Fred's sanitized version. We were speechless. It felt like it had been something he had wanted to get off his chest for a long time, and his interview provided the opportunity to do it. After four or five beers he had sufficient courage to let it out, and he did. His sobering recollection spewed out like a shaken beer, emptying him. Just as I was still haunted by Joan's death, after all these years, he was too, but even more so. I couldn't imagine what it would have been like to have been here, and to have witnessed what he did.

Shortly after Paulin recanted the events surrounding Joan's death, we finished up his interview. By the time he left, we had a new appreciation for him, and were convinced that there was more to Joan's death than met the eye. It was buried under years of beer soaked memories, rumors, and possibly a cover up. I wasn't sure if we would ever really know the truth about her death and didn't know if it mattered. I wasn't looking for justice, I was looking for an explanation to the meaning of my dream and why she kept skydiving after suffering two accidents. There must have been a reason, and it was still out there. As elusive as it was, I was certain she wanted me to find it.

As we were packing up our gear a little while later, we saw Paulin staggering towards his airplane with his *designated pilot.* Out of the clear blue, he turned to me. "That contract will never hold up in a Montana Court of Law," he yelled. He then got into his plane with his pilot, and we stood there watching them take off.

After they were gone, Susan turned to me. "What was that all about?" she asked.

"I have no idea, I said, "but the contract is binding."

To this day, I've never been able to figure out what Paulin meant by his remark. Perhaps he divulged more information than he wanted and regretted it after he had a little time to think about it, or he was warning me that I was getting too close for comfort and people didn't like me snooping around looking for skeletons in their closet. Not that I had been looking for any. My motivation had been to look for cracks in Joan's emotional state that would explain her destructive behavior, and hopefully explain my dream.

We finished packing up our gear and returned to McGregor Lake Resort. Later that evening we had dinner again in their restaurant and discussed the day's interviews. The consensus was that the community was covering for Dave. But why, what had he done? The community adored Joan, and portrayed their relationship as Camelot. Paulin's description of Joan's final jump had been raw and visceral as he relived the moment she had died.

The following day we resumed our interviews, wanting to learn more about Joan and the place she helped create.

DISPUTE

Lost Prairie, Montana: August 21, 2010

On day two of our second road trip, we arrived back at Lost Prairie mid-morning and hung out at The Lounge waiting for Linda and Mike Groarke to meet us as they had agreed. Half an hour later, they hadn't arrived so Susan and I went to their house. The garage door was open and Linda was working on a painting. An artist, and attractive dishwater blonde, in her late fifties, she seemed surprised to see us. We apologized for the intrusion and introduced ourselves. Susan complimented her on her art. Immediately, Linda softened and I let Susan handle the conversation. Explaining that we had thought we were going to meet them at The Lounge, Susan said we had decided to come to their place when they hadn't showed up there.

"Didn't you get my email," Linda said, putting away supplies. "I've changed my mind. I don't want to be filmed. Maybe Mike does. He's down in the hangar you can go ask him if you'd like."

Linda pointed in the direction of the hangar located at the end of their property down near the road.

"Okay, we'll do that," I said, "but why don't you want to be filmed?"

"I just don't want to see myself on film, that's all," Linda said.

"You look great," Susan said, trying to boost her ego.

"Yeah," I said, "you've got nothing to worry about."

"That's not it," Linda said, "it's just that there's some nasty things going on here, business wise, between us and Fred and I don't feel like being filmed. You know what I mean?"

"We know exactly how you feel," Susan said, "Paul and I had a property dispute with our neighbors that lasted ten years. We finally had to settle it in court."

What Susan said resonated with Linda and she relaxed.

"Okay, Linda said, "you can interview me, but no camera."

"No camera?" I said, surprised.

"No, I'll talk, but I don't want to be filmed," Linda said, closing her garage door.

Susan looked at me and said, "Can we do that?"

I deliberated for a moment. "Yeah, I can edit in B-Roll over her voice," I said. "It'll work as long as we can get an identifying shot of her saying her name and where she lives."

"Would that work for you, Linda?" Susan said.

Linda thought it over briefly. "Okay, as long as it's just that, and we do it here," she said. "This whole mess with Fred has really got me angry. He owes us money for using the airstrip for the boogie and his skydiving business. He lives here but he's not a partner. He rents the airstrip and office from us. He didn't like Joanie and she didn't like him. She knew an opportunist when she saw one."

We thanked Linda and told her we would be back shortly with the rest of our crew and equipment. Along the way we stopped at the Groarke's hangar and introduced ourselves to Mike Groarke, who was working on a Piper Cub airplane, and asked if he'd be willing to let us interview him.

"That'd be fine if Linda is up for it," he said, tightening a bolt with a socket wrench.

We explained that we had talked to Linda and that she had agreed to be interviewed, but off camera only.

"Well, then let's do it," Mike said," soon as I finish working on this wing. It shouldn't take more than forty-five minutes. Does that work for you?"

"Perfect," I said, "it'll take about an hour to set up our equipment and then about half an hour or so to do our interview with Linda."

"Good, that'll give me time to finish up here and get cleaned up. Okay, see you then," said Mike, going back to his work.

Susan and I walked over to The Lounge to fetch Mark and Mickey. An hour later we were ready to interview Linda in her quaint backyard. We were about to get rolling when she reiterated that she didn't want to be filmed except for providing her name and where she lived.

We started the interview by filming Linda's intro, and then Mark shut the cameras off and left the set. After a few minutes I departed the set too thinking that Linda might be more comfortable and forthcoming if fewer of us were there.

While Mark and I were gone, Linda talked about her past, telling Susan she had originally wanted to be a pilot, and decided to learn to skydive because she had heard that single-engine planes sometimes crash. It didn't take long for skydiving to grow on her, and she soon became a regular with Joan -- and a Beagle Boogie Babe at Beagle Sky Ranch.

In the fall of 1975, Linda met Mike in Medford when he flew down to winter over with the Ospreys and skydive. She fell in love with him and they married in June, 1977. Living in Calgary, they bought five acres in Lost Prairie in 1979 where they built their house in 1984, and then moved there for good. They both got their pilot's licenses and bought two planes, which they use today for traveling. In the early years, they took turns skydiving and flying loads of skydivers.

When Joan died, Mike and Linda were still living in Canada. They flew to Lost Prairie for Joan's funeral and celebration of her life.

Linda was devastated by Joan's death. She's never had a lot of friends so it hit her particularly hard. "She was a really good friend. It was like losing a star in the sky," she said, holding back tears.

Even though we only recorded Linda's voice, she never seemed to fully relax and spoke in a monotone voice. Perhaps it was just nerves, or maybe she was guarded in her delivery and the context of what she said because of the current infighting with Fred. Nonetheless, I was disappointed that Joan's closest female skydiving friend hadn't been more forthcoming. I was hoping she would open up and reveal some insight into Joan's innermost thoughts, and help me answer the mystery of my dream, but she didn't.

Just about the time we were wrapping up Linda's interview, Mike showed up and stood to the side listening to her. I noticed that his presence made her slightly uneasy and her responses became more stilted than they had been.

Her reluctance to be filmed on camera might have been little more than a lack of confidence. If that was the case, I felt sorry for her. The Joan I had known, and learned about was nothing like that.

Mike was the opposite of Linda. A garrulous and friendly man with hands more befitting a construction worker than a retired marine engineer, he was born and raised in Canada where he did his first jump with a bunch of friends in 1970. Out of that bunch he was the only jumper who kept at it. He got to know the Ospreys through jump meets in Canada and Kalispell. When he heard they were flying south for the winter he quit his job as an engineer in Alberta and joined them. That is where he met Joan, Zimmo, Linda, and the rest of the gang.

Seated in an Adirondack chair, Mike would occasionally rap his knuckles on the arm rests for emphasis as he talked about the formation of Lost Prairie, the old days of skydiving, the reason the Ospreys moved their operation from Kalispell out to Lost Prairie, and Joan's impact on Lost Prairie.

After about an hour we ended our interview with Mike and bid him and Linda farewell. I was relieved that we were able to interview them, considering several hours earlier it had been up in the air. While we were loading equipment into our SUVs, Mickey came up to me. "I think you've really got something here," he said with a smile.

I was surprised and flattered to hear it coming from a veteran of more than a hundred movies and permanent crew member of *Iron Chef.* While his comment was flattering, I was a little disappointed in Mike and Linda's interviews and the fact that I still hadn't been able to interview Dave.

INVISIBLE

Lost Prairie, Montana: August 21, 2010

Before we left Redmond, Susan had called Dave and he said he would be willing to let us interview him, and for us to call him when we were there. Since our second arrival in Lost Prairie, we had tried calling him several times, but there was no answer.

Finally, after our interview with Mike and Linda, I managed to reach him and he said he would meet us at The Lounge in half an hour. An hour passed and no Dave. So Susan and I went to the skydiving office on the other side of the dirt road and Fred called speaking with Dave's wife. "I've got some people here that want to interview Dave," said Fred. "Is he there?"

There was a pause while Fred listened to Dave's wife and then he said, "He's there, well I'll send them right over."

Fred hung up the phone and turned to us. "His house is the third driveway on the left past the Groarke's," Fred said. "He's there now. If you buy him a six-pack, he'll talk your head off."

We thanked Fred and I bought a six-pack of beer at The Lounge. Susan and I then jumped into our Ford Escape while Mark and Mickey hung out at The Lounge filming the interior, and recording ambient sound.

Susan and I drove past the Groarke's and turned up the third driveway after their place. Dave's house was rustic, made from the same roughhewn hand cut lumber as The Lounge and hangar building. Situated on a hillside beneath a sprinkling of pine trees, it overlooked the valley. "Wow, what a gorgeous view," Susan said, as we got out of our SUV.

"Yeah," I said, noticing a backhoe and bulldozer nearby. "I wonder what the deal is with the construction equipment."

"Somebody, I think it was Sam Scott, said he's a heavy equipment operator."

"Ah, a renaissance man," I said, grabbing the six-pack of beer, "he's a pilot, businessman, developer, heavy equipment operator, former paratrooper, and founder of the Osprey Skydiving Club. Is there anything this guy doesn't do?"

"Well, so far he doesn't grant interviews," Susan said, with a grin.

"Yeah, but that's about to change," I said, patting the six-pack, "we've got the perfect enticement."

When we got to the front door Susan rang the doorbell. We waited a moment, and then she rang it again. We listened intently for any sounds of activity inside. Hearing nothing, she turned to me looking for direction. "Maybe the doorbell isn't working. Try knocking," I said. "There's a car here so somebody's gotta be here."

"Yeah, Fred just talked to his wife and she said they were here," Susan said.

"Okay," I said, "try knocking again. Maybe they're in the back of the house."

Susan knocked again, but there was still no response.

"Maybe we've got the wrong place," I said. "Let's go check with Fred."

We returned to Fred's office and Susan confirmed with him that we had been to the right place. Fred tried calling Dave's place again and there was no answer. He hung up the phone. "We'll they must've left," he said. "They like to go to the bar at Lake McGregor Resort on the weekends. You could always check there."

Susan glanced at me. She was getting tired of trying to track down Dave, and I didn't want to push her too hard. She was a great sport, but could get to the point where she would put the brakes on. When it got to that stage, I knew it was futile to push any further. Besides, it was pretty obvious that he was avoiding us, and even if we did manage to find him, I couldn't force him to let us interview him. Consequently, I abandoned the idea, and decided that since we had finished our interviews in Lost Prairie, there were other things we could do.

A short while later, I arranged for Fred to take Mark and Mickey on a scenic flight over the drop zone where Mark could shoot B-Roll while Mickey recorded wild sounds. My plan was to intercut their footage and audio with in-air skydiving video provided to me by Stinky's son Adam who was a skydiver and aerial cameraman.

While Mickey, Mark, Fred and a pilot went up in a single-engine Cessna 152, Susan and I stayed on the ground filming their takeoff and landing. When the Cessna taxied to a stop, Mark and Mickey jubilantly jumped out of the plane. It had been a treat for them and they were appreciative, anything to keep them happy and occupied and from getting bored.

That evening we rehashed the interviews over dinner at the Hitching Post restaurant in Marion which was about seven miles west of Lake McGregor Resort. The food wasn't all that great, but as usual Mark and Mickey ate anything, and never complained.

We turned in early that night because we had a full day of traveling to Medford ahead of us the next day. Unable to fall asleep, I laid awake part of the night trying to imagine what Lost Prairie and Kalispell had been like when Joan was there. It must have been exciting and wild times for her and the Osprey's.

CREATING

Lake McGregor Resort, MT: August 21, 2010

Laying there in the cabin, at Lake McGregor Resort, my thoughts drifted back to taut faced Bill Paulin's interview. He said that in the late 70's, the Osprey Parachute Club had been dropping as many as fifty loads a day on weekends at the Kalispell City Airport, where they engaged in rowdy behavior, loud parties, mischievous pranks, and public nudity.

Moreover, Mike Groarke had elaborated that back then the Osprey's occupied a house and hangar at the airport. The city classified them to be a public nuisance, and told them to vacate the City Airport. He remembered the eviction well. "We were told to get out of the hangar, with a house attached next to it there, where everybody lived in, and the last jump meet we had in the city, we burnt it down. It was a good party," Mike said, bursting into laughter.

I couldn't stop thinking about what Mike had said and how it irritated me like the mosquito buzzing around our room. As hard as I tried, I couldn't imagine Joan being destructive. The person I had spent time with was wild and fun loving, but not violent. Lying there, it dawned on me he had probably been embellishing an image the Osprey's wanted portrayed. If they had truly been arsonists, intentionally setting fire to structures on city property they would have been arrested and jailed. Since there had been no mention during our interviews that this had ever happened, I came to the conclusion the fire must have been an accident, or a controlled burn and he had exaggerated the event.

Relieved, I was able to put my mind at ease and continued reconstructing some of the things we had learned about the creation of Lost Prairie. With no other place for the Osprey's to jump in Kalispell, Joan and the club decided to chart their own destiny and set about looking for land outside the city. Being a banker, they put Paulin in charge of the Osprey's search and acquisition.

It was hot in the cabin. I reached over and grabbed a glass of water from the nightstand. Sipping on it, I remembered Paulin telling us how the club had found their future home: "We were driving down a dirt road and spotted a for sale sign. This was 1978. I called the realtor about a week later and she said*, gosh, there's some acreage here and there's room for an airstrip.* And I said, *hey, we're your people."*

Paulin would further explain that with the exception of Joan and him, most of the other Ospreys didn't work or pay their bills. Somehow though, the two of them -- along with Stinky, Dave, and another partner managed to swing a deal on a tract of 120 acres, promptly selling off 20 acres with the provision it be used for the hangar, lounge, and airstrip. It's unclear who the fifth partner was, because depending who we talked to, we kept getting different names.

Continuing, Paulin proudly told us how they pulled it off. "We put this whole deal together without any money. We had a contract for deed and had owner financing. We were able to get the first portion of the runway, which went up to just past the hangar free and clear and we had the owner Laura and Wilma Maloney encumber each and every twenty -- they financed it to us individually."

Now that the property was theirs, the Osprey Club set about building their own drop zone where they could be free of meddling city officials, congested airspace, and be able to skydive as much as they wanted.

Lumber salvaged from the old hangar building in the city was hauled by Joan and Dave out to Lost Prairie. Work parties of skydivers and friends used it to build a hangar that had two apartments upstairs, and an outdoor latrine and shower facility. On the other side of Lower Lost Prairie road, they used the rest of the lumber to construct a restaurant and bar, and named it *Lost Prairie Lounge,* merely referring to it as *The Lounge.*

During construction, Joan was a fixture at Lost Prairie. Tapping his fingers on his Adirondack chair, Mike Groarke told us, "Joanie was an optimist and always wanted to try something new. It wasn't, this is why we can't do it. Let's try it, let's go and do something different here."

Similarly, Paulin had been impressed by Joan's dedication and hard work. "Joanie was so ambitious," he said. "She was always working. If there was a job to do, she was out there whether it was with a shovel, or hammer and nail, or packing somebody's parachute -- she was that kind of a person."

With the completion of the hangar, Joan and Dave moved into one of its upstairs living quarters. She was now a real pioneer living on the prairie. The unit (probably no more than 300 square feet) included a kitchen, bathroom, bedroom and small living room area that doubled as the entrance. From time to time, visiting skydivers would stay in the other upstairs apartment, or sleep downstairs on the hangar floor. When both filled to capacity, the rest would camp outside and use the outhouse and outdoor shower room which had been built just for that reason, and larger events.

Now that the facilities were finished, the Ospreys were ready to boogie with their friends. Over the years the event continued to grow.

Ironically, Joan would only live to experience one boogie at Lost Prairie.

Traditionally the Lost Prairie Boogie has been held the last week in July, culminating the first Sunday in August in order to coincide with *Heritage Day* in Canada, which is always the first Monday in August. With Canadians enjoying a three day weekend, the Osprey Club's boogie has always attracted quite a few Canadian skydivers who would come down from Calgary and Edmonton to skydive. Over the years, the clubs from up north and the Osprey's developed a special bond, and were part of that *extended family* they loved to talk about.

Sometime after the end of construction, Joan broke up with Dave and moved a used cabin, which she had purchased from Lake McGregor Resort, onto her property. Getting to and from Lost Prairie during spring and fall was a challenge when it rained. "At that time the road [Lost Prairie Road] was a mud-hole from here all the way to the Highway," Sam Scott informed us during his interview.

In those days the dirt road had been brutal and occasionally Joan's Ford Pinto would break down. "She'd be under there fixin' it, and changing the tires," Sam added admiringly, his waxed handle bar mustache glistening in the setting sunlight.

Not only was the road a mess then, so was the grass airstrip. Plagued by poor drainage and mud, it was dangerous. At least one plane flipped on its back when it got stuck in a marshy area near one end of the runway.

Shortly after Joan died in 1981, the original five owners decided to take in another partner named, Syd Torgerson who had some road building equipment. They gave him an ownership position in the airport and he solved the drainage problems, graded the road, and built the runway.

We were told that before her death, Joan's goal had been to move from Kalispell and live at Lost Prairie full time, amongst her friends and to be part of an airport with a successful skydiving operation.

When we interviewed Stinky on our first trip to Lost Prairie, he recalled that, shortly before Joan had died, she had been taking steps to fulfill that desire. "She was looking into her future and it was here with the rest of us," Stinky said. "So I spent a lot of time with her figuring out how to divide her land, where would be the best spots [to locate her house]. She actually drilled a well in preparation of where she was going to put her house."

Shortly before Joan died, she had planned to sell half of her land to Sam Scott to help finance the construction of her house. In the interim, she planned on staying in her cabin.

"Joan owned 20 acres and was planning to sell 10 acres to me and then this accident happened…and it was over," said Sam somberly, his handle bar mustache twitching plaintively.

I took one last sip of water and set the glass on the nightstand. As I did so, my thoughts shifted from Lost Prairie to Medford. A whole new adventure awaited us tomorrow. We had already heard so much about it from Zimmo, and Mike and Linda Groarke. I couldn't wait to get there. Exhausted, I turned off the night light and feel asleep soon afterwards.

HONESTY

Beagle Sky Ranch, Oregon: August 23, 2010

The next morning, we hit the road at 5:00 AM. Sixteen derriere numbing hours later, we pulled into Medford about 9:00 PM, pried ourselves out of our vehicles, checked into a Best Western Hotel on East Barnett Road and went to dinner at the only restaurant open, which happened to be a Black Bear Diner. As beautiful as the drive was, there is only so much that the body can endure and the mind can appreciate before it says, "Are we there yet," as Susan so often asked.

About 9:00 AM we arrived at Beagle Sky Ranch located thirteen miles north of Medford in White City. Situated in the Rogue River Valley, we were now in ranch country surrounded by foothills and mountains. The landscape resembled Lost Prairie, only drier and more populated. I could understand how the transition from Medford to Kalispell could have been an easy one for Joan. The two areas were similar. If she was able to tolerate Medford, she could certainly adjust to Kalispell and eventually Lost Prairie.

Before we drove into the fenced compound, we stopped outside its green metal gate and filmed its sign, which had a parachute on it.

Continuing on, we parked in front of a powder-blue metal hangar that had an open bay door. Getting out of our vehicles I could see a four seat Cessna 182 inside. It wasn't long before a robust man in his late sixties came outside dressed in a “Brakeman Bill” outfit, consisting of a pinstripe shirt, blue jeans, and a khaki colored baseball hat propped atop a light-brown flattop haircut. “George Holberton,” he said, greeting us. “Which one of you, other than the good looking gal here, is Paul Gorman?"

"I am," I said.

George looked over at Susan and said, "Boy, I sure feel sorry for you. How’d you ever get mixed up with a character like him?"

"I’m still asking myself that same question," Susan joked.

George laughed. "My wife has been asking herself the same question all these years too," he chuckled.

Mark, Mickey, and Susan all laughed and so did I pretending to find humor in being the brunt of George’s joke. I’d learned years ago to laugh along with friends when they ribbed me, lest I egg them on.

"Where do you want to film?" George said.

I peered into the hangar. "Can we do it in there?" I said.

"I don't see why not," George said. "While you guys unload, I’ll flirt with this babe."

Mark, Mickey and I set up our gear while George talked with Susan. He was quite the ladies’ man, in a grandfatherly sort of way, and after being married for thirty-two years I wasn't worried in the slightest.

We decided to use the Cessna as background for the interviews. About half an hour passed, and while we were still setting up, George sauntered over telling us that it was a good thing we were doing the filming today because he had just sold the Cessna to pay some bills and it would be gone the next day.

He excused himself to go take care of some business in the hangar's office while Mark, Mickey and I fine-tuned the lighting. Mickey sat in for the talent while Mark set the exposure and focus on his two cameras.

I had scheduled four interviews, including George, to commence at 10:00 AM, and allotted one hour for each interview. The plan was to be finished by 3:00 and out of there by 4:00. Hopefully everything would go as planned and everyone would show up at their designated time.

The first person to arrive was Deborah Kalmakava, getting there right on time -- just as George was coming out of his office. A spry, elfish woman in her early sixties, she bubbled with enthusiasm hugging George like a daughter who had been gone for an extended period of time, and she had. As it turned out it had been years since she had seen him because she had quit skydiving shortly after Joan's death and lived in Ashland about thirty miles south of Beagle Sky Ranch.

Deborah then acquainted herself with Susan and gave her a hug. My impression was: *That's a good sign.* Right off the bat the vibe here seemed more relaxed and less contentious than it had been in Lost Prairie. Maybe it was because they didn't live side by side, weren't fighting over money, and there hadn't been a fatality like there had been in Lost Prairie when we first got there. George and his wife were part of a handful of residents who lived at Beagle Sky Ranch. Like Lost Prairie, it was a private airstrip. Unlike Lost Prairie's asphalt runway, their runway was dirt. Most of Beagle's partners lived elsewhere only storing their planes in hangars they owned.

I introduced myself along with Mickey and Mark to Deborah. She hugged me. "This is exciting," she said. "I've been following your blog. The postings and pictures really bring back a lot of terrific memories. This is such a great thing you are doing for Joanie."

The people in Medford referred to Joan as *Joanie,* while the folks in Lost Prairie predominately called her Joan. It was a distinction that took me awhile to get used to. I was told that the nickname came from a time when Joan had said her nickname in high school had been *Joanie Baloney.* From that time on people, in Medford, referred to her as Joanie.

I thanked Deborah and several minutes later we began her interview.

Dee-Bra, as she was called back then with a joke about her small cup size, was born in Canada, and grew up in Calgary. A friend of hers told her about skydiving in Kalispell and she went there with him. She returned to Kalispell several times and finally did her first jump at the city airport.

During our interview, her description of the experience was so riveting we felt like we were skydiving for the first time too, as she described hanging onto the plane's floor with her butt cheeks, and her legs dangling outside the airplane flapping in the wind. Then, the jump instructor pushed her out of the plane with his foot, yelling, "Go!"

After her first jump, Dee-Bra returned to Calgary. She remained good friends with the Osprey Parachute Club and quit her elementary school teaching job winter break of 1975/1976 to join them in Medford when they wintered over there.

We wrapped up Dee-Bra's interview, hugged her and bid her goodbye. On her way out she stopped to say goodbye to George. He teared up a little and she promised to come visit him more often.

While we were interviewing Dee-Bra, Herb Farber had arrived. A friendly, unassuming man in his late fifties, with curly brown hair and a mustache, he owns his own surveying company. As a graduate of Washington State University, I instantly like him because two of my sisters and my son Patrick had gone there too.

"Go Cougs," I said, starting off our interview with him. Instantly, he relaxed and beamed. Once a Coug, always a Coug.

Known as Ferbie, Herb Farber would say that, in 1971, during college he had tried skydiving with the school's club and liked it. After graduating he took a surveying job in Medford and moved there. It wasn't long before he was looking for a place to skydive and heard about Beagle Sky Ranch. He started skydiving there, in 1974, and became a Beagle Boogie Boy along with Zimmo. Soon thereafter, Joan and Linda McGinty (Linda Groarke now) started jumping there. Not long afterwards, the Osprey's arrived and a friendly rivalry began. One year the Osprey's stole the Beagle Boogie Boy's sign, and the next year they retaliated stealing a montage of photographs and magazine clippings the Osprey's had pasted on the end of a wooden telephone wire spool. Artists they were not.

During his interview, I got the impression Herb wasn't that close with Joan. They had been friends and jumped together, but she hadn't shared anything intimate with him, at least that he talked about. Nevertheless, he had a tremendous amount of respect for her. Five years after he had last jumped with her, he attended her funeral service in Lost Prairie to pay his respects.

We completed our interview with Herb who had to get back to work. I thanked him for coming and promised to keep him informed as to when the film would be finished and where it would be screened.

As he was leaving, Scott Rogers showed up and it was like an old high school reunion between the two former Beagle Boogie Boys. They hugged each other and talked about old times. As Scott informed us during his interview, they used to run into each other occasionally at the Ashland Planning and Permitting Department where Scott worked. Because of his surveying job, Herb's job included getting permits, legal descriptions of properties, and recording surveys. All of that involved him going into the office where Scott worked as a city planner. But now that Scott was retired, it had been a while since the two had seen each other.

As a twelve year old kid, Scott had seen skydivers landing next to Interstate 90 at Issaquah Skydive Center on his way to Lake Sammamish State Park with his family -- while visiting the 1962 World's Fair in Seattle. He was fascinated with the sport. It wasn't until attending Southern Oregon University that he did his first jump at the Ashland City Airport in 1971. He sprained his ankle on that jump and had to layoff skydiving for several weeks while it mended. By the time it healed, the jump instructor had broken his ankle and the skydiving had shifted over to Beagle Sky Ranch, so Scott started jumping there, joining the Beagle Boogie Boys.

Like Herb, Scott who slightly resembles comedian Steve Martin with a gray beard, wasn't intimate with Joan, and more or less had only known her on a superficial level, or so it seemed. In spite of that, he was affected by her fatality and the death of two other skydiving friends. Unlike Dee-Bra, Herb and Scott continued skydiving for some time after the deaths, finally quitting because their lives and interests had changed, not because of the fatalities.

Most skydivers we met were philosophical about skydiving related fatalities and would say their friends were doing something they loved when they died. Another rationale we heard often was that those who died had made a mistake. The implication was that they felt safe because they didn't make mistakes. Eventually the majority of the skydivers we interviewed quit jumping for a host of reasons, mostly though because their lives had changed and they no longer had time to jump, had suffered injuries, or had developed new interests.

We finished our interview with Scott, and he asked if I wanted some old skydiving videos he had shot at Beagle. I replied that I would, and at some point he sent them to me. I used some of the footage in the film, including a jump of Joan free falling in her trademark white jumpsuit.

Our last interview of the day would be with George after we had a lunch break. There was a small grocery store several miles away where we bought sandwiches and soft drinks. We returned to the hangar and ate there. It was getting hot outside. George had a thermometer just outside his building and the needle indicated that it was ninety-five degrees. The forecast called for it to reach 100, which it did by the time we left.

While Mark, Mickey and Susan finished eating lunch, I went next door to an airplane maintenance shop called Steve's Aircraft, and talked with him. George had told him that I wanted to get some aerial footage of Beagle Sky Ranch. Steve owned a single-engine, two seat, Piper Super Cub airplane and was willing to take us up in it.

I offered to pay Steve, but he declined, saying that just putting the name of his company in the credits would be sufficient. I thanked him and informed Mark and Mickey to get ready for another aerial adventure tomorrow. They were excited. It had been a long day so far and they needed something to look forward to. It never took much to boost their morale and the thought of a scenic flight in a Piper Super Cub did just the trick.

Now that we had eaten lunch, and Mark and Mickey's B-Roll flight was arranged, our spirits and energy lifted. We turned our attention to interviewing George, which would be our last interview at Beagle Sky Ranch.

The interior of the hangar was both a workshop and "man cave" for George. The far wall was plastered with skydiving photos, memorabilia, including several photo-shopped posters of skydiving beagles. The concrete floors just in front of his gallery wall had two large rugs, one that was orange and the other that was light brown. Outdoor patio furniture sat on the rugs. It looked like a good place to hang out with buddies, drink beer and watch football games on weekends. The bay doors were translucent so there was just the right amount of ambient light shining in to augment the film lights we had brought.

If Stinky was the underpinning in Lost Prairie, then George Holberton was the Rock of Gibraltar at Beagle Sky Ranch. A burly man with a big heart was who he was. Never mind the teasing he doled out to the guys who skydived at Beagle, he took boys and made men out of them, and coddled the girls like they were his grandchildren. I could tell by the way the interviewees greeted him that he was loved and respected. He treated them like the foster kids he and his wife raised.

In addition to running Beagle Sky Ranch and having been a foster parent, and owning his own construction company, George was a heavy equipment operator evidenced by leathery, blistered, sunburned arms, neck and face from years of working outside. He taught his foster son Rodney to skydive and fly an airplane, which led him to become a commercial pilot.

In the early 1960s George saw the TV show *Ripcord* about a group of skydivers and wanted to try it. He bought a plane with another guy. The two taught themselves how to skydive and they took turns jumping in Ashland. He needed a place to store his plane so he bought land at Beagle Sky Ranch. He then purchased a mobile home and lived in it there while he built a hangar.

The private community was named after an old military base called Beagle that was torn down after World War II.

At the time, the regular jumping was Sundays in Ashland. Both towns lie in the semi-arid Rogue River Valley, renowned for its peaches and pears, and outdoor Shakespearean theater in Ashland. "We'd go to Ashland and the wind would start blowing and everybody would quit," said George. "So we'd come out here and jump and one day everyone said why don't we just stay out at your place on the weekend and jump…and I said okay, and a little drop zone was born -- a little backyard drop zone."

It's unclear whether Beagle Sky Ranch provided the model and impetus for Joan and the Ospreys later on, but the similarities between it and Lost Prairie are striking.

Skydivers at Beagle were a rowdy bunch and occasionally got into trouble. According to George, sometimes they did things that gave jumpers a bad name, but for the most part they got along well together. They didn't fight among themselves, they just hung out and had a good time enjoying each other's company. "It was the togetherness of the group," George said, fondly.

From George's perspective, nobody was better liked than Joan. "I think a drop zone owner would dream about having one hundred Joanie's on his drop zone," George reflected, "because they just came out, they skydived and they were friendly, good to everybody else, and they helped any person they could -- jumped right in and helped them."

George operated Beagle Sky Ranch for nearly 35 years, finally closing the doors on his skydiving business in 2009 due to hard times. He dreams of getting a new plane and starting up skydiving again, and at 68 he just might do it.

"I think to start another drop zone, you'd have to have people with the personality like Joan Carson that would give people the opportunity to see *normal people* jumping," George said, wistfully. "Probably a lot of people have an idea in their mind of what jumpers are like. Some of them are a little crazy. We can be our own worst enemy."

We wrapped up our interview with George and packed our equipment. Meanwhile Susan spent the entire time talking and laughing with him. When it came time to leave, he gave her a big hug and then pointing a finger at me said. "If you ever get tired of that character let me know, he gruffed."

We all chuckled. Susan looked at me. "You hear that, you'd better be nice, or else," she said, jabbing me in the ribs. Once again everybody laughed, including me. I shook hands with George he patted me on the shoulder. "I'm looking forward to seeing the film," he said. "If you want to screen it here, let me know."

"That would be great, George," I said. "I will."

Our interviews in Medford had been fruitful and the people had been very friendly. However, Joan hadn't spent as much time there as she had in Kalispell and Lost Prairie. As such, I came away with the impression that people there never got to know here all that well. She had also been younger then and less settled so she hadn't accomplished as much with her life. Yet it was remarkable that so many people had remembered and still admired her considering it had been almost 35 years since she had left Medford for Kalispell. For most of them it was the last time they saw her alive.

As we pulled out of Beagle Sky Ranch onto Beagle Road, I said to Susan, "I hope George is able to get the drop zone up and running again."

"Me too," Said Susan, taking pictures of the landscape out her window with her cellphone. "It's really a shame what's happened to him."

"Yeah, it meant so much to him," I said as we pulled to a stop at an intersection.

In spite of George's gruff exterior and poking fun, he seemed to lament the loss of his business. During his interview his eyes would occasionally become misty when he talked about the old days.

With the temperatures hovering at 100 degrees we headed for our hotel in Medford to rest up for tomorrow's busy day. In addition to Mark and Mickey's aerial filming at Beagle Sky Ranch, I had scheduled shooting and recording B-Roll in the morning, followed by our drive to San Francisco where we intended to interview Barrie. To our shock, Mark's Grand Cherokee got a flat tire. *Oh no, not now,* I said, under my breath through clenched teeth.

To our good fortune, there was a Les Schwab Tire Center on Hwy 62, just north of downtown Medford, and we stopped there. The bad news was the tire was shot and Mark would have to replace all four tires. It was either that or run the risk of ruining his differential. I was relieved to hear they had the tires in stock, but felt sorry for Mark having cost him a little over $1,000. I hoped and prayed it would be our last bit of bad luck and that the following day we'd make it over 4,000 foot high Siskiyou Summit 17 miles south of Ashland with our overloaded vehicles.

While we were waiting for Mark's tires to be replaced, Susan and I sat in our car talking about the interviews we had just had in Medford, along with those we had earlier in Lost Prairie. Gradually an image of camaraderie between Beagle's Skydivers and the Osprey's developed. Independently they had developed their own cultures. It was a transformational time in Joan's life. During her time in Medford she really began to become an accomplished skydiver and a leader, experiences that would serve her well later.

TOGETHERNESS

Medford, Oregon: September, 1975

George Holberton's drop zone at Beagle Sky Ranch flourished and caught on with some of the male students at Southern Oregon University, like, Scott Rogers. As a skydiver, he remembered it being a conservative male oriented scene at Beagle with a lot of older military types and smoke jumpers practicing.

Rogers had long hair and a beard then, as did some of the other young skydivers, further setting them apart from the older jumpers. It was a culture clash and a changing of the guard.

"This was a male oriented scene out here, and it was always a treat to find women who would be skydivers. It spiced it up and also made us more civilized," said Rogers, grinning mischievously.

The younger jumpers at Beagle Sky Ranch called themselves, *Beagle Boogie Boys* based on the Disney cartoon the *Beagle Boys,* who were a gang of ex-cons that constantly tried to rob Scrooge McDuck.

"We kind of modeled our logo on the *Beagle Boys,*" said Scott Rogers, proudly. "In fact I did a tee-shirt design that had the Beagle Boys from the Scrooge McDuck cartoon, but put parachutes and other things on them."

Jackson County, surveyor, Herb "Ferbie" Farber remembered the *Beagle Boogie Boys* as being a little wild back then. "The events that we had here and when we went other places we were renowned for being a little bit loose," he said, smiling fondly.

It was into this environment that Joan dropped into Medford sometime in the summer of 1974. The exact reason she moved to the Ashland/Medford area is not fully known.

Zimmo's recollection was that Joan came to Medford because of some guy, and it didn't work out between them. His explanation seems plausible because there were plenty of drop zones in the Bay area where she could jump year round, as opposed to the Ashland and Medford area where the weather is hit and miss three to four months of the year. Winters are wet, cold and foggy a good deal of the time.

In fact when it was foggy and they couldn't jump, Dee-Bra told us that they did a humorous exorcism to get rid of the fog. "Roprac was the remnant of a chiropractic sign that the jumpers went out and stole. And it was *the god of Roprac* that they prayed to at night to get rid of the fog. And we had it in Armo's window at 4th and B in Ashland. The window was right on the sidewalk so everybody could see it. But in those days Ashland was pretty loose. And we kept it there until one day in the paper we saw a [picture of a] sign from a chiropractic office that said, *Wanted sign. Stolen sign. Chiropractic sign missing*. And it was really the snake thing that we really wanted, but it came with Roprac, so we called it *the god of Roprac.*"

Regardless of the reason Joan moved to Medford, this much is clear, when she arrived in Southern Oregon, the first skydiver she met was Linda McGinty (now Linda Groarke). As Linda stated in Lost Prairie, she met Joan at Mr. Smith's Bar and Grill in Medford where Joan worked as a barmaid. Linda remembered her as being friendly and always saying hello even though they didn't know one another. In November 1974, the two would run into each other under different circumstances. "About a month later I made my first jump in Ashland," said Linda, "and come to find out she was there too making her first jump after having broken both her wrists."

As coincidence would have it, the jump master wound up breaking his ankle on that jump so Joan and Linda couldn't do any more jumps in Ashland and ended up going to Beagle Sky Ranch where they continued jumping.

Beagle owner George Holberton remembered Joan's arrival well, "One day Joanie showed up…she was a quiet, easy going gal -- just kind of went along."

The *Beagle Boogie Boys* noticed her too. "Joan was atypical at that time for a lot of women because there weren't a lot of women in skydiving, and she was one of the early pioneers into the sport," said Herb "Ferbie" Farber.

Perhaps none of the Beagle Boogie Boys was closer to Joan than the rogue Zimmo. He was just as wild and daring as she. His son had died after falling down some stairs and suffering a brain hemorrhage. Zimmo battled depression and worked though his illness by skydiving. "Some psychologists were telling people with suicidal tendencies to go skydiving because every time you pull the ripcord you reinforce the idea that you don't really want to die," said Zimmo somberly in Lost Prairie. "I did it, and loved it and before too long I really didn't want to die."

When Joan and Zimmo weren't working or skydiving together, they would go camping and swimming with Linda. They talked a lot, and shared their feelings. However, Joan was private and didn't talk much about her past. "I think Joan was drawn to skydiving," Said Zimmo in Lost Prairie. "I don't know if it was depression or boredom or a combination of both. I think she felt that her life wasn't going as fast or big as she wanted it to go and she was going to do something that most people don't do and if she got into it she was going to do something that nobody's ever done, and I think that was her drive and her spirit. She was going to do something really special with her life and she did, I think."

If Zimmo and Joan were kindred spirits then Linda McGinty was her best friend. Not to be outdone by the opposite sex, Joan and Linda, not only started the Beagle Boogie Babes, they designed their own patch to distinguish themselves from the guys, who had their goofy Disney cartoon characters tee-shirt. The babes wore the patch prominently on their jumpsuits to remind the men that they were on a par with them.

Being a Beagle Boogie Babe was a declaration of independence and confidence, after all, it was an era of *Women's Lib*, a time when women stood up to men and demanded respect and to be treated as their equal counterparts. Nobody exemplified this better than Joan.

The Beagle Boogie Boys and Babes made a point of standing out at boogies they attended and those they hosted in Medford. Joan was maybe the biggest show off of all, jumping nude, hanging BAs (Bare Asses), and boasting about how she was going to wing walk someday without a parachute, and so on.

Beagle skydiver Herb Farber remembered Joan similarly. "Joanie was vibrant, but wasn't overly vibrant," said Farber. "She was always up for whatever was going on, and never held back -- just full bore -- that was Joanie."

Clearly, Zimmo knew the wild side of Joan because the two of them, and sometimes, others including Dee-Bra would skydive nude together. And as Beagle Sky Ranch owner George Holberton recalled, it wasn't always when she was skydiving that Joan took her clothes off. "A neighbor told me his side of the story, he came back from town where he had a few drinks with friends, and a lot of them were spending the weekend here -- sleeping right here in the hangar on the ground," grinned Holberton. "Anyway, he returned and sat down with Joanie and Linda, and I think a few others, and they chatted for a while, and then finally he said, *oh, you don't have clothes on.* And so he removed his clothes, and sat down and they all talked. More people showed up. More people removed their clothes 'till it was a pretty good crowd and then they decided they'd go wake me up. And so, they all came into my bedroom. There was like twenty people naked in my bedroom, and they were laughing and shouting, and I said, *Hey you guys quiet down you'll wake the children up.* So somebody said, *oh he's getting mad we better get out.* So they all went outside and I said, *I wonder what they're doing out there.* So I started out after them, and my wife said, *no, no, negative. You're staying in the house those people are naked.*"

Prior to the Osprey's and Dave's arrival, Joan didn't have any boyfriends in Medford -- at least not that any of the jumpers remembered. She just worked, skydived and partied, and was always at the drop zone lending a helping hand.

As helpful and liked as Joan was, she was the quiet one of the bunch. She shared with Linda McGinty her experiences of living in San Francisco and Berkeley, and how in 1973 she would ride her motorcycle sixty-eight miles out to Pope Valley where she would skydive, and where later she broke both her wrists. Joan also told Linda, that because of the injury she had to return home to live at her parent's place in Redmond for a year because both hands required surgery, and it took that long for them to heal.

For Joan, it was a difficult period having to be helped getting herself dressed, going to the bathroom, eating, and brushing her teeth. "It really dampened her spirits when she had her wings clipped," sympathized Linda. "I don't think her mother really supported Joanie's skydiving. I think that was one of the problems when she was in casts on both wrists is that her mother would tell her how much she didn't want her to skydive, and how much she cared for her and she didn't want to see Joanie hurt again. So I think there is a two sided thing that

Joanie just took it as being smothered and she didn't like people taking care of her. She always had a free spirit. She wanted out of there."

By the time Joan moved to Medford and began skydiving at Beagle Sky Ranch, she'd only been jumping for about eighteen months and almost a year of it had been spent recuperating from the two broken wrists. As a result, she was pretty much a novice when she started jumping again, but was eager to learn and improve her skills. "There was a time when she came to me and she said, *I can't seem to close when I'm supposed to*," said George Holberton. "By that I mean one or two other jumpers are falling and a third jumper or fourth, whatever, comes and makes contact with that jumper. Well she wouldn't make that contact, she'd get up close. She was being conservative, and I said, *just go the other way Joanie, be aggressive, slam in take it out a couple of times...crash into them, knock the thing apart, but get that contact you want...I said from now on we're going to call you Killer Carson*...And she did, and she started closing and improving her skills...Everything was going good."

Over the next year, Joan improved her skydiving abilities so much that she and nine other jumpers at Beagle Sky Ranch were able to perform the first ten person star in Southern Oregon. It's a formation, where ten skydivers rendezvous in the sky and hold hands, forming a circle.

"It was because of Joanie that we were able to pull it off," said Beagle Skydiver Zimmo excitedly in Lost Prairie. "She was wearing a reserve on her back right below her neck. We were jumping out of a very small door Beech 18. Every time we tried this before, people would all come in and we'd end up tumbling and falling on each other into what's called a funnel, where you get sucked in like the person in front of you is a vacuum cleaner. They are cutting a hole through the sky. We didn't realize it, but we were all getting there at the same time, so we were creating so much turbulence and burble (dead air), that

that's why we couldn't build this ten man star -- and it was dangerous. So on this one jump, Joanie hit her reserve on the top of the door and that held up everybody, which actually let the base build -- the first few build, and stabilize it. The next came -- because they had to wait for her to get out before they could get out. And so it built slowly, and it built, and we built the first ten man star in Southern Oregon."

Zimmo would go on to say that when they got down, Joan opened her reserve and found bent pins through cones (pins that are attached to the ripcord, which prevent it from opening until the ripcord is pulled). "Her reserve was worthless on that jump. If she had needed a reserve on that jump she wouldn't have had one," sighed Zimmo.

Joan wasn't particularly accident prone because a lot of skydivers suffered broken bones or sprains in those days jumping on round military surplus parachutes. It was just part of the sport. It was at Beagle Sky Ranch where she broke her ankle in August of 1974. "In those days they were jumping round parachutes," said George Holberton. "You landed kind of hard with them."

The day Joan broke her ankle at Beagle, George was there. "So they were gathering her up, putting her in the car, taking her to the vet to get her fixed up," said George with a chuckle. "She turned to me and said, *George remind me to never jump out of an airplane again.* And I said, "Joanie this is all you know how to do. Go heal up for six weeks and come on back. And she did. She even came to me and she said, *You were right, this is all I know what to do, and this is what I enjoy, so I'm happy here.*"

When the Osprey's flew in to Medford sometime in the fall of 1975, Stinky and Dave had just bought a WWII designed twin-engine Beech 18 aircraft for the club. Used by the Army and Navy during WWII, as a light transport and for hauling cargo, it could hold 10 jumpers. "That fall there were five or six of them that decided they were going to take off for the winter and get out of the cold weather," recalled Stinky, sitting about one hundred yards north of the Osprey's homemade hangar during his interview in Lost Prairie.

Stinky who didn't go, continued. "They ended up going to the Reno Air Races, which are in mid-September, hung out there for a few weeks and partied and jumped…And then they went a few other places and ended up at Beagle Sky Ranch in Medford."

The Ospreys and Beagle's skydivers hit if off almost immediately. Zimmo, who had been going to school at Southern Oregon University and jumping at Beagle remembered it well. "We didn't know them and they didn't know us, but for some reason you're automatically community. It only took a few skydives before we were all family. We helped them out, shared our apartments with them and before too long they said, *yeah we're going to get an apartment in the same building because we're going to stay* -- and every night when you get off work, guess what, you would head off and do something -- the whole group of you."

During that time, Joan was working in Medford and Zimmo was unemployed. "I needed a job so Joanie says, *I'm working for a cabinet shop. I'll ask my boss.* She called me and said, *yeah they'll hire you.* On the weekdays we were working together and on the weekends we were playing hard together," said Zimmo.

By the time the Osprey flock landed at Beagle, Joan was a fairly accomplished skydiver and well respected member of Beagle Sky Ranch. She was not intimidated by the older and rowdy Osprey's when they arrived at Steve (Armo) Armitage's recommendation to come join him in Medford. "Armo had been jumping in Montana, and started jumping here at Beagle," said George. "So Steve called his friends in Montana and said, *Hey, we're having a great time, come join us.* And one day they all showed up.

"I was working for a company up in Calgary at the time. And I said that's it, I quit, I'm going skydiving and that's where I met Joan, and

Linda and the rest of the gang," chuckled Mike Groarke, when we interviewed him in Lost Prairie. "Joan and Linda had to work, but the rest of us were free and easy,"

The winter of 1976 is when a second flock of Ospreys arrived in Medford, including Lost Prairie Boogie organizer Fred Sand and Canadian school teacher Dee-Bra who remembered her first night in town vividly. "We drove for two days, it was winter, so when we got into Oregon we came up into the high desert north of Bend and it was blue sky and winter wheat and was just beautiful - something that I'd never seen in the winter before because I'd always lived in the northlands," she said. "And we showed up in Medford late one night and drove to somebody's house named Joanie Carson, and she had a little beige Beetle parked in the front of her duplex, and I had no idea where we were, or who she was, and I don't even know how Fred knew her, but we stopped at Joanie's and partied a little bit and then she said, *I guess we're all going to Ashland.*"

"So we all drove, whoever was with Joanie," continued Dee-Bra, "and our truck full and showed up at Armo's house. And so there was already a party going on there, it must've been a Friday night, and we showed up and the party got bigger. Pretty soon we all went up to a place called the Beau Club which was about three blocks away. It was a bar where the jumpers who had come down previously spent every night. And so we went up to join them and partied, partied, and partied, and the next morning half of us woke up on Armo's floor. Some people were other places, I have no idea where. I thought, *I have no idea what's going on but I'm sure having fun.*"

While Medford was larger than Ashland it was a blue collar working town. Ashland, on the other hand being home to Southern Oregon University and the Shakespearean Festival, was the sophisticated little sister. There was much more going on there culturally speaking so the jumpers tended to party there since some were students there. But, once the skydiving had moved from the city's airport to Beagle Sky Ranch, they tended to partying there too -- sometimes spending the night camped out on the drop zone.

Joan and Dee-Bra hit it off, she soon become the third Beagle Boogie Babe behind Joan and Linda. Together, they did their best to hold their own against the Beagle Boogie Boys, smokejumpers, and ex-military types that jumped at Beagle.

It wasn't long before Canadian Dee-Bra fell in love with Armo and stayed behind with him when the Osprey's migrated back to Kalispell in May or June of 1976. Eventually, she married him and has lived in Ashland ever since. As a retired school teacher, she spends her time gardening and volunteering at a preschool.

The two skydiving clubs were well suited for each other in more ways than just maintaining a friendly rivalry. When Mike Groarke and Linda McGinty also wed, and Joan and Osprey leader Dave became a couple they became blood.

Whenever the groups got together, they'd see which club could be the grossest. "We kind of learned from each other, said Beagle skydiver Herb "Ferbie" Farber. We found that we were compatible, and oftentimes had competitions to see who could be more-gross than the others. When we were at the same place together it was even worse."

The gross-out contests became more extreme and finally culminated with the Osprey's taking the show public. "There was a restaurant in Medford called Kim's, and we had a few parties out there," said Beagle Boogie Boy Scott Rogers. "I think it was the Kalispell group in particular who would moon us on the other side of the room in the restaurant."

George Holberton, did his fatherly best to put it all into proper perspective. "People partied and had a good time," he said. "There wasn't any violence, there wasn't any property damage, they just mostly talked and laughed, and told jokes, had a few drinks -- they just were together. I guess that was it. It was the togetherness of the group."

In May, 1976 Joan decided to attend a jump meet at her old stomping grounds in California. She invited her fellow Beagle Boogie Babes, Linda McGinty and Dee-Bra, to meet her there. "There was a jump-meet in Pope Valley that she and I decided we would go to," said Dee-Bra. "I don't remember much about it except that she had a little Beetle Volkswagen, and she sold it to buy this very cool van -- a Volkswagen Van. And she drove it down to Pope Valley -- Pope Valley is in Northern California in the Napa Valley -- a little bit north of the Napa Valley. And I thought, *man she is just so brave.* And she took off for Pope Valley by herself. And another friend and I drove down and met her there -- hung out together. It was really fun. I thought, *man, I could be at home teaching. Here I am in California and it's warm and it's only May. This is the life.*

Today, Pope Valley Horseshoe Ranch is a mere relic of its illustrious past. Founded by Curt Curtis and his wife Ann in 1970, it was considered to be the best drop zone in the world at the time. It was where the U.S. National Skydiving Team trained year round.

Located about 80 miles north of San Francisco, Pope Valley was populated with farms then. As you wound down the narrow road entering the valley, there was a general store, post office, auto repair garage, creek and clusters of oak and a scattering of pine trees. About a mile east is where the drop zone was located. It had its own motel, swimming pool, restrooms, shower room, and restaurant with a bar -- a first for the time back then. Today, the valley's farms have given way to Vineyards, and the motel and restaurant are boarded up and dilapidated, so is the old general store. Only the auto repair and towing business is still operating. In 2013, Canadian investors purchased the former drop zone and plan to turn it into an airport for private jets flying in for wine tours.

Joan and her Beagle Boogie Babes spent several days skydiving in Pope Valley and then she visited friends in the Bay Area while the rest of the clan headed back to Medford. On her way back, a big snowstorm hit the Siskiyou mountain range, closing the pass and forcing Joan to re-route from I-5 over to Highway 101 along the coast. The coastal route wasn't any better due to a rainstorm that caused a slide and blocked the road. She finally arrived back about a week late. Upon returning, she eased her fellow Babe's worst fears, and enthralled them with stories about her adventure.

In addition to the three official Beagle Boogie Babes consisting of Joan, Linda and Dee-Bra, there were two honorary members. "To be a Beagle Boogie Babe you had to be with two other Beagle Boogie Babes and kiss them both," said Zimmo. "I think I became Beagle Boogie Babe number five."

According to Linda, George Holberton was the other honorary Beagle Boogie Babe, making him number four.

Shortly after Joan returned from Pope Valley, she left for Kalispell with Dave and his flock of Ospreys. "We made Dave buy us a six pack of beer. We were laughing that we sold Joanie for a whole six pack of beer," quipped Zimmo.

So with Joan and Linda going to Kalispell, and Dee-Bra staying in Ashland, the two clubs did kind of a flip flop with the women. To this day, the Ospreys think they got the better end of the deal because they got two women while the Beagle Boogie Boys only got one.

Zimmo and Dee-Bra didn't see much of Joan after she left. The only time they saw her was during the summer boogies in Kalispell. But Joan's death five years later would have a lasting impact on everyone at Beagle, especially Dee-Bra who fought back tears as she recalled what she and Armo had been doing when they got the news. "I do remember Fred calling us to say that Joanie had gone in. We were working on a little concrete border in our yard in Ashland. I still remember exactly where we were when the phone rang. We went running in and it was Fred, and it was like...the spark had just left."

Then two more of their Beagle friends perished in skydiving accidents within six months, one on Labor Day and the other Thanksgiving weekend. Their deaths were mind numbing, and left some of them questioning whether skydiving was worth the risk. "We were no longer invincible," said Dee-Bra somberly.

For Armo and Dee-Bra the loss of Joan and their other two friends ended up being life changing. They quit the sport after only 28 more jumps.

Ten years later Dee-Bra attended a boogie in Lost Prairie where she had to make one last jump to pay homage to Joan and her other two fallen Beagle friends. It was an emotional experience for her. "I had to make one more jump," she said, her eyes watering. "So I did it with my good friends from Kalispell. It was very exhilarating. It was probably one of the most fun jumps I'd ever made. I wasn't scared. Fred and Lannie and Garfield were on the load and I thought, *Oh my brothers are with me I'll be fine.* And I was. I couldn't even walk I was so full of adrenaline when I landed. It was crazy."

SCHEDULING

Lost Prairie to San Francisco: August, 2010

While we were on the road between Lost Prairie and Medford, and then Medford and San Francisco, it had been difficult to stay in contact with Joan's brother Barrie, primarily because he was on vacation in Costa Rica and wasn't due back until the day before our scheduled interview. Consequently, I was worried as to whether or not his interview would happen. I tried not to let Susan, Mark and Mickey know my concern. I'm pretty sure they did though, and to their credit, they didn't bring it up. At that stage, I think they were just as engrossed in the story as I was and wanted to see it through.

Prior to leaving on our road trip to Lost Prairie/Medford/San Francisco, I had been in touch with Barrie, via email, informing him about the progress with the filming, and trying to arrange an interview with him.

For the next nine days I heard nothing from him while he was vacationing in Costa Rica.

Finally, on Sunday, August 22, 2010 I got an email from Barrie as we were driving from Lost Prairie to Medford, and was relieved to hear from him on one hand, but frustrated on the other. His schedule was so tight that it was going to make it difficult to interview him. His flight from Costa Rica was arriving at 7:00 PM Tuesday, and the next day he was flying to the Midwest. He didn't have a specific time yet, and was hoping we could do the interview the evening he got in, or early Wednesday morning.

The following morning I sent an email to Barrie:

We arrived late last night in Medford. I really want to make this work with you. Thus far, we have ten great interviews including today and 2-3 more in Seattle.

The only missing piece is what you can provide about Joan's childhood and family.

Our schedule is flexible on Tues and Wed. Please let me know where and what time works for you and we'll be there.

As we pulled out of Medford on Tuesday, August 24, 2010, I was stressed, having dealt with the flat tire the day before and still not having a firm date, time and location for Barrie's interview. Nonetheless, I decided to continue on to San Francisco. If Barrie wasn't available, or was unwilling to be interviewed, it would be on him, not me. My integrity was on the line and I intended to honor my commitment. Not to mention we needed to get Mickey to SFO airport on Wednesday.

I don't recall exactly where we were when I got Barrie's email, but suffice to say we were somewhere in Northern California when I was able to finally pull it up on my cell phone.

Barrie's message was good news. His travel plans had changed. He would be available on Wednesday afternoon, after 1:00 PM. He proposed using a conference room at his office in Fremont for the interview.

I sensed from Barrie's email that he was conflicted about doing the interview. Maybe it was because he questioned my intentions, or because of his own insecurity. Whatever the case may be, he downplayed his insight into Joan's childhood saying he was four years younger than she. Likewise, he felt her skydiving friends might have already covered that phase of her life in depth, even though he was the only family member to ever visit her in San Francisco and Kalispell where he made twelve jumps during several summers.

He ended his email by suggesting that Joan's older sister could probably add a lot.

I was ecstatic and let out a whoop for joy and then told the crew. That evening I sent Barrie an email from my sister's place in San Francisco doing my best to ease any concerns or fears he might have:

That's great news Barrie. Fremont at 1:00 PM tomorrow will work well. The conference room sounds perfect, but if you can't get it then we'll need a quiet parklike setting outside.

We're looking forward to meeting you and I'm sure your perspective and stories will add a lot to our project. If you have photos we could use, it would help. We brought our scanner.

That evening I recapped in my journal about the events of the past few days and the big day tomorrow. Weary and excited my mind was swirling with contradictory thoughts and feelings as I began second guessing myself:

We departed Medford about 10:00 PM and were soon climbing the Siskiyou. Our Ford Escape faithfully chugged its way to the summit and a short time later we were in California. It was all-downhill from there, but the temperature kept rising, hitting 104 at a Shell Station in

Corning. Even though our vehicle had AC, I was sweating it. We had an interview tomorrow in San Francisco with Joan's brother, Barrie. It had been difficult scheduling the interview because of his tight schedule, so the last thing we needed was another car problem, like we'd had with Mark's flat tire, to stop us cold and postpone or permanently derail our interview with him.

Along the way I began having second thoughts about the project. I felt that something was missing...Sure the story was interesting and unique, but where was the conflict? Thus far we hadn't found any. Joan loved skydiving, was a hard worker and everyone loved her, that's what we kept hearing.

But the truth was that after 11 interviews, two road trips and nearly 3,000 miles I was just as perplexed now as I had been more than 30 years earlier as to the reason Joan engaged in a risky sport called skydiving...not to mention the reason she had left the sophistication of San Francisco for the redneck scrub of Medford, and later finally settling in the remote wilderness of Montana. Admittedly, I was at a low spot, unless we found out soon what motivated Joan, there wasn't much point in continuing on. I had tried my best, but her essence was elusive. Maybe somebody else would be able to unlock Joan's past, but for me it just wasn't happening.

My patience was getting thin and so was my wallet. One more interview to go and then time to call it quits. I would've called it quits right then, but that would be rude and heartless. Truth was, I had resurrected intense feelings and memories of Joan and was responsible for what I had stirred up. I owed Barrie the decency to interview him...Afterwards I could tell him that Joan was still remembered and loved by everyone who had known her, but unfortunately, enough wasn't known about

Joan to make a movie about her. I was pretty sure I could say it in such a way that he would understand -- at least I hoped so.

We arrived in San Francisco at approximately 6:00 PM. What can you say about a place that's been written about, sung about and talked about more than maybe any other city in the U.S., if not the world? It is the quintessential American City, golden, seductive, and beguiling. Joan loved the place, and so did I. It seemed fitting to wind up our interviews in the city where my involvement with her began 37 years earlier.

My sister, Dorothy, lives in San Francisco and offered to put us up. It was great to be in a real home again, where we could eat real meals and sleep in a real bed. After almost a week of being on the road, we were tired of traveling, tired of imitation food, and wanted to stretch our cramped legs and get a little space from each other. We were able to do all three there.

The morning of Barrie's interview, Susan, Mark, Mickey and I rose early. After breakfast we left, setting out to film the spots that in 1973 Joan and I had passed through and spent time in.

Our first stop was Market and Powell Street where Joan and I had caught the Powell - Mason cable car. At that location we filmed the cable car arriving, turning around and then departing.

Next we rode the cable car up to Chinatown where we got off and filmed vegetable markets, overflowing sidewalks, and storefronts. Joan and I hadn't spent time there, but she had worked at a pharmacy in Chinatown so I wanted some shots of the area.

From Chinatown we walked up to North Beach and shot the iconic honkytonks, Big Al's and Carol Doda's and other sleazy dives. All the while, Mickey recorded ambient sound. Joan and I also hadn't spent time there, but it was so iconic that I felt I might be able to use it in the film. As it turned out, I never did.

Lastly, we walked up to Little Italy and filmed the exterior and interior of the U.S. Restaurant, where Joan and I had eaten dinner, and then Molinari's where she had shopped for after dinner snacks.

Although the U.S. Restaurant had moved several doors down, I still reflected on eating at its original location with Joan in 1973.

GENEROSITY

San Francisco: June, 1973

When Joan and I got off the cable car at Columbus and Stockton in the heart of North Beach, we were in the Italian section of town. It felt like I was in Italy, not that I had been there before. The air smelled of garlic, and awnings advertising the names of restaurants written in Italian checkered the buildings on both sides of Columbus Street.

As we walked down the sidewalk Joan drew double-takes, smiles and whistles from lecherous men admiring this vixen. I'm sure they were wondering; how did that gangly wimp end up with such a knock-out? *Eat your hearts out,* I gloated silently, even though all the attention made me feel uncomfortable.

We arrived at the U.S. Restaurant and stopped outside. It was a mustard colored pie-shaped building with an arched, red, white, and green awning that wrapped around the 'V' shaped' corner of the building.

"Very cool building," I said. "It kind of reminds me of some buildings in Pioneer Square -- in Seattle."

"This is my favorite restaurant in San Francisco," Joan said, beaming. "They've got the best Italian food in the world. You wanna eat here?"

"Sure," I replied, smiling. "You can't do any better than that."

Joan nudged me with an elbow playfully. "You're gonna eat your words," she laughed.

"I'm so hungry I could eat anything," I joked.

Joan smiled. "Let's go inside then," she said.

I opened the door and held it open for Joan. I glanced up at a neon 7-Up sign and the words U.S. Restaurant above the door as were entered. Inside, the place was packed, and bustling, with servers scurrying around carrying plates overflowing with more varieties of Italian food than I knew existed. The Kitchen was fully exposed, running the length of the counter. Pots and pans clanged and boisterous voices barked out orders in Italian, fighting to be heard over the cacophony of conversation coming from customers.

The floor was a repetitious pattern of small mosaic black and white tiles, and the walls and water stained ceiling were a yellowish cardboard color. I wasn't sure if it was the original paint or if it had yellowed over time because of a constant haze of cigarette smoke that filled the room.

A waitress dressed in a powder blue uniform resembling a nurse's outfit arrived. She grabbed two menus from a rack attached to the counter and then turning greeted us.

Joan hugged her like a family member. "Hi Anna, this is my friend, Paul from Seattle," she said. "We went to high school together. He's visiting for a few days."

"Nice to meet you, Mr. Paul…Any friend of Joan's is a friend of ours," Anna said, with an Italian accent. "Come right this way, I've got a romantic table just for the two of you by the windows." Anna led the way followed by Joan and then me. We arrived at our table on the far side of the restaurant.

Anna helped Joan seat herself and then I sat on the opposite side with my back to the windows, which was great because I was able to watch the entire restaurant from my spot and it was a good show.

Meanwhile, Joan asked Anna about her parents. "How are Luigi and Maria?"

Anna gestured to the kitchen. "Busy, they're in the kitchen cooking," she said. "Maybe you will see them when you leave."

"I hope so," Joan smiled, "I miss them and this place."

"We miss you too, Miss Joan. Can I get you something to drink?" Anna smiled.

"Yes, bring us a carafe of Burgundy, please," Joan said.

"On its way, Miss Joan," Anna said, writing our order in her receipt booklet.

Anna departed and Joan told me that before she had moved to Berkley she had lived several blocks away and had eaten here frequently. The restaurant was family owned and run and they welcomed her like one of their own. Since Joan's mom, dad and three siblings lived in the Seattle area, the Borzoni family and their relatives who all worked in the restaurant were like a surrogate family for her. I didn't realize it then, but years later I would learn how important the concept of creating a family-like community was to Joan.

I studied the menu, but other than spaghetti and meatballs, most of the items were unfamiliar to me. My mother made spaghetti with meat sauce and that was about the extent of my knowledge of Italian food.

"Get anything you want, it's on me," Joan said, looking up from her menu. "You don't have to pay for mine," I protested.

"I know, but I want to," said Joan. "Now, what would you like to eat?"

I glanced at the menu again and pointing at my selection said, "I'm gonna have the Spaghetti and Meatballs".

"Good choice," Joan said, smiling.

A short time later Anna arrived with our wine and a baguette. She took our order. Joan ordered Veal Parmigiana for herself, and sides of steamed zucchini and artichokes for the table. I ordered my Spaghetti and Meatballs, which came with a bowl of Minestrone soup.

Anna wrote it all down and headed for the kitchen. Joan raised her glass of wine. "Welcome to San Francisco. I'm glad you're here," she toasted.

"Thanks, so am I," I said, while still clinking glasses.

We each swallowed a sip of wine and then Joan excused herself to go the restroom. I watched her weave her way through the tables, occasionally saying hello to some of the customers. She disappeared around a corner and I glanced about at various customers who were engaged in lively conversation while eating mounds of pasta, and gulping red wine in between bites.

Yellowed Venetian blinds, partially shuttered on the windows behind me, cast stripes on the light colored clothing of some of the customers. A cloud of cigarette smoke, and overhead open-faced fluorescent lights, combined with the venetian blinds creating a film noir' movie set.

Anna arrived with our orders and placed them on the table. "Miss, Joan is special," she said. "She's one of our favorites. You are very lucky to have her as your girlfriend."

I was taken aback by what Anna said, but didn't want to set the record straight and disappoint her that Joan wasn't my girlfriend. "Yes, I know," I said, nodding.

Anna left and Joan showed up soon afterwards with Anna's sister, Anita. Dressed identically to Anna, it was hard to tell the two apart except that Anita was thinner, and slightly taller.

Joan introduced me to her and Anita smiled nervously as I stood to shake her hand. I too was nervous and was getting the feeling that I was on display -- Joan was showing me off to her *family*. I was flattered, but all of the attention did make me feel uneasy.

Joan hugged Anita and then she turned and walked away. We sat down and I saw Anita stop and whisper to a busboy that looked over at our table and grinned. Joan poured more wine into our glasses and raised her glass. "Bon Appetito," she said. We clinked glasses and gulped it down.

The food was delicious. I had never had meatballs before and they melted in my mouth. They were slightly sweet with a hint of fennel and loaded with garlic. And this was the first time I had ever had fresh pasta and it wasn't chewy like the dried pasta my mother used to prepare. It was so much better. Joan offered me half of her Veal Parmigiana because she was getting full. It was delicious too, and another first for me. She explained that the meat was thinly sliced, breaded, and then fried and topped with Tomato sauce and melted fresh Mozzarella cheese.

We had just about finished everything when I saw Anna bringing a plate full of green colored pasta to a nearby table.

"What kind of pasta is that?" I asked, nodding in the direction of the table to my left.

Joan turned and remarked, "It's pesto pasta, you want some?"

"Uh, no thanks, I was just curious, that's all."

Anna was turning to leave their table when she glanced over and Joan caught her attention. Anna leaned towards her. "Yes, Miss Joan what can I do for you?"

"Anna, bring Paul an order of Pesto Pasta, please," Joan winked.

Anna smiled and then left.

"Joan, I'm getting full," I said, rubbing my stomach.

"We can take it home, if you can't finish it," she said. "Besides, you need to put a little meat on your bones."

We laughed. She was right, I was skinny.

As it turned out I ate the entire order of Pesto Pasta.

Joan had ordered Spumoni Ice Cream and I had chosen Flan. I hadn't had it since I was in Spain in 1969.

I finished my flan and Joan offered me the rest of her ice cream. "You've got to try it. They make it themselves. There's nothing like fresh Spumoni Ice Cream. She scooped a spoonful of the rainbow marbled ice cream on her spoon and held it out. “Open wide," she laughed.

I opened my mouth and Joan fed me a spoonful of the creamy desert. "That's it. There, isn't that delicious," she smiled coyly, and I nodded. "Another bite?” she asked.

"No, no. No thank you…I mean yes, but not right now," I said, smiling. Fully aware of her innuendo, I tried my best to not eat more and not offend her.

Apparently my response worked because Joan laughed. "Yes you can get Spumoni Ice Cream here anytime,” she said. “Are you ready to go?"

“Yeah, I’m so stuffed that I need to walk,” I said. Joan left a tip and we got up to leave.

Twisting our way through tables and servers we arrived at the door. Joan paid the bill and Luigi and his wife Maria came out of the kitchen to say goodbye to her and meet me. They hugged her and shook my hand before we left.

After we were outside we were walking past the Golden Spike Italian Restaurant when Joan noticed the owner through the windows. She waved and he came outside and they hugged. She introduced me to him and we shook hands. *Man she knows everybody in the city,* I thought. The two hugged again and exchanged goodbyes.

We continued walking down Columbus Street, with Joan drawing looks from passing men. Stopping outside a storefront named Molinari Delicatessen Joan grabbed my arm. "Come on let's go inside, I want to get a few things for tonight."

I followed Joan inside and spent my time pretending to look at copious olives and cheeses. Meanwhile, Joan pranced around the inside of the shop grabbing several bottles of wine, a baguette, cheese, a chub of salami and olives while two male clerks gawked at her. It was as if Marylyn Monroe had dyed her hair brown and had just strolled into their shop. The clerks did a double-take at me and then at each other and shook their heads in disbelief. *What was this hot pepper doing with a wimp like that?* Little did they know I was asking myself the same question when she came up with a shopping bag full of goodies and smiled. "You see anything you want?" she asked.

The clerks looked at me long faced. "No, I think what you've got is more than enough."

"Good," Joan grinned, handing me the grocery bag. "Let's go home then."

We rode the Powell Street Cable car down to Market Street and hopped on the Muni 'F' bus headed to Berkeley. In those days the busses were GM "Old Look" transits painted Shamrock Green and white. They had sliding windows with two jelly bean shaped mini windows above every two seats.

The bus was packed with commuters. It was like a sauna despite every sliding window being open. Joan and I stood in the aisle holding onto the overhead stainless steel handrail. It wasn't long before the salami in the paper bag I was holding began to smell and people started looking at me. Joan giggled under her breath holding back her laughter. When we finally got off the bus, the two of us burst out laughing.

"Hey salami-breath," Joan teased. You sure made a good impression on all those commuters. She chuckled and I grinned. Even though I felt uncomfortable being the center of attention on the bus, I didn't mind her teasing me about it and laughed along with her. It was the least I could do. After all, she had paid for everything over my protestations. It had been a wonderful day so far, and the evening was still young.

I couldn't imagine then that nearly forty years later I would be filming inside the U.S. Restaurant where Joan and I had eaten, and would be making a film about her. Mark, Mickey, Susan and I packed up our gear just outside the U.S. Restaurant and headed for our 1:00 p.m. interview with Barrie in Fremont.

REALIZATION

Fremont, CA: August 25, 2010

That afternoon, we arrived at a business park in Fremont to interview Joan's brother, Barrie. Admittedly, I was nervous, and Barrie seemed so too. I had never delved deeply into another person's personal life, and to make it even more awkward, I really didn't know him. I was also nervous about what I planned to tell him afterwards. As for Barrie, I suspected that his anxiety stemmed from stage fright, which is quite normal.

When we pulled into the business park it was nondescript like many other businesses parks. Laid out in building clusters, it was hard to tell one from the other. It took us several drive-throughs before we figured out the address lettering scheme and were able to locate Barrie's office. We stopped in the "Visitors" parking area and I called him on my cell phone. A short time later Joan's younger brother emerged from the building and beckoned us to pull our rigs closer to the door, which we did.

I got out of our Escape and extended my hand. "Hi, I'm Paul Gorman. You must be Barrie Carson."

"That I am," Barrie replied, aloofly.

I introduced the rest of the crew to Barrie. After everyone had shaken hands, Barrïe pointed at the building entrance. "There's a conference room to the left just inside the doors," he said. "I think it'll work. Come on, I'll show you."

"Okay, let's go," I said, beckoning to Mark and Mickey to come along, while Susan offered to stay with the vehicles and keep an eye on the gear.

The room was minimalistic. Aside from having a conference table, chairs, a potted plant, several vases and shelves on one end of the wall that was it. There wasn't a lot of set dressing to work with. *Oh well, it'll have to do,* I thought.

"Will this work, Mark?" I inquired.

"As long as it has enough outlets," Mark said, walking around the room counting the number of wall outlets. "Looks like we've got three. We need four, three for me and one for Mickey."

"How about you Mickey, is this okay?" I asked.

"Yeah, as long as we can turn off the air conditioning in the room," Mickey said. "My mic will pick it up."

I turned to Barrie. "Any chance we can turn the AC off and run a power cord into the hallway?" I queried.

"There's a switch on the wall over there that controls the heat and AC, as for the power cord that's a no, no," said Barrie, "it would be a trip hazard."

"We can tape it down," Mark reassured, "and run the cord along the wall."

Barrie stroked his goatee thinking it over. "Okay, "he said, "but if the facilities guy sees it he'll be mad and will tell my boss."

We promised Barrie that we'd take the blame for it, and then went outside to bring in our equipment while Barrie went back to work.

Before he left he instructed me to move our vehicles after we were done unloading in the "Visitor Parking" area, and to come get him when we were ready.

After we were finished setting up, I went looking for Barrie amongst a maze of five foot high Herman Miller styled cubicles in a large open space.

Having worked many years in an engineering environment it looked familiar and stifling to me. The partitions were low enough that employees having hushed conversations sprouted above them randomly throughout the room. They were also low enough that I could see people working away at their computers. They would look up and watch me walking past. I was a stranger in a land that I was happy to no longer belong. Barrie had given me a visitor's badge, so if they wondered who this unaccompanied foreigner was they probably thought I was a vendor, which was commonplace in engineering firms.

I finally located Barrie after asking several people directions. He was on the phone and mouthed to me that he would be there in a minute.

When I re-entered the conference room Mickey was sitting in for Barrie while Mark adjusted the lighting. Mark had done a good job set dressing the bland room by bringing in an indoor plant from the lobby, putting it and several vases behind where Barrie would be sitting.

"Looks good, Mark," I said, glancing around the room. "The plants and vases add a good touch. Barrie said he'll be here in fifteen minutes. Are you guys about ready?"

"Just about," Mark said adjusting the position of his 1K rim light that would be used to backlight Barrie.

I looked over at Susan who was studying her questions and said, "How about you, are you ready?

"Did you want me to ask him about Joan's relationship with Dave?" Susan asked, looking up at me from her chair.

"Yeah, the more we know about him the better," I said, "since he won't let us interview him."

"Anything else?" Susan said.

"Ask him if he knows the reason Joan moved to Medford," I said, "so far, nobody knows definitively."

Susan jotted down several reminders to herself.

"Alright guys, we're only going to get one shot at this so let's get it right," I said, stating the obvious, which always annoyed Mark, but let him know that I was still unhappy about letting him talk me into shooting the film in 3-D with two cameras.

About ten minutes later Barrie came in, explaining that he had been busy getting last minute things done before leaving on his business trip that evening.

Wearing a meticulously pressed light blue dress shirt unbuttoned at the neck, exposing a white V-neck tee-shirt, Barrie was attired *business casual.* A handsome man in his mid-fifties with a tanned face that was virtually wrinkle-free, he looked at least ten years younger than his age. If it weren't for the flecks of gray in his goatee and temples of his light-brown hair, he could pass for someone in his late thirties. He resembled Joan only slightly. His eyes were hazel while hers had been brown, and her hair had been dark brown. When he smiled though, you could see the family resemblance. He had the same warm, broad, charismatic smile as hers.

During the interview, Barrie would tell us that he was the youngest of four children and Joan was four years older than he. Not only had he been the nearest sibling in age to her, but he had been the closest to her emotionally. They bonded on a variety of things, including the anti-Vietnam War movement that was happening then. They connected on music and the counterculture movement too. He looked up to her as his big sister. His older sister Janet was almost seven years older than him and his brother Bob was eighteen months older than Janet, so growing up he really didn't interact with them all that much.

Employed as a software sales engineer, Barrie lives in Los Gatos, California. An unmarried man, his two twenty-something daughters live with him. As a member of the tennis team at Redmond High

School he still plays competitive tennis, which by the looks of it has kept him in great shape. He also is a drummer in a band, playing parties and fund raisers.

My impression of Barrie was that he had an easy going charm and sensitivity about him, was articulate, handsome, had a killer smile, and female audiences would love him if the film was ever screened.

Meeting a family member of Joan's felt a bit like a kinship for me. I've never been superstitious or religious; having attended Catholic school for seven years cured me of that, and never believed in ghosts or conspiracies, but at that moment I felt a connection I can't explain.

Despite the bond I felt, I don't think Barrie felt it towards me. If anything, I think he was suspicious of my intentions and wondered why I was making the film. He wanted to know how I intended to portray Joan. I can't say I blamed him. Having four sisters of my own, I would've done the same thing. However, I got the impression that he wasn't only protecting Joan, he was guarding his reputation, his family name, and the idealized memory he had of her.

I told him about the experiences I had with Joan in San Francisco, about sleeping with her, and that nothing had happened. “That’s cool,” Barrie, said, shrugging it off. Then I told him about the dream I’d had. I explained that after she had died the dream haunted me for years and that occasionally over the years I had the same dream. For me, making the film was a quest to understand the meaning behind my dream.

Having said that, Barrie seemed to relax and lower his guard. From that point on, he was honest and forthright. "Do you want to hear the sanitized story, or do you want to hear the nitty gritty one?" he said.

I was ashamed that all of us, myself included, said in unison like a gaggle of reporters, "the nitty gritty story." *Yes, give us dirty laundry.*

Barrie paused, then exhaled deeply. "So Joan got pregnant when she was eighteen, and had a child, and she gave that child up for adoption. So I think at that point, she wanted to leave, to go find herself a little bit, because she had not really found happiness at home, she got pregnant, had to give up her daughter, and didn't really have a lot of support through that from her parents -- pretty disapproving. So for her, I think she might have had that instinct or desire to move on anyway and go find herself and maybe part of that would've been moving. At the time it was '69, 1970 and a lot of stuff was going on. It was a time of change, revolution, questioning, protests -- it was just part of that environment. She decided to go to San Francisco. But it was very much, I think, about her leaving the pain of that and wanting to find herself."

Suffice to say Barrie delivered a bombshell, which totally caught us off guard, yet explained everything. Explained why Joan had left Redmond, Washington shortly after high school and moved to San Francisco. Explained the reason she had possibly taken up skydiving and why she gravitated to drop zones around the country, and explained what she ultimately was searching for. Everything made sense now to me.

What a difference a day and an interview had made. Twenty-four hours earlier the project was floundering, but today it was alive, stunning, and layered with so much emotion, purpose, joy, heartache and meaning. The essence of Joan had been found and her spirit was alive in that room when Barrie so eloquently explained Joan's past.

Mark, Mickey and I glanced at each other in astonishment at the moment of crystallization. We were humbled by Barrie's eloquence and sorrow and by the gift we had received. It was as if Joan herself was speaking to us. It was magical and we captured it on film.

Beagle Boogie Babe was alive and I was going to finish it. I had crossed the Rubicon and there was no turning back, not that I wanted to, not that I could. Barrie had bestowed the ultimate gift of his family upon me, and for that I was grateful and indebted. I vowed to him then that I would try my best to complete Beagle Boogie Babe and honor Joan.

We wrapped up Barrie's interview about an hour later and he left us to go back to work while we loaded our vehicles. After we were finished, I went looking for him to let him know that we were ready to leave.

I spotted Barrie standing inside his cubicle talking to a co-worker in an adjacent cubicle. I made eye contact with him to let him know I was there. He seemed slightly perturbed. I wasn't sure if it was because I was interrupting him, or that he had time to reflect on my candid conversation about my experiences with his sister in San Francisco, or if he was just too busy at the moment to deal with me. Whatever the case may be, I waited uncomfortably several minutes for him to finish his conversation. I cleared my throat to get his attention, and then said, "Hi Barrie, we're all packed and ready to go."

"Did you turn the AC on and put everything back the way it was?"

"Yeah, everything is just the way we found it," I said.

Expecting him to want to see for himself and also to say goodbye to Mark, Mickey and Susan, I stood there for an awkward moment.

"So you're done here then?" he retorted, distantly.

"Yes, we're finished," I said. "Thank you for the interview and for letting us film here. It was great meeting you."

I hesitated momentarily not sure if I should hug him or shake his hand. Barrie's coolness wasn't helping me decide, so I extended my hand. He looked at me inquiringly then shook my hand weakly. I couldn't tell if he was regretting the interview, or if he was emotionally exhausted. Admittedly, I was bothered by his abrupt distance and was embarrassed when I went outside and the crew asked me why he hadn't come out to say goodbye.

"I don't know," I said. I was just as dumbfounded as they were and couldn't think of anything else to say. If Mark, Mickey, and Susan were bothered by it they never let on. It had been a great day and we still had to get Mickey to the airport for his flight home to L.A. Later that afternoon we dropped him off at SFO, returned to my sister's house and celebrated.

The next day we headed home to Seattle, buoyed by our time in San Francisco and our interview with Barrie. Beagle Boogie Babe was alive and thriving.

DISTURBING

Kalispell, Montana: October, 2010

On October 20, 2010, two months after interviewing Barrie in San Francisco, I returned to Lost Prairie and Kalispell with Mark to shoot B-Roll and to interview a woman named Sharon Tousey.

The day after we arrived in Lost Prairie, Mark and I went to Kalispell City Airport. I wanted to get some shots of it because it had been the Osprey's original drop zone, and where Joan had lived for four years in her motorhome with Dave -- upon arriving from Medford.

While filming there we happened to run into Bill Paulin, who we had interviewed in Lost Prairie in August. He was there buying parts for his airplane. We talked briefly about the progress of the film, and then he invited us to join him that evening at his friend Rick Wilson's place to drink beer and talk about Joan. Wilson had been a skydiver and had worked at the Osprey's favorite watering hole in town, Moose's Tavern. Paulin also said that Wilson had lots of pictures of Joan and the old jumping days. It sounded too good to be true, so I agreed to be there at 6:00.

Just as the sun was setting, we arrived at Wilson's, and Mark parked his Grand Cherokee in the gravel driveway. Getting out, we went around the side of the house to a detached garage where Paulin had instructed us they would be.

I knocked on the door and Paulin opened it holding a beer in his other hand. "Come in," he said, and then gulped on his beer. "This is Rick Wilson. It's his man cave. He's king here and can do whatever he wants."

Holding a spatula in one hand, Rick Wilson a balding unassuming man somewhere in his mid-sixties, turned from a wood burning stove where he was frying something. He extended his right hand. “Hi, I’m Rick but folks just call me Wilson,” he said, with a friendly nod and wink.

"Nice to meet you, Wilson," I said, shaking his hand. "I'm Paul and this is Mark."

"Which one of you is the director?" Wilson asked, stirring a skillet of onions and sausages on the stove.

"I am," I said. "Mark is my cameraman."

"So you're the one who knew Joan," Wilson retorted.

"Yeah," I said, "I went to high school with her and then spent a little time with her in San Francisco."

"She was a great chick," Wilson said. "Always was my favorite."

"Ol' Wilson had a big-time crush on her," Paulin chimed in, handing Mark and me beers. "Problem was nobody dared cross Dave. Having been a Special Forces paratrooper in 'Nam, he could kill you a thousand different ways.”

I took a big gulp of beer and swallowed hard at the sobering thought, while Paulin’s taut face tightened.

"Shame what happened to her," said Wilson, stoking the stove… "I wasn't there -- working at Moose's, but I heard all about it. You never use somebody else's chute, and you don't jump drunk."

"Was she drunk?" Mark probed.

"We were all drunk that weekend," said Bill, guzzling down the rest of his beer. "We didn't drink while we jumped, but we were all hungover from the night before. That's the way it was whenever we had a jump meet."

Paulin popped open another beer and chugged down a big blast like he was reliving the weekend.

Wilson asked several questions about the progress of the film. Then Bill inquired who was financing it. I was a little taken aback by his question, and was momentarily speechless. Mark picked up on my reticence and told Bill that I was financing it. Bill was incredulous, which further confounded me.

In hindsight, since Bill had been a banker, and taken several filmmaking classes in college, he knew how expensive film production could be, and that no bank would ever loan money on a film project. From that perspective his question made perfect sense.

For the next hour and a half we drank beer, ate fabulous local sausages slathered with grilled onions, and laughed at Mark's witticisms. He was quite the joke teller and kept us entertained. I was glad he was along.

Wilson showed us some of the black and white photos he had taken. They were nice pictures but most of them were taken before Joan had gotten to Kalispell so were of little use to me. He said he had more that we could look at tomorrow but we were leaving town then. I gave him my email address and asked him to scan any of Joan and email them to me. As it turned out, he never did.

When we were about to leave, we stepped outside with Paulin. By this time he was intoxicated and swaying.

"Dave was so handsome, so charismatic, a womanizer, oh how the ladies loved him, they all wanted him, he could have any of them, and he did," said Paulin. "But Joan was his match, she wouldn't put up with his womanizing and his drinking. She's the one that got away -- broke up with him. He couldn't handle it. Women never dumped him; he threw them away like yesterday's garbage."

Paulin swilled on his beer, burped and continued. "Crazy drunkard, that's what Dave was. Joanie left him and it enraged him, pissed him off. He punched her in the face. That's what happened."

I was stunned. We had heard rumors about a *fight* that weekend, but I had never thought it could be something physical.

Before I could respond, Paulin said, "Have you talked to Dave?"

"We've tried, but he won't talk to us," I said.

“He's avoiding you then," Bill said, polishing off his beer. "You need to talk to him, that's what you need to do. It's all there. That's your story. Talk to Dave."

With that, Bill said he had to go and got into his pickup truck and took off. He was so intoxicated that I wondered whether he'd make it home, and so did Mark. "I hate drunk drivers," he said, shaking his head.

"Good thing you're driving then," I said as we headed back towards Mark's Grand Cherokee and then to our hotel in Marion, where we planned to shoot more B-Roll in Lost Prairie the following morning before interviewing Sharon.

That night I lay awake and couldn't get the thought out of my mind of Dave supposedly punching Joan in the face. So many questions: If it happened, when did he do it? Did he knock her out? Did it impair her jumping ability? Did she pass out while jumping? So many questions and so few answers.

Maybe it was just a superficial wound and Joan had defiantly borrowed somebody else's parachute and jumped anyway just to piss off Dave. That was it, it was all an accident. It wasn't Dave’s fault any more than Joan's. It was nothing more than a lover's quarrel, a fight that had escalated to the point where both had made poor decisions -- a domestic argument, the kind that happens thousands of times every day in the U.S. Yeah, that's what it was, just a lover's disagreement.

Maybe, or maybe not. If a thorough investigation was ever conducted by the Flathead County Sheriff or County Coroner, I was never able to obtain it. Shortly before Mark and I had gone to Lost Prairie I had contacted the Sheriff, and was told I would need permission from the family to obtain any records. By this time, my relationship with Barrie was a little strained and I didn't want to ask him for their authorization. So that left Dave or somebody else who had been there and seen what had happened to talk about it.

The problem though was nobody wanted to talk about it on camera; it felt like they were all protecting Dave, or were too scared to say anything. It took Paulin getting drunk to talk about it, and he never said the punch in the face she sustained might have contributed to her death. But he implied it, and obviously was bothered enough about it to bring it up; albeit after seven or eight beers. But when it got right down to it, the only person who knew for sure was Dave and he wasn't talking.

The following morning after breakfast, Mark and I shot some B-Roll in Lost Prairie then headed into Kalispell to interview Sharon Tousey, who I had learned about shortly after returning from San Francisco and interviewing Barrie.

HOMELESS

Kalispell, Montana: October 22, 2010

Before Mark and I had left for Lost Prairie in October to shoot B-Roll, I had wanted to know more about the circumstances of Joan's death. In addition to contacting the Flathead County Sheriff and Coroner, I inquired with the Kalispell Library asking for any newspaper reports about her fatality. Several weeks later, I received two copies of articles in the mail that had appeared in the Flathead Beacon news about her death. One of the articles indicated that at the time she died she was residing at a home in Kalispell owned by a person named Sharon Tousey. I found Sharon's phone number online, called her, and arranged an interview.

The morning after drinking beer with Paulin and Wilson, Mark and I arrived at Sharon's gray and rust-red trimmed double-wide manufactured home. Getting out of my Escape, I tried to imagine Joan's Tioga motorhome parked in the grassy yard beneath the canopy of two rows of pine trees. During my phone conversation with Sharon, she had informed me that Joan was homeless and had parked her motorhome alongside her home, spending the last year of her life living there after breaking up with Dave. By the looks of it, she had parked her motorhome between some trees about fifteen feet away from Sharon's double-wide. Sharon would say later, during her interview, that Joan had hooked up the motorhome to her septic, power, and water, and paid her rent and split the utilities with her.

I knocked on Sharon's door and was greeted by two young children and a teenage boy. My initial reaction was that it wouldn't work having the kids running around inside while we tried to interview Sharon. My concern was quickly alleviated when a woman in her early sixties came to the door, introduced herself as Sharon and told the children they would have to go outside and play for a while.

Wearing a purple V-neck pullover over a white blouse, Sharon invited us in through the kitchen. A warm hearted and modest woman who looked a bit like actress Jane Stapelton, I immediately liked and felt comfortable with her. I could see why Joan had stayed at her place. Sharon's former husband, Tim, had been a skydiver and through him had met Joan at jump meets. Sharon had never been a skydiver. Her older son was Tim's and her's, and the younger children were foster children she was raising. Deeply involved in her church, she supervised cleaning at Emanuel Lutheran Home, an assisted care facility in town.

Having never been interviewed or filmed before, Sharon was anxious, but settled down quickly as Mark and I humored and complimented her. In no time she was telling us everything she remembered about Joan' stay at her place.

It was spring of 1980, when Joan broke up with Dave, that she moved her Dodge Tioga into Sharon's Kalispell yard.

Sharon remembered Joan as being, polite, intelligent, quiet and very private. "She really never did talk about any of her personal life, skydiving or any personal thing," said Sharon.

While living at Sharon's, Joan supported herself primarily by working as a Pot Tender at the Anaconda Aluminum plant in Columbia Falls, approximately 17 miles north of Kalispell.

In its heyday, the plant employed up to 1,200 locals -- Joan being one of them. The work was dangerous. "It was pretty dirty work," recalled Sharon. "She would work late afternoons, or maybe it was eleven o'clock at night and go until seven or eight in the morning, and then they would do another shift -- maybe it would be a day shift for a week and then she'd have a week off or so."

On her days off Joan would drive her Ford Pinto out to Lost Prairie to work on her property and skydive, or do things around town. "She did not just hibernate in her little trailer [motorhome]. She worked, she visited, she went up to Lost Prairie," said Sharon. "I'm sure she had other friends that she visited -- and work related people."

But when Joan was home she didn't have any visitors and spent most of her time by herself in her motorhome writing poetry, or in the yard playing with Sharon's kids who adored her, and she adored. Every now and then Joan would go inside Sharon's home and the two would do homey things together like baking and sewing. "She got me started on decaffeinated coffee," said Sharon, wagging a finger. "To this day I still can't drink real coffee and stay up all night like I used to -- darn her."

Sharon taught Joan how to knit, which resulted in her making a sweater for her nephew (Janet's son).

Unaware about the daughter Joan had given up for adoption, Sharon felt that Joan was sad before she ever broke up with Dave. "She just had a little sad quality about her," said Sharon. Sharon also believed that the cause of Joan's breakup with Dave was because of another woman. "She never really talked about it," Sharon said, "but I just know that there was another involvement there."

Even though Bill Paulin and other people had characterized Dave as being someone who was charismatic, ruggedly handsome, a womanizer, and heavy drinker, his relationship with Joan lasted the better part of five years, with some friends saying they had a lot of fun together. That being the case, the breakup was particularly hard on Joan.

"I think that she was really heartbroken because she had given her whole self into her relationship with Dave," said Sharon. "She was just the type of person that would give all of herself to whomever, and whatever she was going to do -- she gave it all, and I just think it was hard on her."

Joan rarely had visitors while she was living there, but Sharon did recall Dave visiting her once. Other than that, she lived a pretty solitary life outside of work and skydiving.

I asked Sharon whether Dave was violent towards Joan. "Not that I know of," Sharon replied. Then I told her what Bill Paulin had purported about Dave punching her in the face and giving her a black eye the weekend she died.

Sharon gasped, bit her lower lip in disbelief, but didn't deny that it could have been possible.

I then asked her if Joan had ever said anything negative about Dave and Sharon said, "She never did really talk about any of her personal life, skydiving, or any personal thing, and the only time that she ever said anything derogatory, I guess, against Dave is that she said, *I'm taking him off my life insurance policy at work.* And she did."

Later, I obtained a copy of Joan's probate Inheritance Tax settlement from Flathead County Records, which showed her life insurance indeed had been passed on to her estate, naming her father as Executor.

When Joan died, it was a shock to Sharon and her children. It was surreal to have someone living at her home and suddenly that person was dead. Having Joan's empty motorhome parked there was strange and a daily reminder that she was gone.

Within a week, Joan's family came to retrieve her belongings. Sharon was as helpful and sympathetic as she could be, endearing herself to Joan's mother, Edna. They became friends and for many years wrote each other up until recently. It wasn't long ago that the letters abruptly stopped coming, and Sharon wondered what had happened.

While wrapping up Sharon's interview I explained to her the reason the letters had probably stopped was because Edna had Alzheimer's and was institutionalized. Sharon was saddened by the news and felt sorry that Edna never fully got over Joan's death. I asked her if she still had Edna's letters, but unfortunately she said she had just thrown them away.

As Mark and I were leaving Sharon's place, I gave her a hug and wished her well on her plans to retire in two years. Outside, I stopped to take one last look at where Joan's motorhome had been parked, while Mark filmed the area. I suddenly felt sorry that Joan had spent the last year of her life living alone in her motorhome in a friend's yard.

I still couldn't get over how the direction of her life had changed since San Francisco. She seemed so vibrant, teaming with life and full of possibilities when I spent time with her there.

I had totally expected because she was living in Berkeley that she would go to college there, end up with a professional career, get married, raise a family and live happily ever after – the American Dream. There was no reason for me to have thought otherwise at the time.

Living in Sharon's yard in her motorhome, on the other hand, seemed like the end of the road. The more I tried to imagine Joan's motorhome parked alongside Sharon's manufactured home, the more ominous it felt. There was a solemnity to it. Sharon alluded to it, not so much by what she said, but how she said it. Several times she mentioned that Joan had a sadness about her, a sadness that was there even before she broke up with Dave. As wonderful of a person as Sharon was, I felt sorry that she had to deal with Joan's death, and that this was how Joan had lived out her final days.

Although Joan's living arrangements seemed depressing to me, perhaps she was not depressed. She was still active with work, friends, skydiving, and was developing her property in Lost Prairie. Maybe she had a plan and would one day move on.

Apparently Sharon felt that way, because during our interview she said that even though Joan wasn't going to school she felt that she was bigger than Kalispell and someday would move on. I came away feeling that what Sharon was really saying was that she couldn't understand why Joan hadn't left years earlier.

After Mark and I left Sharon's place, we drove to Columbia Falls -- seventeen miles northeast of Kalispell. I wanted to film the aluminum plant where Joan had worked before she died.

DEPRESSING

Columbia Falls, Montana: October 22, 2010

As a small company town, Columbia Falls was in a state of decline because of the recently shut down Columbia Falls Aluminum Company (CFAC) aluminum plant. When Joan worked there it was owned by Atlantic Richfield Company and was known as the ARCO aluminum plant. As we pulled into an empty parking lot sprouting weeds, an ominous plant surrounded by barb wire topped chain-link fencing came into view. Located alongside the Flathead River and shadowed by hulking Teakettle Mountain looming directly behind it, it looks more like a prison than factory. Just beyond the fence, a large reader board tracked the days since a LTA (Lost Time Accident) -- a sobering reminder to the employees on how dangerous it was to work there as they entered the facility.

While we filmed the plant, I kept wondering whether Joan had been depressed and possibly suicidal at the time of her death. After all, she had given up her baby, broken up with Dave, was living in a friend's yard, and was working a dangerous dirty job at a factory that looked like it was straight out of the former Soviet Union.

I had asked Barrie and Sharon the same question, and the consensus was that she was not depressed -- moody maybe, but certainly not depressed enough to take her own life. When we had interviewed Zimmo in Lost Prairie, we had asked him the same question, and as a Psych major in college, he said something that made sense. "She was spontaneous, but she was always kind of quiet and reserved…but willing to try anything, and I mean anything, which made her kind of like she was bipolar, not bipolar, two personalities. There was the quiet calm Joanie, and the let's go raise hell Joanie."

Having witnessed Joan's abrupt personality shifts when I spent time with her in San Francisco, Zimmo's analysis made sense to me.

Shortly before Joan's death, Lost Prairie had just been getting started, and she was getting her life together. She had purchased twenty acres, put a cabin on it, drilled a well, and was looking to subdivide her land to finance building her dream home there. She had a lot to live for.

If that weren't enough, according to Sharon Joan had a nephew she absolutely adored. She might have been lonely and sad at the time, but it seems unlikely she was depressed to the point of taking her own life. Nonetheless, unhappy people sometimes do things they know they shouldn't do, which I believe was the case with Joan. If anything she was fearless and defiant. From my experience with her, and from what many others said, you didn't dare tell her she shouldn't or couldn't do something, because she would turn right around and do it to prove you wrong. On the day she died, if she had been hit in the face and somebody said she shouldn't jump, she would go right ahead and jump, even if it meant borrowing somebody else's parachute.

Mark and I finished our filming at the aluminum plant and headed out to Lost Prairie to get some shots of the hangar, the airstrip, and the sun setting over the valley, which I planned to use in the film along with voiceovers.

Afterwards, Mark and I went to dinner at our motel in Marion and talked about all of the things we had experienced that weekend.

When I got home to Redmond after our third trip to Lost Prairie, I called a person named Mike Klinke. His name and phone number had been given to me by Bill Paulin, while at Wilson's place, saying I should interview him because he was in Lost Prairie the weekend of Joan's death, had been good friends with her, was a skydiver, and now lived in Seattle.

DEATH

Lost Prairie, MT: Memorial Day Weekend 1981

In talking to Osprey skydiver Mike Klinke on the phone in late October, 2010, he characterized the weekend Joan died as being a wild event of all night partying involving heavy drinking, 4x4 off-roading, ribald displays of sexuality, gross out contests, and non-stop skydiving -- not unlike most other Osprey Parachute Club events of the time -- and now.

The weather was particularly sunny and warm that weekend, and coming off a relatively mild winter and warm spring, everyone was in a festive mood to boogie. Nothing could be better than partying with your skydiving family at the newly created Lost Prairie drop zone where you could do as you damn well please and nobody would complain about it, mainly because hardly anyone lived there, and the last thing they were going to do was call the sheriff. Montana had always been Libertarian, and somewhat lawless, but Lost Prairie was like the wild west, you made your own rules, shot your guns, drank heavily and barreled around on a Bronco -- Ford that is. It just didn't get any better than this for the skydivers. It was skydiving utopia -- heaven on earth. It was Freedom. Even the Osprey's pet rat got into the fun, skydiving in a plastic tube mounted atop a helmet. When it died of old age it was given a hero's funeral – being buried beneath the dropzone's pee-gravel circle.

On Friday May 22, 1981, skydivers began arriving in the afternoon from Montana and Canada. Cottonwood seeds of friends drifted in and were welcomed like long lost family members with bear hugs and handshakes, and alcohol, finally plopping down on blankets that checker boarded the verdant prairie grass. The party was just getting started and was not unlike any other raucous skydiving event hosted by the Osprey Parachute club. You partied until you passed out, or right up until you jumped the following day.

But that would all change; Joan would be dead within 48 hours, and the party would abruptly turn into a dirge on Sunday, May 24, the day before Memorial Day. Joan's death had a sobering impact on those who attend the gathering that weekend at Lost Prairie. It wasn't an official jump meet. It wasn't an official club sanctioned boogie, it was a semi-spontaneous jump meet. After all, it was only May in Montana and you couldn't count on the weather there. But since it was sunny and warm, it was time to call your skydiving friends and jump at Lost Prairie. You had to jump when you could because it might become socked in for weeks or months.

Typically, jump meets stop only momentarily after a fatality, but it was different this time.

"Joan's death had a huge impact on the people," said, Osprey skydiver Mike Klinke. "We sort of cancelled everything we were doing that day. Other jump meets that I've attended when there's been fatalities it has hardly ever shut down the entire operation. And Joan's death pretty much shut down the entire operation."

That night the Osprey's spent their time drinking heavily at McGregor Lake Resort's bar, where they grieved and cried, drawing looks from lumberjacks, who frequented the spot, wondering who all the weeping people were.

Less than twenty-four hours later clouds had moved in and skydivers from all over Western Montana would hear the bad news about Joan and show up to mourn with the *family* who had been present when she died.

Once the Osprey's had collected at Lost Prairie, they decided to do a memorial jump to honor Joan. Klinke was on one of the loads. "I went up with Joan's boyfriend Dave," said Klinke. "I believe Fred Sand and Stinky [were] on the load with us…And I believe Bill Paulin was the pilot of the airplane…We were very concerned about Dave at that point, he was very despondent over the death of Joan. We had questioned the wisdom about having him jump with us on that particular load, but Dave has a strong love of life so our fears were unfounded."

The grief and shock of Joan's death was felt beyond Lost Prairie.

Barrie told us during his interview, that he had learned about Joan's death when he got a phone call from his father telling him about the accident. Nearly thirty years later he still had a hard time talking about it. "When I learned of Joan's last jump and her death, I was in Santa Cruz with my wife, and it was Memorial Day weekend. And I had never experienced anything like that. I was very close to my sister, and I was devastated – absolutely devastated."

Meanwhile, further up the coast in Medford, Beagle jumpers learned of Joan's death as word spread.

"I think Joan was the first, and it was sad," said Beagle skydiver Scott Rogers. "I got the word, I'm not even sure how I heard about it other than just the buzz on the drop zone, but everybody was talking about it."

For fellow Beagle cadre Zimmo, Joan's death was like losing a family member. "I got the phone call and I was devastated. I lost a sister. It's like losing your own sister," he said when we spoke with him in Lost Prairie.

The fact that the jump meet at Lost Prairie had come to a standstill the day of Joan's death and caused so much grief to the Osprey's and their extended skydiving family is no surprise. She was beloved by everyone who knew her. She didn't have an enemy in the world. She epitomized the fraternity and love of the sport in a manner that few have ever achieved. Joan Carson was the matriarch, the Amelia Earhart, the Beatles, of skydiving in Montana and Medford. Yet, she was unaware of her stature, as was virtually every other skydiver outside of her immediate skydiving circle. Joan was skydiving's unsung hero, which is beauty unto itself. The purity of her spirit is that she never did it for money, fame or recognition, she loved skydiving because it fed her soul, and eased her pain.

Ann Curtis, one of the founders of Pope Valley Parachute Ranch is the only other woman who comes close to that distinction. Several years later I met her in Pope Valley and showed her *Ride the Sky*. Afterwards she said, "Even though Joan jumped at Pope Valley I didn't know her. But your film could've been about me. I was just like her, except for the baby." She went on to say that somebody was planning to make a film about her.

I had gone to meet Ann Curtis to ask her to endorse the film, but after hearing about her film, I didn't have the nerve to ask her.

ALCOHOLISM

Kalispell, Montana: 1964 - 1976

Skydiving is an addiction for some. Those who do it regularly will tell you that it's the rush, the sense of community that goes along with it, the striving to get better at it that keeps you going. For some, it becomes a passion and a way of life. They live to skydive and skydive to live, travelling from boogie to boogie around the country, camping out at dropzones, they reconnect with old friends, and make new ones.

"It was such a passion," said Osprey skydiver Bill Paulin, who started skydiving in 1964 continuing until 1976. "It was like alcoholism. It was such a rush. You wanted to do it again as soon as you landed."

When you jump out of an airplane, you are already travelling at close to 100 mph. Immediately you encounter 100 mph air resistance. It's like you were shot out of a canon. Because of this, the rate of decent initially is reduced due to forward momentum, and there is very little sensation of falling. As your forward thrust ebbs and the tug of gravity takes over you start falling faster. You are not aware of it though, because after 10 seconds the air resistance is 110 mph -- only 10 mph more than when you jumped out of the aircraft. You continue falling faster. The faster you fall downward the more air resistance upward. Eventually you reach a balance. You are still falling but you have reached terminal velocity of about 120 mph. Since there is nothing around you as a reference point, you have no perception of speed. It's as if you are floating on a cushion of air, but you are falling 1,000 feet every six seconds. The average free fall lasts only about sixty seconds in which time you will have fallen about 8,000 feet before your main parachute inflates. Assuming you jumped out of an airplane at an altitude of 10,000 above ground level (AGL) you might have experienced temperatures 35 degrees colder than when you left the ground.

At terminal velocity the rush of air past you is fast and furious and loud. Buffeted by the high speed airflow, your face distorts ghoulishly. With your head up, back arched, legs spread slightly, lower legs bent forty-five degrees upwards, arms bent at the elbows and your forearms out in front of your torso; you resemble a person riding a chopper motorcycle in the sky. You navigate using various arm and leg movements by changing the airflow around your body. By deflecting air, you can turn, go forward, go backward, slow down your rate of decent, and speed it up. For example: If you want to turn right, bank your right arm downward and your left arm upward. More air will spill off the left side of your body creating a right turn. A left turn can be accomplished by doing the opposite. To stop the turns, return to the neutral position where both arms are in the same plane. These maneuvers take practice and over time allow you to join up (dock) with other skydivers in the air to create formations.

Skydivers wear altimeters on a wrist, telling them their altitude above ground level. The United States Parachute Association sets 2,000 feet as the minimum opening level for experienced skydivers and 2,500 feet for less experienced jumpers. Since it takes between 600 and 1,200 feet of free fall for most main parachutes to fully open, that means an experienced skydivers should deploy their main parachute at 3,200 feet just to be safe.

In the event the main parachute is unusable, this will allow enough time to perform a cutaway, and deploy a reserve chute. Reserves can open in less than 400 feet after deployment. The minimum altitude to deploy a reserve and still land safely is 700 feet.

Today most experienced parachutists deploy their parachute by reaching back and pulling a small pilot chute stowed near their butt in a pouch at the base of the container on their back. They toss the pilot chute off to the side into the airstream. The pilot chute fills with air. Attached to it is a seven to ten foot line called the bridle leading to the deployment bag stowed inside in the container bag/harness assembly. When the pilot chute is filled with air, the bridle pulls the deployment bag out of the container. The pilot chute continues pulling. It stretches the steering lines that had been rubber banded beneath the deployment bag. When these lines are taut they pull the risers out of the deployment bag. Once there is tension on these items, the pilot chute pulls the canopy out of the bag and it inflates with air. To keep it from inflating too fast, causing injuring to the skydiver or damage to the parachute, a device called a slider holds the lines close together near the base of the parachute. As air fills the canopy the lines spread forcing the slider downward.

When the parachute is fully inflated, the skydiver checks to make sure that it is not damaged and is properly inflated. Satisfied that the parachute is in good shape the skydiver reaches up, a little more than head high, and detaches the steering toggles from the left and right risers. The skydiver then checks the steering. By pulling on the right toggle the parachute goes right, and by pulling on the left toggle it goes left. The last thing the skydiver checks is the flare. This is accomplished by pulling down on both toggles simultaneously. Flaring slows the parachute and is important when landing. Airplanes do this by putting their flaps down thus creating drag.

In the event that the parachute is damaged, or is not functioning properly the skydiver needs to assess whether or not the situation can be corrected in time. If not, can the parachute be flown safely as is? If neither one of these are true then the parachutist will do a cutaway and fly using the reserve parachute.

A cutaway is accomplished by pulling a handle on one of the shoulder straps, thus activating 3-ring releases on both risers at the same time. Once this happens, the skydiver falls out of the main parachute and is freefalling. Now that the parachutist is safely separated from the main parachute to avoid entanglements, the reserve parachute is deployed one of two ways: Either by means of a reserve static line that pulls out the reserve when it cuts away from the main parachute, or manually by pulling a second handle.

In the case of Joan's double malfunction, it was reported that her main parachute never came out of the deployment bag. *Bag lock,* is caused when lines become wrapped around the bag during deployment, or the mouth of the bag is locked. Unable to use her main parachute Joan then did a cutaway. For unknown reasons, her reserve parachute never fully deployed and became a *streamer,* meaning it's out or partially out of the deployment bag but it is failing to inflate fully. Streamers can be caused by a damaged parachute, uneven line deployment, line entanglement or slider hang-up.

Falling at 120 mph with the streamer above her, onlookers said Joan never gave up. She fought it all the way down by yanking on the reserve's risers, trying to get the streamer to inflate.

Oddly, both of Joan's malfunctions were similar in that they could have been caused by line entanglements or twists. Spinning, instability, or being upside down at the time of deployment, increases the risk of line entanglements and twists. According to the United States Parachuting Association's, "The Skydiving Handbook," the two main factors in parachute malfunctions are:

1. Equipment related: Faulty equipment due to damaged equipment or equipment that was improperly packed.

2. Body position: Improper body position or instability at the time of deployment could cause the pilot shoot to become entangled on the skydiver thus stopping the deployment, or an unstable opening could cause the lines to become entangled or form a knot preventing the parachute from fully inflating.

Because of the similarities between Joan's double malfunctions, it's possible they were caused by her being out of position or unstable. If this indeed caused her malfunctions, the real question is why would an experienced skydiver with more than 700 jumps not be in the proper position twice on the same jump? With that many jumps under her belt, it wasn't the first time she had done a *cutaway.* When we interviewed Zimmo he told us about a time he had seen Joan do a cutaway with another jumper, "They opened the parachutes at the same time," he exclaimed. "The next thing I knew they did cutaways at the same time, went into freefall, and then pulled their reserves simultaneously. It was like it was choreographed. It was like a ballet."

ORGANIZING

Redmond, WA: January through March, 2011

After my phone conversation with Mike Klinke, I spent several months working at our home in Redmond on a rough edit of the film, looking for holes that needed to be filled and plotting my next round of filmmaking. I was wrapping things up.

Almost immediately after deciding to take on the project, I decided to film scenes re-enacting my experience with Joan in San Francisco and Berkeley, and wrote a script about it.

Now that I was getting a handle on the rough edit I had more time on my hands and in January, 2011, I placed an online ad for two actors -- one to play Joan and the other to play myself. I auditioned ten actors, five men and five women a month later in February at New Discovery School in Seattle.

During this time Susan kept pushing me to interview Joan's sister, Janet. As far as I was concerned then, Barrie had done such a good job covering all the bases that I didn't feel it was necessary to interview her. Susan finally convinced me that the preponderance of the film was males and it would be good to include another female voice in the film, especially since the film was about a woman, and was the sister of Joan. I finally acquiesced, and am glad I did.

Several days after the auditions, I cast Megan Ann Jones and Jesse Lee Keeter to act in the reenactment scenes and scheduled to shoot them on Saturday March 19, 2011. I also scheduled an interview with Mike Klinke for that Sunday, and planned to record my narration that Friday. I already had arranged to have Mark, Mickey and Susan as my crew.

It just so happened Mickey's mom, who lived on nearby Bainbridge Island, died shortly before the weekend of the shoot, which cast everything in doubt. Would he be available and want to work then?

I didn't know, and wouldn't have blamed him if he declined. I left it up to Mark to check with Mickey being as they were best of friends at the time.

Mark checked in with Mickey and then informed me that he was up to it. On March 8, I booked a flight for Mickey to Seattle from Los Angeles. I arranged it so he would arrive on the Thursday of the weekend shoot, and then depart on the Tuesday after it. This would give him time to spend with family members living in the area before and after the shoot.

Having nailed down a day for shooting the reenactments, and confirming Mickey's participation, I set up an interview with Mike Klinke for that Sunday, and then reached out to Joan's brother Barrie, sending him an email about scheduling Janet:

It has been a while and I just thought I would give you an update on Beagle Boogie Babe. This weekend we are recording the narration, and filming 3 or 4 reenactment scenes and then the last of the interviews. Speaking of which, I would like to interview your sister. Hopefully she is interested because it would really be great to get the perspective of another family member, particularly a sister, and will provide some material to intercut with your interview. Please let me know if she is interested. I will need to know this week, because I have scheduled interviews for this Sunday (March 20), at New Discovery School in Seattle, but can accommodate her on Friday or Monday if that works better for her. Sorry for the short notice, but it's been hard getting my audio guy up here from L.A...

After this weekend, the only filming left will be to shoot some skydiving footage in Lost Prairie. However, this won't happen until the weather gets better there -- probably late April or May. At this stage I am still editing the film and have trimmed it down to 96 minutes from 153 minutes. I hope to get it down to 90 minutes when it is completed. I am really excited about this project and believe it has enormous potential. I still plan to screen it this summer at Lost Prairie; however I might have a test screening in Seattle before then. If I do, I will let you know.

Later that same day Barrie emailed me back. He appreciated the update, provided me with Janet's contact information, and said she was looking forward to helping.

That evening I called Janet to arrange an interview and was nervous about it.

I always hated calling someone out of the clear blue I didn't know and having to adequately explain who I was, and what I was doing in thirty seconds lest they hang-up up on me. I rehearsed what I was going to say for about an hour then finally dialed her number. My trepidation was particularly high due to the stilted goodbye I had with Barrie after his interview seven months earlier.

Two or three rings after I called, a woman answered the phone. "This is Janet."

Beagle skydiver Dee-Bra had commented during our interview with her in Medford, that when she had gone to Joan's funeral in Lost Prairie she had heard Janet's voice. "I heard her sister talking to someone and was amazed at the remarkable similarities between their voices. Oh, this is so sad, I can hear her but she's dead. It was terrible," Dee-Bra lamented. "It was the first friend that I had lost. It was hard."

I introduced myself, and then based on what Dee-Bra had said, focused on Janet's voice trying to tell if it sounded like Joan's. It had been so many years since I last heard Joan's voice that I wasn't sure. In any case, it was a good distraction from my nerves. I'm sure I sounded like a complete idiot though as I tried to carry on an intelligent conversation with her.

"Oh yes, my brother Barrie talked to me about you and your film about Joan," Janet said. "It sounds great. How can I help?"

"I'd like to interview you if that's okay," I said.

"What would you like to talk about?" Janet inquired. "Barrie was much younger and closer to Joan than I was."

Suddenly I was feeling inarticulate, and mumbled, "I'd like to get your perspective from a sister's standpoint about -- benign questions you know, about growing up -- nothing too serious."

If Janet noticed my inability to express myself she didn't let on, filling in my train of thought, she said, "About the baby?"

"Yes, about the baby," I exhaled with relief.

"I can do that," Janet said. "When and where do you want to meet?"

I told her that I would like to do the interview at New Discovery School in Seattle on Sunday, March 20 at 2:00 PM.

I mentioned I had arranged to interview another person, earlier in the day, named Mike Klinke, who had been a skydiver in Kalispell and Lost Prairie when Joan was there, and now lived in Seattle.

Susan was the founder and director of New Discovery School and had offered to let me use it that weekend to interview them and film the reenactment scenes too. On Saturday, March 19 we shot the acted scenes, and then the next day we filmed the interviews with Janet and Klinke.

Janet arrived right on time for her interview. I introduced myself, along with Mark, Mickey and Susan. As the owner of Sammamish Montessori School, Janet was relaxed, confident and friendly, and immediately hit it off with Susan being the founder and director of a preschool herself.

FRIENDLY

Seattle: March 20, 2011

Dressed smartly in a white blouse with black flecks and a black cashmere cardigan Janet was an attractive 63 old blond. Like Barrie she looked at least ten years younger than her age.

As a former flight attendant, Janet left home soon after high school and was gone traveling so much that she rarely saw Joan. It wasn't until Joan came to visit her in Minneapolis that they were able to connect on a level outside of parental confines.

After Janet moved back to the Redmond area, Joan who was living in Kalispell would fly over in the plane that she and Dave owned and visit Janet. She adored Janet's son, bringing him baby clothes and toys.

The day Joan died Janet was home in Sammamish from her stewardess job. "It was one of those surreal moments," she said. "My dad called me up and said he had gotten the message…and he said there had been an accident and that Joan had died."

Pausing briefly to compose herself, Janet continued. "I know she knew she was going to die," she continued, "you can't not know. You have two parachutes and neither one is opening…I don't think she ever looked down. I just think she just kept looking up. And from what I can gather from what people have said, that's exactly what she did."

Janet told us later she regrets that she never took the time to see Joan in her skydiving world.

Janet was no stranger to tragedy in her life. Seven or eight years after Joan’s death, her father died, twenty years after Joan’s death, her son was killed in an auto accident in 2001, and then she's had to deal with her mother Edna's Alzheimers disease.

All in all, our interview with Janet lasted about an hour. She was composed, cheerful and articulate, although she did become emotional when she talked about getting the news from her father about Joan's death, and when she talked about the funeral. Overall though, her interview complimented Barrie's almost flawlessly. Combined with his, a portrait of Joan's family life emerged.

CHILDHOOD

Mendocino, CA to Redmond, WA: 1950 - 1969

Joan Margret Carson was born on December 28th, 1950 in Mendocino County Hospital, the daughter of Canadian immigrants Herbert Barrie Carson and Edna Carson.

The rolling green hills of Mendocino County, located about 60 miles north of San Francisco, are scattered with oak trees and majestic horse ranches sectioned off by white fences. The sprawling ranches finally succumb to vineyards and wineries the closer you get to Napa County.

Amongst other things, Joan's early years were spent moving multiple times.

"My parents moved to Redmond in 1962," Barrie said, when we interviewed him at his company in Fremont. "Prior to that, my family had moved almost every year – sometimes even twice a year."

Barrie's father, Herbert worked as a chemist and when he finally got to Redmond the family made it clear to him that they were tired of moving and wanted to stay there, and they did.

In part, Barrie felt that Joan's sense of adventure came from their dad. "My Father had wanderlust and was constantly looking for a place where he wanted to be," Barrie said. "And part of that was moving and changing jobs and trying to find that place where he wanted to be."

Joan was creative growing up. She danced ballet and tap for four years with Janet while they lived in Shelton, Washington.

Janet, who was three years older than Joan, didn't connect all that much with her because when Joan was in elementary school she was in junior high. When Joan was in high school Janet was away at college, and then flying for the airlines. But Janet did remember the dance lessons with Joan during elementary school as a time when the two connected and were at their closest. She especially remembered how much they enjoyed stopping for ice cream cones afterwards as a reward.

"She loved to do art," said Barrie about Joan. "She drew and painted -- played music a little bit...She was always kind of the artistic one in the family. She never really developed or took it anywhere, but to me it kind of reflected her personality -- that need to express." By the time the family moved to Redmond, Joan was in 5th grade and attended Redmond Elementary. Two years later she moved on to junior high, and started expressing herself.

During those years, Joan channeled her dance training and creative energy into being a cheerleader at Redmond Junior High, and later would continue cheerleading at Redmond High School. "I don't recall her enjoying it really a lot when she got to high school, but she just kept doing it because that's what she did," said Janet.

"She was really popular and it was her way of connecting and being part of the high school," recalled Barrie. But he also remembered her as being quiet while living at home. "Joan was always kind of quiet in the family, that was kind of her role in the family, but I don't think that's who she really was."

Quietness would be a trait of Joan's that others would notice later on. By all accounts though it seems reasonable to assume that she expressed herself physically, whether it was dance, cheerleading, or skydiving, she communicated to the world physically through her actions.

Surprisingly, she was not much of a risk taker growing up. "She went up skiing with us," said Janet. "She was adventuresome, but she was actually a little more shy about stepping out and stepping into doing things -- that kind of came with time and experience. And it came from getting away from our family and just being on her own."

The birth of her baby and the subsequent adoption would transform Joan, channeling the pain and possibly anger into a self-reliant and determined person.

TURMOIL

Redmond, WA: 1969 - 1971

In the winter or spring of 1969, when Joan learned she was pregnant, her parents forced her to move out of their house. She lived with a couple in Seattle until giving birth to a baby girl and putting it up for adoption. "I think Joan wanted to keep the baby, but my parents weren't pro that, they were all about image," said Janet. "And if you knew Joan she wasn't into image at all."

The father of the baby, whose name neither Barrie nor Janet were able to remember, or didn't want to divulge, was incapable of providing help financially or emotionally, so Joan had to shoulder the burden all on her own, and ended up never wanting to see him again. The way Barrie and Janet portrayed him, he was never somebody she was serious about.

While Joan was in the hospital, the nurses made the mistake of handing her the baby and she bonded with it, which made giving up her daughter all the more painful.

At the recommendation of her parents, the adoption was a *closed adoption* so Joan never knew anything about the adoptive parents, or her daughter, and always wondered about her. "I think it was a difficult time in her development," said Janet.

After giving the baby up for adoption, Joan attended Bellevue Community College briefly before dropping out of school.

Soon afterwards, Joan left the Seattle area and moved to San Francisco. It was 1971. The Vietnam War was still going on. It was a time of revolution, protest and change and she was drawn to that and decided to go to San Francisco and be at the center of that movement.

REBORN

San Francisco: 1971

"When I visited Joan she was actually living on Green Street in San Francisco and working at a pharmacy in Chinatown," said Barrie. "I don't think she was doing anything other than paying the rent. She was not career motivated. She was out there just trying to find herself."

Prior to working in Chinatown, Joan worked in Mill Valley for Bank of America as a teller, just as she had done in Bellevue, Washington before she left.

Despite the fact that Joan worked in Chinatown, she loved the North Beach area of San Francisco where she was a regular at the Italian delis and restaurants, eating there often.

"She really liked being in San Francisco and the adventure of it, but she got really excited about this skydiving thing," said Barrie, grinning, remembering the happiness and enthusiasm it gave Joan.

While still living in San Francisco, a male friend had invited her to go skydiving. By June of 1973 Joan had relocated to Berkeley taking a job as a waitress at Raleigh's Pub on Telegraph Avenue. Even though she wasn't a student at the University of California, she expressed to me, when I stayed with her in San Francisco, that she had moved there because rents were cheaper, and she had a girlfriend living there. As an added bonus, moving there made it easier to get to drop zones at Antioch, Livermore, Byron, and Tracy. Living in San Francisco and Berkeley she started taking chances that she hadn't done growing up. Her skydiving journey had begun.

According to Barrie and Janet, as happy as Joan was to start skydiving, the pain of having a baby, and then being forced to give her daughter up for adoption would never leave her. But she rarely discussed it -- even with family members.

Maybe it was because of her conservative upbringing, or because her family almost never talked about their feelings. Joan was very tight lipped about the adoption. Nobody we interviewed, other than Barrie and Janet, ever mentioned it.

In later years when she flew home to visit Janet, she did talk about her feelings a little. "I think she always had some regrets," said Janet. "I remember one time that Joan did tell me that she was sad, and she always thought of her daughter."

PEACE

San Francisco, Medford, Lost Prairie: 1973 -- 1981

By all accounts it would appear that skydiving gave Joan direction and purpose, and eased her anguish -- at least temporarily.

"When she was up in the air everything that mattered was right there with her. She didn't think about her problems. She didn't think about the earth. All she could think about was how beautiful it was and how freeing it was to be up there," said Janet, as if fully comprehending for the first time the significance of her younger sister's need to skydive.

In 1973 there were several drop zones in the San Francisco Area. In addition to Antioch and Livermore, there was the newly opened Pope Valley Parachute Ranch north of Lake Berryessa being the most prominent, and Joan's favorite. She jumped at all of them before she broke her wrists.

But for Joan, in spite of her injuries, skydiving was well worth the risk. Not only did it provide her with peace of mind, but it gave her the *family* she had been desperately seeking.

"Once she got into skydiving it was the skydiving community that drew her, said Janet. "All of the towns she ended up in were small, even though when she left Redmond she wanted something bigger.

When Joan ended up in Medford, she wound up being in another small town but this time in a small town where she had a common group of people that she just adored. I can remember her talking about skydiving and telling me how wonderful it was to have that connection from a varied group of people with a common interest."

Joan's parents were less than thrilled about skydiving; in particular her mother Edna disliked the sport. After Joan had her accidents there were occasions when Edna tried talking her out of it, Joan would cite statistics, such as it was safer than driving a car. And regarding her broken wrists, Janet said that Joan would become defensive, “the next time I won’t put my hands behind me.”

If there was anything positive that came out of her injuries, it was that it gave Joan time to spend with her mother and see relatives and travel. While Joan was recuperating at home after breaking her wrists, her mother took her to England to visit an uncle and do some sightseeing.

However, as soon as Joan had healed from her injuries, she went right back to skydiving. All of this made an impression on Barrie who couldn't understand how something that could give her so much pain, could give her so much joy.

Curious about the sport, Barrie jumped several times with Joan in Kalispell in the late 70s. He did it to experience what his sister was so crazy about, but quickly realized after landing on a chain link fence at Kalispell City Airport, that skydiving wasn't for him, and never jumped again. In spite of his close call and Joan's death he was philosophical about the sport.

"I don't think Joan's death taught me that skydiving is something to avoid," Barrie said. "Everything in life has risks. Skydiving has risks, going to the grocery store has risks...The question is, is how do you live your life, and what's the value to you of what you do, and what you are passionate about. There are things in life that are risky. The alternative is to live a safe life, and I think that's not living. I don't think Joan for a second ever took a safe path in her life -- ever. And that's one of the things that made her unique. I think that's one of the things that people were drawn to with Joan, is that she lived life that way…people saw that…that's a very attractive thing -- it's very powerful."

Jumping in Kalispell would not only give Barrie a better understanding of the impact skydiving had on Joan, but it provided him with and explanation of the allure skydiving had on her and others which he talked about during his interview.

"When I was in Kalispell visiting Joan, I spent a few late nights after a few beers talking to people trying to understand this thing called skydiving," said Barrie. "It never made sense to me…because I did it…loved it on one level -- feared it mostly though. And I wanted to understand what drove people to continue to do it. I don't think there's any one thing that anybody said, but what I walked away with from this conversation was kind of a view of life that divers were willing to roll the dice every time they got in an airplane -- that's how they lived their life. I think you could look at that and think it was almost a death wish -- like you had a death wish. I think for me I ended up looking at it as a life wish -- that if you're so passionate about what you're doing that you're willing to risk everything for it -- you're definitely living life to the fullest."

Joan's last jump would not only have an adverse effect on Barrie and the rest of her family, it also left a lasting impact on her friends and fellow skydivers. One skydiver in particular who was there the day she was killed was deeply disturbed by what he experienced. He talked about it in Seattle the same day we interviewed Janet. That person was Osprey skydiver Mike Klinke.

SADNESS

Seattle: March 20, 2010

Mike Klinke arrived at New Discovery School for his interview. A balding, cherubic man with a ruddy complexion, he owns a printing business in Seattle. I had already spoken with him on the phone about the events leading up to Joan's death. Having been there that Memorial Day Weekend in 1981 he had characterized it as being out of control.

I wanted to interview him again, only this time on film. My hope was to learn more about Joan's fatal fall, and the events immediately following it.

When Klinke met Joan, somewhere around 1976 or 1977, she was living in her motorhome at the Kalispell City Airport with Dave. As a college student at the University of Montana in Missoula at the time, he spent his summers, and holidays jumping and partying with the Osprey's at the city airport and in Lost Prairie when it got up and running.

He told us some of the crazy things they did like cramming twenty people into Joan's motorhome during the winter for a holiday party, lighting toilet paper on fire and sticking it between their naked butt cheeks while everybody else hooted and hollered at the spectacle of somebody trying to keep their ass from going up in flames. But more than anything, he remembered the day Joan died.

"I was walking along the road, and looked over and saw someone under a streaming parachute," Klinke said, his voice quavering. "I remember calling out, *pull your reserve, pull your reserve,* but that was her reserve. She'd already done a cutaway and now had a streaming reserve. When we got there, Joan was on the ground, pushed into the ground a bit. I did the mouth to mouth resuscitation."

Klinke broke down, reliving the horrible tragedy for the moment, forcing us to stop so he could compose himself. Susan slipped into her school office, grabbed some tissue, ran back out and handed it to him. Apologizing profusely, he dabbed his eyes until they were dry, while Susan comforted him. In the meantime, Mark, Mickey and I looked the other way and did our best to appear busy. While interviewing, we had seen three or four people break down and it was always uncomfortable.

Fellow Osprey jumpers, Bill Paulin and Fred Sand had been present too when Joan died and had given their side of the story. According to Fred, a certified rigger, Joan had done everything right. When her main parachute failed to deploy she had done a cutaway, jettisoning her main chute, and then pulled her reserve which failed to come fully out of the bag it was packed in. Paulin's account was similar to Fred's with the exception of seeing a streaming reserve. With more than 8,000 jumps under his belt, Fred who has had about 30 cutaways while jumping was cavalier about it. “It’s just part of the game; that’s why we take two parachutes – just in case.”

When we interviewed Paulin in Lost Prairie, he solemnly recalled that he had been walking on the dirt road just outside The Lounge with a person named Bob. Similarly, Klinke had been walking down the same dirt road when Joan’s shoot didn’t open. Their stories are so similar Paulin might have mixed up Bob with Klinke, or vice versa. It doesn’t really matter because the result was the same.

After Joan hit, Paulin ran back to call 911. "I don't even know if it was 911 in those days," he said, his voice nearly a whisper. "But anyway, we called the helicopter and it started out. And they [some jumpers] came back and said she was dead. So we called them [the helicopter] off, and then somebody came in and said she was moving and we called them again. We didn't have the communications that we have nowadays. And so they came out, but she was gone."

The cause of Joan's double malfunction remains a mystery. Her fatality was investigated by the FAA. "The FAA didn't find anything. They found nothing wrong with how it was packed, what happened. They just said it was just that, an accident," said Joan's sister, Janet, when we interviewed her in Seattle.

But to this day rumors persist that somebody else had packed Joan's parachute and that she had used borrowed equipment during that jump. When we spoke with Zimmo in Lost Prairie, he said, "I was told that she had borrowed a parachute, and borrowing any gear anytime when you're skydiving always has an extra risk because you're not familiar with the gear."

Sam Scott corroborated what Zimmo had said when we talked with him in Lost Prairie. "There were just rumors that she was using gear that she wasn't really used to…but I don't know if that was true or not."

Another report is that Joan's reserve was not packed by a certified rigger -- a definite no-no as far as skydiving common sense is concerned and illegal by FAA (Federal Aviation Administration) rules.

Many experienced skydivers pack their own main parachute rather than pay a rigger to do it. Not only is it cheaper, but it is legal. Back in the days when Joan was jumping, FAA regulations mandated that reserve parachutes be opened, inspected and repacked by a certified rigger every 12 months. Today they must be re-packaged every 6 months even if they were never used.

"You can't pack your own reserve unless you're a licensed rigger," said Zimmo a former skydiving instructor, "which means you have to go to school and get rated by the FAA to pack pilots' rigs and sport's parachutist's emergency reserves. You can't have a guy who may not understand what he's looking at packing it. This is a life saving device now. We're not having fun when we start using this. We're trying to save our lives. So it makes sense. You want somebody who understands every aspect of what's going on, whether it's worn, this needs to be replaced, everything, whether there's a safety issue about your particular rig, other people reporting this problem, you don't know that, but he does. He's getting the bulletins all the time in the mail. Yeah, you've got to have a licensed rigger do it."

According to the United States Parachute Association, there was an average of 34.1 skydiving deaths per year during the 1980s. The fact that Joan's fatality was a double-malfunction makes it even rarer. Since the probability of having a double malfunction is about one in a million. It goes without saying that if she was using borrowed gear, or if her reserve wasn't packed by a certified rigger, the probability would increase.

Continuing our interview with Mike Klinke, he choked up as he recalled having to call Joan's father after cleaning her blood from his face due to the mouth to mouth resuscitation he had performed. "The sheriff needed to contact her parents. Dave was not up to the task of talking with them, so I broke the news to her father," said Klinke, fighting back tears, still haunted by the experience.

Only Dave knows why he was not up to the task.

We finished our interview with Klinke and I promised to let him know when the film was finished and to invite him to the premiere screening. He apologized for breaking down and I reassured him that it was okay, and that he hadn't been the first. He shook my hand, then left somberly, head hanging low and shoulders slumped. Having recently lost his wife to cancer it helped explain his breakdowns. However, I'm sure I would have broken down too if I had gone through what he did, and had to deal with it all these years. I felt particularly sorry for him and so did Mark, Mickey, and Susan, as we watched him leave.

By 4:30 PM Sunday, we were emotionally drained from a weekend of shooting the reenactment scenes, recording my narration and Klinke's and Janet's interviews earlier that day. We stood there in silence too numb to say anything. Finally, we packed up our gear, and Susan and I said goodbye to Mickey who was going to spend a few nights with Mark before heading back to L.A.

While driving home, I thought about how many people were still saddened by Joan's death thirty years after she died. As affected as they were, they seemed to find solace in saying, "She died doing what she loved." Perhaps so, but if she had known the impact her death would cause so many years later would she have changed it if she could? The Joan I knew was a generous person so I believe she would have.

What ever the case may me, by all accounts when Joan arrived in Kalispell she was jubilant, and death was probably the furthest thing from her mind. She was in love, had new friends, was having the time of her life, and it all revolved around skydiving.

GYPSY

Kalispell, Montana: May, 1976

Pulling into Kalispell, sometime in May of 1976, Joan parked her motorhome at the Kalispell City Airport alongside the Osprey Parachute Club's hangar and house, which she used as her mailing address. It was their home base, where they packed their parachutes, hung out, and partied until the sun came up the next day, which was pretty much every weekend regardless of whether the weather was good and they were jumping. She made it home for almost four years.

"The old days for us it was a far more social activity," said Osprey skydiver Mike Groarke during his interview in Lost Prairie. "We used to travel together; a lot of us lived together. The house in Kalispell is where a lot of the jumpers lived for a while -- Dave, Stinky, Joanie, a bunch of them all together."

It was April 1977 when Joan started work at the Anaconda Aluminum Plant in Columbia Falls. Shortly thereafter she bought a Ford Pinto, using it for commuting to and from work, running errands, and seeing friends. Little is known what she did for work prior to working at the aluminum plant. Zimmo mentioned something about her working at a plywood mill, so it's possible she did, being as there was one in Columbia Falls. Suffice to say, Joan was ambitious and did whatever it took to pay her bills, skydive, and take flying lessons.

While living at the City Airport, Joan took flying lessons with Mike Klinke, Linda McGinty and several other skydivers. "I remember we would go out whoever was up on their flight lesson -- coming in to land, and we really liked doing this with Joan -- was standing alongside the runway to make them nervous on their landing and count how many times they bounced down the runway," said Klinke, chuckling. Joan was unflappable though, eventually earning her pilot's license. Upon obtaining her license she earned extra income by dropping skydiving students from the club's single-engine Cessna 152.

Klinke also remembered that after big parties in Joan's motorhome at Kalispell City Airport, they would all head a mile to their favorite watering hole, Moose's Saloon in downtown Kalispell. The pizza was cheap and so was the beer and the floor even then was always littered with peanut shells discarded from the free bowls of peanuts Moose's handed out. It was a good place to play pool, throw darts and hang out with the Osprey's and their friends after a day spent jumping.

The jumpers had a tradition at Moose's; after your first jump you had to stand on a table and tell everybody about it while they laughed, teased and peppered you with barbs and peanuts. It was boisterous, and was all in good fun. The Osprey's might have been a rowdy bunch, but they didn't fight amongst themselves. The only trouble they had was with outsiders trying to make names for themselves by picking fights with them. The Osprey's were well known around town so they were an easy target. And in those days, Kalispell was a rough and tumble sort of town. With a population of about ten thousand, its economy relied heavily on lumber, cattle ranching, farming, aluminum production, and tourism. Glacier Park and several world class ski resorts were about 30 miles away.

For the most part, the Ospreys kept to themselves at the city airport, until they were booted out. The move didn't seem to faze Joan though, being forced to move wasn't too much of an inconvenience because she could park her motorhome in a friend's yard, or the aluminum plant parking lot. It was her home on wheels. In a way she was a skydiving gypsy.

BREAKUP

Kalispell, Montana: May, 1980

Other than Sharon Tousey, Mike Klinke was the only other person we interviewed who talked about Joan's breakup with Dave. When we interviewed him in Seattle, Klinke told us that Joan and Dave had an up and down relationship with a lot of good times and conversely some not so good times.

"A year prior to Joan's death, she and Dave were on rocky times," said Klinke. "Things had gotten so bad between Joan and Dave that Nancy [Sharon Tousey] had offered to let Joan come in and get away from Dave -- that they needed this time apart, and that she had offered up that space. I would have to say most of us thought that would be a good idea, that Joan needed space away from Dave."

Mike Klinke's explanation of another woman being the cause of the breakup appears to support Sharon Tousey's account, whose yard Joan lived in the last year of her life, but he was more philosophical about it. "Back then we had our share of soap operas of times where people hooked up and broke apart," he said. "We were a pretty free spirited bunch back then. Joan and Dave seemed to stick together pretty well...Conversely there would be some conflict as well, which was not unusual for any group of jumpers at that time."

But Joan's sister Janet never really saw Joan's relationship with Dave as being anything more than about skydiving, planes and Lost Prairie because Joan never talked about him with her.

It seems safe to say then that in Joan's mind she had ended her relationship with Dave. She had moved out, taken him off her life insurance, hauled a cabin onto her property, was taking steps to subdivide her land and build her own house there. And, according to Sharon, she only had Dave over once while she lived in her yard. For Dave though it was a different story. At the funeral and for years to come, he would give the Carson family the impression the two of them had still been a couple when Joan died. "It was very hard for me to hear Dave talk about Joan," Janet said when we interviewed her in Seattle. "But was harder to hear that there'd been a split before, and the impression I got was that they were still together. That was hard for me because I wasn't sure what was legitimately true about what he was telling me."

In spite of Joan's breakup with Dave, Klinke felt Joan would find her way in the world. "I believe that Joan would have been successful at anything she did," said Klinke in Seattle. "I think she would have found the right guy and settled in...She would have moved on. This was not her ending place, this would've been a stepping off spot because she had it all and she knew when she needed to move on to bigger and better things and she would've."

As spring of 1981 rolled around and the weather improved, Joan spent more and more time out at Lost Prairie skydiving and working on her twenty acres, which she was excited about and proud of. If Joan had a plan to move away from the area, she didn't share it with anybody. But, some people felt she would move on, and maybe she would have. Since Joan didn't talk much about her personal life, her actions must have communicated the notion for some to think that way.

MEMORIAL

Kalispell, Montana: May, 1981

The Carson family arrived in Kalispell several days after getting the news of Joan's death. They stayed for a week, making arrangements, collecting Joan's belongings at Sharon's, and attending the memorial services. The funeral was held at Weatherford Funeral Home in Kalispell on Thursday May 28, 1981. The service was in the evening and started at 7:30 PM.

Joan's sister Janet attended the funeral and fighting back tears had this to say about it, "I was still thinking it wasn't true...because they had her body cremated...It created the idea that it wasn't real."

That weekend, a "celebration" of Joan's life took place in Lost Prairie, with the local Osprey Parachute Club hosting the event. Skydivers who had known Joan flew in from all around the Northwest. "It was the most warm, loving, thing I think I'd ever been to," said Janet.

Dee-Bra, Herb "Ferbie" Farber and several other jumpers from Medford, Oregon were among some of skydivers who had flown in. George Holbertson's son Rodney, who was the first person I spoke with on the phone about Joan, was their pilot. "We flew through a thunderstorm like I've never in my life flown through before and I thought, *if we're going to a funeral we're probably not going to die because somebody has already died*," reasond Dee-Bra.

Joan's ashes were spread in the sky above Lost Prairie by Dave and Joan's younger brother Barrie from one of the Osprey club's Cessna. The planes then flew an asymmetrical formation and a solo fly-by representing the missing person, which really made an impact on Janet along with the function that followed. "The potluck and party, if you want to call it, afterwards was all about joy and celebration and the impact Joan had on their [skydivers] lives."

Janet continued that at some point during the event, her father Herbert, a scientist, went around asking questions as to what had caused his daughter's malfunctions. "My dad wanted to go around and find out if there was a reason why didn't the chute open because somebody else had packed it -- and neither chute opened," said Janet. "If he learned anything beyond that he kept it to himself and never discussed it or Joan from that time on."

After the celebration, a group of Joan's skydiving friends went to McGregor Lake Resort several miles away to let out their emotions. "We got wild and crazy that weekend," Dee-Bra said, still feeling the pain. "I remember mooning. I think eleven of us mooned up against one of the bars on the lake outside of the drop zone that we always drank at. And we leaned up against the windows and I thought, *Oh my god this is going to be such a mess if something breaks here because all of us are going to have glass shards in our asses -- it's going to be so awful.* Nothing broke. We just partied and partied and tried to cheer up."

Herb "Ferbie" Farber had this to say about the memorial when we interviewed him at Beagle Sky Ranch, "We paid tribute to Joanie because everyone had a lot of respect for her. Anytime we lose someone in the skydiving community we're a close knit relationship and have a bond between all skydivers. We did drink a fair amount of alcohol, beer, whiskey or whatever was available. It was good and kind of a cleansing thing to go and do that and to say goodbye. I guess they call it closing."

As heart wrenching as Joan's death was for her skydiving friends, if anything positive came out of it, it was something Sharon Tousey said at her home that struck me. She felt that it made the Ospreys question how they choose to recreate. "I think it made them more cautious," Sharon said. "I think it made them realize that life is pretty damn short – it could be gone in an instant as it was with Joan. I think it maybe made them realize that they could be gone at any time."

Likewise, Barrie managed to find something good in Joan's death in spite of, "a pain that never goes away," he said, at his office south of San Francisco. "It was difficult to go to Joan's service in Kalispell. Our family collected there and it was the last time I saw Joan's friends...But I think the thing I was left with out of that experience, of going to Joan's funeral, was a couple of things is -- it was the first opportunity my family really had to see Joan's friends and her life. And if there's a silver lining into that experience it was that my parents, my brother, and my older sister got to see the impact Joan had. It was an incredibly difficult time, but somehow that experience ends up in my mind being something that I have positive feelings about."

Although, overcome with grief at the time of Joan's death, Janet was introspective about it at her interview. "I'm a believer that you have a time, and sometimes that time is cut short, and sometimes it's when it's meant to happen," she said. "I do know that if she had to die, this is the way she wanted to die. So as hard as it was, the one thing I'll say about Joan's death is she went the way she lived."

ROUGHCUT

Redmond, WA: March through July, 2011

Now that we had shot the reenactment scenes and filmed the interviews with Janet and Mike Klinke, I concentrated on the rough edit, and fulfilling the kismet I was increasingly feeling that I was meant to make a film about Joan. By following my intuition, things had turned out pretty well.

From that point onward I spent two weeks sitting at our dining room table looking out over Ames Lake, watching spring arrive, as I edited the reenactment scenes, and then put them in the film as a flashback montage. From that sequence, I created a trailer using just those scenes.

In early April, 2011 I contacted Barrie by email:

Below is a new trailer for Beagle Boogie Babe. The scenes are from a flashback sequence of my experiences with Joan in San Francisco during the summer of 1973. We filmed these scenes two weeks ago at my wife's school in Seattle the day before we interviewed your sister, Janet. I enjoyed meeting her and will be editing her interview later this week.

At this point I am still working on the edit. I will also be working on making arrangements on where and when to screen the film in Kalispell/Lost Prairie this summer. My goal is to have those arrangements finalized and to notify everybody by the end of this month.

Hope you enjoy the trailer!

Barrie never responded to my email so I assumed he liked my portrayal of Joan, and continued editing.

For the next three months I worked on the film, sometimes sixteen hours a day in the same room. Weekdays, I would start in the morning, at 8:30, right after Susan left for work. At noon, I would take a short break to eat lunch, and then get back at it. Usually, around 4:00 I would stop editing, take our Yellow Lab Sadie for a walk, and then grocery shop in Redmond. When I got home around 5:30 or 6:00 I would go back to work. Susan would generally get home around 7:00, and I would fix dinner then. After eating, I would start up again and keep going until midnight and sometimes two in the morning. The more the film developed, the more I reflected on how much it had changed from my initial expectations.

When I had started the project, I wondered whether there was anybody out there who still remembered Joan, and was pleasantly surprised to track down twelve jumpers, two family members, and friends who not only remembered her, but remembered her well.

In the process of interviewing them, I learned something about a sport I had very little knowledge about, and marveled at the creation of Lost Prairie by a group of recalcitrant hippie skydivers in the wilderness. I enjoyed the adventure of retracing Joan's footsteps across Washington, Oregon, California, and Montana. And when Barrie told us in San Francisco that Joan had a baby out of wedlock and had to give it up for adoption, I felt like I had finally unlocked the riddle of my dream. I finally believed that I understood the reason Joan had become a skydiver, why she had taken the risks she did, and was so adventurous. Skydiving provided an escape for her.

I couldn't help but think that the chance of everything coming together the way it had so far was slim, along with the fact that her story was unique and interesting. I could have easily discovered that she had died having lived a boring life. On the contrary, Joan was anything but boring and I was lucky to be making a film about her, further persuading me that the dream I'd had was a premonition, and was my destiny.

I had a lot to be pleased about, but was bothered by revelations by Sharon Tousey, Mike Klinke, Bill Paulin and whisperings of others about Dave. What I had regarded as being youthful shenanigans had abruptly turned into something much more serious and possibly dark.

It bothered me that Dave had probably cheated on Joan, purportedly punched her in the face, and then had not been man enough to break the news about her death to her father.

It bothered me that Joan had felt compelled to take Dave off her life insurance.

It bothered me that somebody else had possibly packed her parachute, or that she had borrowed somebody else's. It bothered me that Dave wouldn't let us interview him.

And it irritated me that so many people seemed to be protecting Dave, by portraying a fairytale image of his relationship with Joan. So many things didn't add up -- actually in my mind they did, and they weren't good.

I wasn't prepared to deal with the possibility of something so dark. Outside of the police, I had no idea where to go for help. But even if I did, I had no proof that any wrongdoing had occured, and even if something had, it was surely past the statute of limitations. This was Montana, the Wild West where road signs were pockmarked with bullet holes. For all I knew there was a good chance Dave and his skydiving buddies were friends with the police who would side with him.

The cops would take one look at my report and laugh me out of the office: "You want us to investigate a possible crime that happened thirty years ago? What crime was committed? What evidence do you have?"

"None," I would tell the police, "just hearsay, and a strong suspicion and a feeling in my gut that Joan would probably still be alive today if she hadn't allegedly been punched in the face the day she made her last jump."

I could just hear them say, "Okay, Mr. Gorman thanks for coming in. Next."

So, I had solved one mystery and in the process had possibly uncovered another. As much as it nagged at me, I put it aside and worked on the rough edit. What else could I do? Nothing. I had a deadline to make. I had better get busy in order to screen the film at the Lost Prairie Boogie in July -- in time to commemorate the 30th anniversary of Joan's passing.

Off and on, Mark and I experimented with combining footage from the two cameras into a merged 3D image. Eventually, I came to the conclusion that it wasn't worth the effort. The two cameras weren't color balanced, making it nearly impossible with my limited color correcting experience to have the colors match perfectly, and I didn't have the budget to have it done professionally. There was also the time limit factor. I barely had time to cut the film once, let alone twice. Even if I was able to do everything, there was the projection issue. In order to enjoy the 3D experience, I would have to provide special glasses (blue and red) to the viewers. I informed Mark of my decision to release the film in 2D. Since he had pushed for releasing it in 3D, I didn't want to offend him and assured him that if the film *took off* we could then release a 3D version. Mark was comfortable with the compromise I proposed, and relieved, I think.

I still wanted to trim the length of the film to no more than 90 minutes. As a filmmaker, I had always made films that were fully scripted, which provided a road map. This was my first documentary and I was in virgin territory. All together, we had filmed about twenty hours of interviews and ten hours of B-Roll. With so much footage it was very difficult for me to decide which scenes to cut. The biggest problem was that I liked everything, and put way too much in it. It was like eating something delicious and you can't stop. The first draft was 153 minutes long. As hard as I tried, it was challenging for me to step back and be objective, so I invited Mark to watch it. He ended up falling asleep about half way through the rough edit -- *not a good sign.* I stopped the film where he had dozed off and went through it scene by scene asking myself whether or not it moved the story along. If it didn't, then I cut it.

My biggest supporter and critic was Susan. She watched the film countless times giving me feedback on what needed to be explained better and what I should cut. Gradually the film took shape and I managed to get it down to 96 minutes.

During all of the head scratching, I contacted, Joseph Seserko, a composer I had worked with years earlier. Originally, I had met him when my son Kelly was acting in a children's community theater musical. Joseph composed and then performed all of the music live at the play. I was really impressed with his music and got his contact information afterwards.

Several years later I was making a teaser for a feature film called *The Last Mirage* that I intended to screen at the Cannes Film Festival Market (MIF) in 1997, and needed a composer. I reached out to Joseph and asked if he was interested in doing the music for it, and he said he was. So I sent him a copy of the rough edit and he composed the music. Immediately I was hooked. His score fit perfectly and was just what I had imagined. Good sound and music are vitally important. The better they are, the better the film. In my earlier years, I hadn't been focused on audio quality and regretted it later. Those hard lessons made me appreciate how important it is to have good quality sound in a film. It's half of the film.

It had been fourteen years since I had spoken with Joseph, yet nothing had changed. He was still the same concise person he had been before and always made me feel a little uneasy talking to him. I told him about *Beagle Boogie Babe,* and asked him if he'd be interested in doing the original music score for it. He was interested but wanted to see the film first without any scratch (temporary) music, and then he would decide.

I liked Joseph, and for the most part found him easy to work with. However, as a music-major from the University of Washington, and teacher, he could be very much the perfectionist. He wanted to know exactly where I wanted music to begin, where I wanted it to end, what type of music I wanted, the mood, the instruments, and the mix I was looking for. Did I want it behind the voices, over the voices, did I want it to swell and fade out, and then resume again, or to end abruptly, and so on.

"Just do whatever you think will sound good," I finally said. From that point on Joseph worked on it independently. I don't know if he was angry at me, or was glad that I had turned him loose, so to speak, but I didn't hear much from him until the evening we went into the studio to lay down his music.

Having worked with Joseph before I knew how exacting he was and how perturbed he could get if anything in the film changed, so I made sure to send him a copy of the film that had the *picture locked* (frozen). As it turned out, a few changes were made in post-production and Joseph had to improvise on the spot to make things work. He seemed a little irritated, but the changes were so minor that he got over it quickly.

In addition to Joseph's original music score, I had obtained Rock music from a band called Child. Excited to get their music, I posted about it on my blog:

All of the Rock songs in Beagle Boogie Babe are unreleased material by Child, widely regarded as one of Seattle's best bands during the 1970's. Back then they played the same circuit as a band I was managing, which sent me to San Francisco to land them some gigs. It was during that trip that I spent time with Joan Carson.

Several years ago I came across some of Child's music on YouTube, and thought it still sounded great, so I contacted them about using their songs in the film. They agreed to have their music used in the movie. Yes, things have come full circle.

At first I was a little underwhelmed by the music Joseph had composed. But, before long it grew on me and I loved it; combined with Child's rock 'n roll songs it made a great soundtrack. Overall, the music and sound ended up getting more compliments than just about anything.

By the first of May 2011, the structure of the film was nearly done. The picture was *locked* and the runtime was now 93 minutes. I only had two months to complete the film in order to screen it at the Lost Prairie Boogie. The boogie ran from the last week of July, through the first Monday in August.

In mid-May, I started looking for a colorist to do the grading, and a recording studio to do the sound mix. In the past I had used Victory Studios in Seattle to color grade the teaser I had made for *The Last Mirage*. They were really good and really expensive, so I more or less scratched them off my list.

Susan's cousin, Kevin, had used a widely known Seattle colorist for his film *Back to the Garden*, and loved his work -- so I contacted him. He was too expensive and besides he was booked. I was striking out, and beginning to panic.

It just so happened, I was grocery shopping, when a grocery clerk named Travis saw me. He was talking to a customer. Travis knew about my filmmaking and introduced me to Peter Barnes, who coincidentally was the owner of Clatter and Din recording studio in Seattle. I had heard of the facility before, and they had been on my short list of studios to contact about the sound mix.

Peter was a friendly and energetic guy. I gave him a quick summary of where I was at with the film. "Here's my card," he said. "Send me a link to your film. I'm sure we can work something out, and we can also do your color grading."

I have almost always been an optimist and feel things happen for a reason. I sent Peter the link that evening and a day later I got a return phone call from him.

"Hi Paul this is Peter Barnes at Clatter and Din," Peter bubbled on the phone. "I watched your film last night and think you've got a really cool project there. We'd love to be part of it. Why don't you come in so we can discuss the scope of it with my team."

On May 16, 2011 Mark and I met with Peter, his colorist Matt, and Recording Engineer Brendan Hogan. We discussed the extent of the work that needed to be done, and the schedule. We came up with a start date of June 22, 2011. I would have preferred starting it earlier, but Clatter and Din's schedule was full and I was going to be out of town the week before that.

Four days after meeting with Peter, I still hadn't received an estimate and sent him an email. Later that day, I got an email back from him explaining his father had died in the morning and he would be out of town all next week. He wouldn't be able to get me an estimate until

Monday or Tuesday of the following week. "Would that be okay," he asked.

“Sure, Peter, that's fine," I said, "Do whatever you need to do. I can wait until next week."

When Thursday of the following week came, I still hadn't gotten an estimate from Peter and was starting to worry. Time was running out. Things better get moving with the project right away, or I would have to screen it the way it was, which wasn't all that bad, but wasn't great. The biggest problem was that I didn't have a soundtrack other than a few Child songs and music I had pirated off the Internet. Joseph had wanted to record his score live at Clatter and Din with studio musicians. I wasn't too excited about the idea because it would add another $1,000 to the budget. I was relieved when Joseph said he was unable to schedule the musicians he had wanted. So, he wound up playing all the instruments and recording the score himself at his home. In the end it worked out well and saved me money.

On June 2, 2011, I sent Peter an email inquiring about the status of the estimate.

That afternoon I got a call from Peter apologizing for not getting back to me sooner because he had just gotten back the day before. He said he had the numbers for the estimate and read them to me over the phone.

"We really like helping independent filmmakers and normally we'd charge approximately $17,775 to do everything and I'm willing to do it for $10,665 -- that's 40% off," Peter said. "How does that sound?"

"Let me talk to my wife about it, and I'll get back to you, "I said. “It’s more than I expected."

"What's your budget," Don't worry you can't offend me, I've been offended so many times that the only thing that pisses me off is a compliment," Peter said, laughing.

"$8,500 is all I can afford," I replied.

"Alright, Paul $8,500 dollars it is," Peter said. "We try to help local filmmakers anyway we can. How soon do you need your film done?"

"Since I'm screening it in Montana on July 29th," I said, reminding him. "I'd like it a week before that, if possible."

"Hold on, let me look at my schedule real quick," Peter said, "things have changed significantly since you were here last."

I could hear Peter's muffled conversation with somebody else and then he got back on the line with me. "You're in luck, man, I can put Matt on it starting the twenty-second as you requested, and will bring in Brendan to do the mix," Peter said. "It's gonna be tight though because your project is going to take two weeks, and that's if there aren't any changes to the film. Also, if a full-rate client comes along in the meantime, we have to give them priority. Are you still up for it?"

"Yes," I said. "Let's do it. What do you need from me?"

"I'll schedule a meeting with Matt for tomorrow at 2:00," Peter said. "You can go over everything with him and he'll fill you in on what they need. Does that work for you?"

"Sounds good to me, see you tomorrow," I said, hanging up the phone.

I returned to our dining room of our house and sat down at my IMAC. It was a little before 2:00, the sun was shining, the lake looked beautiful, Susan was still at work in Seattle and would not be home until around 7:00. I decided to treat myself and take the rest of the day off and go for a long walk with Sadie along the Sammamish River trail in Redmond.

The film had taken a toll on me in more ways than one. Not only had I gained weight, I was also having trouble sleeping at night. Scenes and things I needed to do would race through my mind, keeping me awake. *You need to do this, you need to do that, don't forget to add the part where such and such says this about that, and make sure to get a shot of this.* It felt like I was on a hamster wheel, and would go on like that for hours while I tossed and turned until I finally got up and took half of half a milligram of Lorazepam and fell asleep.

But it was all worth it. I loved what I was doing and *Beagle Boogie Babe* was its own living entity. I couldn't wait to see what happened next. To me making a film was much more entertaining and satisfying than watching a movie, so much so in fact that I wasn't much of a movie buff. I rarely watched movies.

During my twenties, I had been somewhat of a *cinephile* tagging along to theaters with my two film school friends watching art house films by Truffaut, Fellini, Kubrick, Kurosawa, Bertolucci, Buñuel, Herzog, Nichols, Yves Robert, Lina Wertmuller, Coppola, Woody Allen, amongst others. I can't say I loved or understood all of their films, but I went anyway and am glad I did.

What I took away from those filmmakers, was that it wasn't about the money, the stars and being famous, it was about getting your film made no matter what it took. It was about feeling so passionate about something that you would mortgage your house, live in your car, sell your blood, eat cat food, and wear multiple hats to get your films made -- whatever it took.

What I also learned from those directors is to not force the story, let it unfold on its own. Let the story come to you. Sometimes it worked, and sometimes it didn't. When it did it was great and the result was art.

I felt relieved to get the color correcting and sound mix settled to where I could move on to other things that needed to be done. Things were unfolding on their own.

ROADBLOCKS

Redmond, WA: April - July, 2011

While Clatter and Din was color grading the film and doing the sound mix, I was busy designing a poster, and a postcard to send to the interviewees. I was also making arrangements for the screening in Lost Prairie.

Complicating matters was that Fred Sand was no longer in charge of the Lost Prairie Boogie. The owner of the dropzone on the valley side of the airstrip and structures sold the actual landing site to a guy named Tony Hanks. The corporation (Mike and Linda Groarke et al) who owned the airstrip struck a deal with Hanks to run the boogie, thus ending Fred's tenure as boogie organizer.

Linda Groarke alluded to this possibly happening when we interviewed her eight months earlier in Lost Prairie, but I didn't realize it was so imminent.

Unaware of the change, I kept emailing Fred updates thinking he was the *man in charge*, and not knowing that I needed to negotiate with Tony, the owner of Wilderness Meadow Skydiving.

I first started hearing rumblings that Fred had possibly been ousted in early April on one of the forums at Dropzone.com. Some skydivers were saying he was out as organizer of Lost Prairie LLC, and others were saying that he was staying on as the organizer for Wilderness Skydiving. The result was confusion for me and skydivers who were trying to decide whether there was going to be a boogie, and if so whether or not they would be going. Some of the veterans said that if it was true Fred was out they wouldn't be going out of loyalty to him.

There was only one way to find out who was running the boogie and that was to ask Fred directly. On April 11, 2011 I sent him an email.

I am hoping you are still interested in screening Beagle Boogie Babe at this year's boogie. I've heard mention of a competing boogie at Lost Prairie, and don't know anything about the dynamics, but wanted to give you first shot at it because you are in it [the film] and helped us. I will need to know by April 22 because I want to mail invitations by the end of this month.

If I don't hear from you within the next few days then I will call to check that you received this message.

A day later I received an email back from Fred that only said: "Got it. Let's do it."

Five more weeks passed. I hadn't heard back from him so I went ahead and mailed *Save the Date* postcards to all of the interviewees and crew as a reminder that I was still planning on screening *Beagle Boogie Babe* at the Lost Prairie Boogie.

I then emailed Fred:

I mailed invitations [save the date postcards] on Friday (yours should arrive in several days). I will call you tomorrow to discuss the details of how, where and what time we screen Beagle Boogie Babe.

As I mentioned, I would like to have two screenings. The first would be on [Friday] July 29, and would be for family, friends, cast and crew. The second would be [on Sunday] for those attending the boogie.

Later that afternoon Fred called me explaining that he was no longer running the boogie and I would have to make arrangements through Tony Hanks at Wilderness Meadow Skydiving.

So the rumors were true, Wilderness Meadow Skydiving, a newly formed company had indeed taken over the reins of the boogie and Fred was out as its promoter.

It must have been quite a blow to Fred after organizing the boogie for about forty years. Online at Dropzone.com longtime skydivers who had been regulars at the boogie over the years were sympathetic to him being let go.

"How dare they fire Fred. If it weren't for him the boogie wouldn't be what it is today." Other skydivers that knew him wished him well.

And I'd have to agree with them, if it weren't for Fred's organizational and promoter skills, the boogie probably would have died many years earlier.

I told Susan, Mickey and Mark about the developments. They all remembered Linda's assertion during her interview about Fred not paying them their fair share. Mark defended him, "Fred deserved more money than all of the others because he's the one that did all of the work."

Of course, Mark didn't know Fred any better than I did, but he'd been around the block in L.A.. “There are shakers and movers that get things done,” he said, “and then there are people who sit around and bitch and moan about them getting all the money and acclaim -- and that they are getting robbed.”

Now that it was confirmed Fred was no longer in charge of the boogie, it was time to reach out to Tony and make arrangements. When

I had spoken with Fred on the phone, he said he had informed Tony about the film and my desire to screen it at the boogie.

Fred would go on to say Tony was receptive. That was good to know, at least I wouldn't be cold calling him. Fred had given me Tony's phone number and a day later I called him. Tony was friendly on the phone and willing to help but vague. Other than planning on having a 40 ft. party tent with chairs and tables, he couldn't guarantee anything else. Tony did say, though, that doing a private event there for the interviewees and crew was out of the question. The purpose of the tent was so skydivers could eat, hang out and share their videos on a yet to be determined big screen TV. If I wanted to have an *open to the public* event there that was a different story.

Tony and I came to an agreement that a good time for me to host the public screening would be on Sunday, July 31st at 11:00 AM. Tony reasoned, by that time most skydivers would have already been up for several hours, finished with their morning jumps, be ready to eat lunch, and could mosey over to the tent and eat there while they watched the film. Better yet, since it was still morning, they wouldn't have started guzzling beer and wouldn't be rowdy. I liked the idea. "I think it'll work," I responded to him.

By the looks of it, I had a venue secured for the *public screening.* However, the fact that he couldn't be exact about the big screen TV and sound system made me uneasy.

No offense to Tony, but he was a neophyte as far as the boogie business was concerned. He had stepped into the big leagues of skydiving trying to put on one of the longest running and most influential skydiving boogies in the country -- perhaps even the world. People from all over the US, Canada and world flocked to jump at the Lost Prairie Boogie.

Lost Prairie was like a Grateful Dead concert. It was *The Last Waltz* of skydiving -- the Holy Grail of boogies. If you were serious about jumping out of airplanes, you had to say you had been there, and jumped at least once. In so doing, you also had to boast you had been to one of the late night raunchy displays of debauchery, featuring either the *Cock Chorus*, or *Crack Chorus*.

As a long time skydiver, Tony had jumped into this maelstrom and was getting an initiation by fire.

This being his first time organizing the "boogie", I wouldn't be surprised if he was inundated with legitimate requests and bullshit, which would help explain why he didn't seem to have time or interest in my film. Besides, there was nothing in it for him other than just being nice.

I felt somewhat better having found a venue for the public screening, but still hadn't come up with a suitable place for the private screening. The Lounge was out of the question because it was closed. Owned by Stinky and Dave's wife Jenny, we were told that they were locked in a lawsuit over somebody owing somebody money.

The hangar was another possible venue for the private screening. But it was not feasible because skydivers would be using it during the boogie to pack chutes.

That left only one other place close to the boogie, and that was McGregor Lake Resort. I called them and spoke with the owner, Marge. She said they could accommodate me and agreed that the best time to do the private screening would be on Friday afternoon because it wouldn't be too crowded. Perfect, I could screen the film there for the interviewees and Joan's family.

Marge also said they did catering and could set up a buffet. The only catch was that their big screen TVs were mounted over the bar and were hard wired into a satellite dish on the roof, making it difficult to access any hookup, let alone repositioning any of the flat screens.

Further, she explained that their customers liked to watch sports and probably wouldn't be interested in watching a documentary -- even if it was about Lost Prairie. As such she ruled out me using any of their

TVs and recommended I rent one in Kalispell. I could appreciate her point of view.

I called around several rental shops in Kalispell and the rental prices I was quoted were more than I was willing to pay.

I had a large Panasonic flat screen TV at home and a small Onkyo stereo system with audio inputs that I had used during the flashback auditions at New Discovery School. The TV weighed a ton, but it wouldn't cost me anything. So I decided to bring it, my stereo, and a DVD player. I could also use them at the boogie screening if they wound up not having a TV system or if it was inadequate.

Now that I had solved the public and private screening issues, and post production work was progressing nicely, it was time to send out formal invitations to the interviewees and family members.

MARKETING

Redmond, WA: July, 2011

With the boogie less than a month way I wrote a Press Release letter and on July 2, 2011 sent it along with the trailer to newspapers in the Kalispell area:

I am a filmmaker from Seattle and have created a film ("Beagle Boogie Babe") about a skydiver from Kalispell named Joan Carson who died in a tragic skydiving accident at Lost Prairie in 1981. Ironically, Joan died on the very drop zone she helped create. Today, the airfield at Lost Prairie is named in her honor.

This year marks the 30th anniversary of Joan Carson's death. A special screening of the film will be held at 11:00 AM on Sunday, July 31 at the Lost Prairie Boogie and is free to the public.

"Beagle Boogie Babe" retraces Joan's life from before she was a skydiver up to her death, and explains what drove her to continue skydiving even after suffering two serious accidents. The film features interviews from Kalispell area skydivers, shedding light on their

involvement with the Osprey Parachute Club and their rowdy behavior, which led to the formation of Lost Prairie.

I would appreciate it if you would share this information with your readers, or provide me with any assistance that you can.

Three days later, Flathead Beacon Writer Dan Testa responded to my email saying that he had watched the trailer for the film and wanted to do a feature story on it. He went on to ask if I would be available for a phone interview later in the week.

I was surprised and elated by his response and admittedly a little nervous.

I had been interviewed several times before with the release of my film *Broken Frame - The movie that took 22 years to finish*, and never felt comfortable doing it. I had heard and read that in order to give a good interview you had to be interesting. You also had to be careful what you said because like a court deposition, which I had been through several years earlier involving our property dispute, it could be used against you. I found the best thing to do was to drink a couple of beers -- I would then be relaxed, but wouldn't sound intoxicated.

After a couple of brews, I called Dan Testa and gave what I thought was an interesting interview, answering all of his questions concisely and energetically without elaborating too much. It must have worked because on July 11, 2011 an article appeared in the Flathead Beacon News titled: ***Revisiting Lost Prairie's Early Days -- New documentary examines life of Joan Carson, and her fatal jump.***

I sent the article to family, friends, interviewees, Joan's family, and posted a link to it on my blog. The consensus was that it was a great article. I was thrilled. Everything was coming together perfectly.

As good as the article was I never got a response from Barrie. In fact, in spite of also mailing save the date postcards, and formal invitations later, I hadn't heard from Barrie since the first week in April (nearly three months earlier) when I had sent him a rough edit of the flashback scenes. I was wondering if the scenes had offended him.

Finally, on July 9, 2011 -- just twenty days before the private screening date, I got an email from him saying that he was planning on being in Kalispell on July 29 and wondered if I was going to have some type of event to show the film.

Relieved and puzzled, I sent Barrie an email the following day:

Glad to hear that you will be there!

I've sent several postcards, but maybe you didn't receive them. I'm glad that you emailed me.

I am planning on having two screenings. The first one is a private event for the film's participants and will be held on Friday, July 29th at 2:00PM at Lake McGregor Resort. Lunch will be provided. The second screening will be held on Sunday, July 31st at 11:00AM at Lost Prairie, and will be open to the public.

I'm trying to get a head count for the food. Do you know if Janet is coming, and how many guests will be in your party?

That same day Barrie emailed me back explaining that he had seen the first postcard but had never received the second one with the details. He confirmed he would be there on Friday with his daughter Abbie, and that Janet would be there Friday too with her daughter Allison. They were looking forward to seeing the film, Joan's friends, and us.

I was glad that Barrie and Janet were coming and was looking forward to seeing them again and showing them the film. I emailed Barrie thanking him and recapping the weekend's details:

Susan and I are looking forward to seeing you guys there! My cameraman, Mark Anderson, will be there too, but I'm not sure if my sound guy Mickey McMullen will make it. I invited all of the interviewees and several of Joan's friends so keep your fingers crossed. I did not invite Dave because he did not respond to our interview requests. However, if you and Janet would like him to be there then please let me know and I will invite him.

On another note, Fred Sand is no longer organizing the boogie. After 40 years of running it, a guy named Tony Hanks (Wilderness Meadow Skydiving) is now doing it. Tony has agreed to let me screen BBB in Prairie Skydiving's 40' x 60' tent on Sunday July 31 at 11:00AM.

The following link is to an article about Joan which appeared in yesterday's Flathead Beacon newspaper: I think it's available in print too, so you might be able to order copies.

Lastly, attached is a photo of the Lost Prairie Lounge which Joan helped construct. Unfortunately it has just closed! Lots of changes at Lost Prairie this year...

So everything was set: I had sent invitations, designed a poster, had a write up in a local newspaper, reserved the venues, booked a hotel room for Susan and me, and one for Mark and his teenage son Evan who was going to help us, and ordered food for the private screening. All that was left to do was to do the final mix at Clatter and Din with Joseph Seserko and Recording Engineer Brendan Hogan. I would then pick up DVD copies of the film on July 26 three days before the first screening.

MIXING

Seattle, WA: July, 2011

Surprisingly, the final mix went smoothly. Joseph was flexible and upbeat, and Brendan was complimentary, saying that it had been a fun and interesting project to work on. He wished us well in Lost Prairie. "I think people there are going to love the film," he said, sitting at the recording mixer.

"I hope so," I said.

"Why wouldn't they?" Joseph interjected.

Privately, I had always had some concern about the sexual nature of the reenactment scenes. True as they were, they revealed a side of Joan that contradicted the Pollyannaish characterization of her by the interviewees and people we talked to. Other than Zimmo, who alluded to her wild streak, everybody else portrayed her as saintly, so much so that we wondered amongst ourselves why they didn't nickname her Saint Joan. But as Osprey skydiver Mike Klinke had explained when we interviewed him in Seattle, skydivers were too busy living in the present and future to talk about the past. It was the perfect environment for Joan.

Warts and all, I felt that showing Joan's sexual proclivities helped explain who she had been, how she had had a child out of wedlock, and showed a pattern of risky behavior she continued pursuing even after having to give up her baby. True, she became monogamous after settling down with Dave, and probably even before, which would explain the angelic impression her friends in Kalispell/Lost Prairie and Medford had of her. As earnest as their observations of Joan were, it was only half of the character arc that Joan had traveled. And, as a filmmaker, I felt it was my responsibility to accurately show the entire scope of her life -- good and bad.

In any event, my decision making didn't ease my concern. I was pretty sure those scenes were going to be a surprise to a lot of people. I turned to Joseph and said, "I'm worried about the sex scene, how people in Lost Prairie and Medford will take it."

"Big deal, that's the way she was then. She liked sex, who doesn't," Joseph said, dismissively.

Brendan nodded in agreement. "I don't think you have anything to worry about, Paul," he said. "It's a good film."

Joseph was right. It wasn't a big deal. Sex was a part of life, and who didn't like it, I rationalized. I thanked Joseph and Brendan and said goodnight.

Leaving Clatter and Din I walked to my car. That evening was warm and clear and I was only three blocks away from where Spike's truck rental business had been located on 4th Avenue South, and where thirty-seven years earlier I had dropped Joan and Spike off after giving them a ride. I decided to drive past the old location on my way home.

As I pulled to a stop in front of the old space I was suddenly overwhelmed by a wave of nostalgia and emotion. Not only had I last seen Joan at this location, I had worked upstairs managing Mojo Hand, driven trucks for Spike up and down the coast to their sattelite yard in Eugene, listend to the 1st moon landing pulled over somewhere in the lunar landscape of Eastern Oregon while picking up a one-way rental, washed trucks on weekends in the potholed yard, and retrieved a stolen Ford Econoline van in Pope Valley of all places.

Now, almost four decades later I was on the precipice of screening a rough draft of a film that in a way had started here. It was here I got deeply involved with Spike and he had *arranged* for me to stay with Joan in Berkeley. What a strange and interesting trip it had been and it wasn't over yet. I had a screening in several days and couldn't wait to see what the reaction would be.

On July 28, 2011 we left Redmond for Lost Prairie, our cars packed to the hilt with camera gear, posters, computers, flat screen TV, stereo, clothing, and food. Susan and I followed Mark and his son Evan.

Mickey and several interviewees had RSVP'd that they couldn't make it. That left about nine other invitees unaccounted for. In the event they showed up and brought a guest, I went ahead and ordered enough food for all of them. At this point it was the least of my concerns. If we ended up with leftover food, so be it. We were on the road again and that was the most important thing.

PREPARATION

Lost Prairie, Montana: July, 2011

On Friday morning July, 29 I posted on my blog site to let everybody know that we had arrived in Lost Prairie the day before:

We arrived at Lost Prairie around 5:00 PM. Our cars are covered in dust about an inch thick due to the Montana Outback shortcut we took...which consisted of 35 miles of dirt road. We won't try that route again.

A lot of changes have occurred at Lost Prairie this year, but there are still a lot of familiar faces in the crowd. Isn't that what Lost Prairie is supposed to be all about.

Joan Carson's dream was to create a place where skydivers could live and congregate and enjoy skydiving and each other's company. That hasn't changed. Everywhere we looked there was a smiling face, handshakes, high fives, hugs and the sound of laughter. Joan's dream lives on even 30 years after her death.

Upon arriving in Lost Prairie I introduced myself to new boogie organizer Tony Hanks. He then showed me the big screen and sound system in the tent.

Unfortunately, the "big screen TV" Tony provided was standard definition and was awash with glare due to its curved screen -- thus hard to see. It would be okay at night for skydivers wanting to watch the aerial footage they had shot earlier in the day, but less than satisfactory for screening *Beagle Boogie Babe* during the day.

Also, his sound system was a PA system with XLR and 1/4 inch phone jack microphone inputs. I didn't have RCA converters that would enable me to hook up my DVD player. As such, using his PA system was pretty much out of the question. So, I decided I would use my TV and stereo system for Sunday's screening.

We spent the next hour handing out postcards advertising Sunday's screening of *Beagle Boogie Babe,* and putting up posters supplementing the half-dozen posters that Fred Sand had already put up.

Shortly before we left, we stopped by and said hello to Fred at the old manifest building he still used as his office for his tandem skydiving business. I also wanted to discuss the arrangements he had made with Stinky's son Adam to shoot some aerial footage for us on Sunday. At this stage, I fully anticipated that after the screenings there would be changes to the film. I could then insert Adam's aerial footage into the final cut of the film.

We thanked Fred for his help and left. Next, we stopped at McGregor Lake Resort and discussed the logistics for the following day's screening with Marge and checked out the space at the rear of the bar where the actual viewing would take place. The area had a small stage several feet high. Mark and I concluded that if we put a table up there it would make a good platform for my TV.

The owner then showed us the alcove to the right of the stage where she would set up the food. It was private and set aside. I was relieved; it all looked like it would work just fine, provided it wasn't overly crowded with boisterous customers. But she had assured me that it didn't get busy on Fridays until after 4:00 PM. She seemed sincere, friendly, and trustworthy. At this late date there really wasn't anything I could do about it anyway.

Susan and I departed for the Red Lion Hotel in Kalispell and Mark and Evan headed for their hotel a few miles down the road in Marion. There was a restaurant there where they could eat and I would then reimburse Mark.

After checking into our hotel, Susan and I went to an Italian restaurant in downtown Kalispell. It was the best meal we'd had in Kalispell.

That night I didn't sleep well. Other than the few people who had RSVP'd, I still hadn't heard from any of the others. I didn't know what to expect. Would anybody show up and if so how many people would it be? It was the uncertainty that was driving me crazy. I tossed and turned all night long. On one hand, I would imagine everybody showing up along with their spouses, and then there would be nobody except for Mark, Evan, Susan and me -- not even Barrie and Janet. I hadn't heard from them since Barrie's last email more than two weeks earlier.

I assumed they were coming, but after the experience I had trying to pin down Barrie's interview in San Francisco I wasn't sure. As for Janet, she had arrived on time for her interview, but Lost Prairie was nearly five hundred miles away from where she lived, and was a dangerous drive. Maybe she had changed her mind.

The morning of the first screening, Susan and I drove out to McGregor Lake Resort where we met Mark and Evan for breakfast. Afterwards we went up to Lost Prairie. Mark, Evan and I shot B-Roll of the two de Havilland jump planes taking off and landing at the south end of the runway while Susan hung out at our SUV watching the skydivers, and nursing a sore knee.

Satisfied that Mark and Evan had a handle on things, I wandered over to Joan's old cabin. Listing on a hillside several hundred yards from the end of the runway in calf high prairie grass overlooking the valley, I tried to imagine Joan living in it. As hard as I tried, I just couldn't wrap my mind around the idea. As beautiful a setting as it was, the cabin was primitive compared to the duplex in San Francisco where I had stayed with her.

The front door was open. I glanced in the direction of a house about 100 feet away to make sure I wasn't being watched. Satisfied I wasn't, I stepped inside the one room cabin. Vandalized and disheveled as it was, I was surprised to see that it had wiring, baseboard heat, and two sinks that had fallen through a rotten counter top.

Stacked next to the sink were four snow tires. I presumed they belonged to Joan and fit her Ford Pinto. She had probably been storing them there for the summer.

On the other side of the cabin was an old car battery and lying on the fir floor next to it were two toddler outfits. I assumed Joan had bought them for Janet's baby with the intention of either sending them or taking them to her.

The cabin needed hookup for power, and water. It also needed a foundation. From what we'd heard, she had planned on doing all those things, and more. And according to Stinky, before her death she had drilled a well. But, as this time capsule revealed, life had ended abruptly for her.

Upon her death, the cabin and 20 acres she owned became part of her estate, eventually going to Janet's son who died in 2001. Fred would tell me during one of our phone conversations that the Carson family had sold the property around 2006. As far as I could tell, the new owners hadn't done anything with it in the five years they owned it.

On the way back to where Mark, Evan and Susan were, I reflected on how Stinky had also said that Joan had felt that she was getting on in life, and it was time to settle down -- and had decided to make Lost Prairie her home. It struck me odd when he said that because from the perspective of someone who had just turned sixty, thirty didn't seem old at all. But the more I looked back on it, when I turned thirty, I felt like I was getting up there and was taking steps for my future too.

When I got back to Mark, Mickey, and Susan, they were filming a memorial built to four skydivers and a pilot who died when their plane crashed shortly after takeoff and burned in 2007. It was a cold reminder of the risks involved with the sport. It seemed ironic that a valley so pristine and peaceful could have witnessed so much suffering. Joan's fatality was the first skydiving death there, a distinction marked by a bronze memorial plaque inset into a stone pedestal just outside Fred's office in the old manifest building. This was ground zero for the Osprey's. *Sacred ground.* It was here that they signed up for their loads, packed their shoots, dirt dived, boarded planes, and watched their friends free fall through the deep blue sky and land in the freshly bailed prairie grass. It was here that they had seen Joan die.

It seems fitting that they would choose a spot to honor Joan where they had so many memories, and where she had been so instrumental in creating their experiences. Inscribed on the plaque is a poem she wrote while living in her motorhome in Sharon's yard:

"FLY"
What can I say about something I love so much?
It's the love of my life, the beat of my heart.
It cleanses my soul.
The freedom of flight can do more
to change one's perspective on life
than any earthbound freedom.
JOAN M CARSON

On our way to the screening at McGregor Lake Resort, we were walking back to where we had parked our vehicles, when a morbid thought popped into my mind. By the description of what Osprey skydivers Bill Paulin and Mike Klinke had said during their interviews, we were in the vicinity of where Joan had impacted the ground. I wondered whether there were still fragments and DNA of her embedded in the soil. I tried desperately to get the thought out of my mind and concentrate on the screening that was going to happen at McGregor Lake in three hours. As hard as I tried, the thought would linger with me off and on the rest of the time we were in Lost Prairie.

ANXIETY

MacGregor Lake Resort, Montana: July 29, 2011

By 1:00 PM, Mark, Evan and I had everything set up. We had put a four-top table on the stage and my flat screen TV on top of it. On either side of the TV, we placed my stereo speakers on bar stools. We had also arranged enough tables and chairs to accommodate twenty people. It looked functional and cozy especially with the pine wood paneled walls, and antlers on the walls. It seemed appropriate to do the private screening there.

The Lake McGregor Resort had been there since the 40s and had been one of Joan's and the Osprey's hangouts. So much so that some of the old timers still frequented the joint. As coincidence would have it, while Mark, Evan and I had been setting up, Susan had been making the rounds, checking with Marge on the progress of the catering, and talking to the bartender who was curious about the film. During her conversation with him, she happened to mention Dave's name. The bartender leaned over and whispered to her that he was sitting at the bar.

Upon hearing that, Susan came up to me and said Dave was there.

I was stunned. "You're kidding me," I said, incredulously. "Are you sure it's him?"

"That's what the bartender said. You should go talk to him."

"About what?" I asked.

"Invite him to the screening," said Susan.

I hesitated for a moment remembering Barrie's email to me, several weeks earlier, saying he and Janet didn't have a problem if I invited Dave to the screening. Not wanting to go against their wishes, I decided to go talk with him.

"Alright, where is he?" I replied, getting up from my chair.

"He's the guy wearing the plaid shirt sitting at the bar," said Susan.

"Okay, wish me luck," I said, suddenly feeling meek.

"You'll do just fine," Susan reassured.

Working my way over to Dave, my mind was bombarded by a multitude of emotions ranging from:

1. Suspicion: Dave's fight with Joan and alleged punch in the face might have contributed to her death.

2. Jealousy: He had been Joan's boyfriend -- not that I had ever really made an effort to be, but I was vested in her now and felt like her protector

3. Fear: He had been portrayed to be a godlike, charismatic cult leader who would totally destroy me.

I sidled up to the bar next to Dave who was talking to an overweight man with gray hair planted on a barstool next to him, his butt cheeks hanging over the seat. I took a deep breath to relax myself. "Are you Dave?" I asked, fully aware that he was.

He turned to me, my first thought was a line from a movie I'd heard somewhere. It seemed fitting for the moment: *You don't look like much to me.* I had expected a bigger man, not that Dave didn't look fit because he did. It was just that he didn't look mean or ominous. Instead, there was a sweetness about his handsome face and posture. His eyes were sorrowful. Immediately, I felt sympathy for him. Both Klinke and Zimmo had said how remorseful he was that he never got to apologize to Joan for the fight they'd had before she died. He looked like he was still regretting it.

Dave sat there with a blank look on his face like he had seen me before, and maybe he had. There were photos of me on my website, and I had been all over Lost Prairie filming.

Before Dave could respond to my question, his friend interjected, "Yes, that's Dave. He's my friend who are you?"

"My name is Paul Gorman and I'm a filmmaker from Seattle," I said, stuttering slightly.

"Oh really, well I'm a pilot for Alaska Airlines and I fly there all the time," said Dave's friend nursing a bourbon. "I flew out here for the weekend to see Dave."

The guy was getting on my nerves so I decided to change the subject, and pulling out a postcard with Joan's picture on it I handed it to Dave. "I'm making a film about Joan Carson," I said. "People have said that she was your girlfriend. We're screening the film here today. Barrie and Janet Carson will be here and would like you to come to it, if you can."

Dave studied Joan's picture somberly and then tucked it into the left pocket of his shirt. "What time is the screening?" he said, staring at his beer. "Two o'clock," I said. "And if you're interested, we can interview you afterwards."

Nodding pensively, Dave mulled things over. I couldn't tell if he was on the verge of tears or was about to go postal on me. After several seconds his airline pilot friend broke the silence. "Come on Dave, let's go up to the boogie," he said, nudging Dave.

The two got up to leave. I shook Dave's hand. His grip was weak and his palm was clammy. "Hope you can make it, Dave," I said, still shaking his hand.

I watched them leave as Dave's airline pilot friend swayed a little, and hoped I would never have to fly with him.

Mark, Evan and Susan were standing around near the stage when I returned. "Well how did it go?" inquired Susan. "Is he coming to the screening, and will he let us interview him?"

"I don't know, he didn't say," I said, sitting down on a barstool.

"He won't come," Mark said. "He doesn't want anything to do with this film. There's nothing in it for him other than making himself look bad."

"We'll see," said Susan. "There are two sides to every story, and he deserves the benefit of the doubt until we hear his side."

Susan was right. Dave deserved us not rushing to judgement until we heard his side of the story. The problem was that he had been reluctant to tell it, and that made him look guilty.

With about fifty minutes to go before we screened the film, I decided to go for a walk outside. Susan asked if I wanted her to come along. "No thanks," I said. "I'd like to be alone for a while."

It was a pleasant afternoon outside. The sun was shining. Robins and finches were chirping happily as they flitted in the trees and pecked for food in the grass. I strolled down to the lake. The lapping water calmed my choppy nerves from the encounter I'd had with Dave, and the upcoming event.

I kept second guessing myself about Dave, wondering whether I had scared him off. Maybe he had come to watch the film and visit with the Carsons. Several weeks before we left for Lost Prairie, Susan had phoned him and left an invitation on his answering machine. Then again, maybe he had just been there to have a beer with his friend.

Whatever the case may be, his unexpected presence had rattled me. More relaxed now, I headed back inside.

Upon reentering the bar, Mark and Evan were seated, engrossed with their cellphones, and Susan was helping the owner Marge put the food out in the alcove on the pool tables. The food looked tasty and was nicely displayed. About the time they were finishing, Janet arrived with her daughter, Allison and niece, Abby (Barrie's daughter). It was now 1:20.

Susan went over and greeted Janet with smiles and hugs. The two had hit if off nicely in Seattle, sharing a love for children and the same careers. Smartly attired in blue jeans and a white and black mottled blouse, I gave Janet a hug and thanked her for coming. They had driven over the day before from Sammamish. Abby had just returned from two weeks in Amsterdam and had flown into Seattle where she met her aunt. The girls, both in their twenties, were excited to learn something about their aunt Joan.

I asked Janet whether Barrie was coming.

"Barrie doesn't tell me what he's doing, so you know as much as I do," Janet said, laughing.

I sensed Barrie's ultra-privacy and aloofness annoyed her and she didn't want to talk about it so I changed the subject asking her if she and her daughter were going to the boogie. "We were just there," Janet said. "Wow that was an amazing experience."

"So are you going to do a tandem jump?" I teased.

"You'll never catch me up there, I prefer having both of my feet firmly planted on the ground, thank you very much," Janet said, laughing at herself, along with the rest of us.

At that moment I noticed that Osprey skydiver Sam Scott had arrived wearing his black ten gallon hat. His freshly waxed handlebar mustache glistened in rays of sunlight streaming in through a window. It reminded me of horns on a longhorn steer. I greeted him and thanked him for coming, then introduced him to Janet and the girls.

Barrie wandered in moments later dressed in blue jeans, black polo shirt, and light grey sport coat. He stopped to talk with Janet, Allison, and his daughter, Abbie. I waited a moment, then sauntered over to him to say hello.

"Hi Barrie, thanks for coming," I said.

"How's it going," he asked. "Getting a little nervous," I replied.

"Just work through it," Barrie said, grinning. "That's the way to do it."

"So how was your flight?" I said, shifting gears.

"Fine, I just got in," Barrie said. "I haven't even had time to change. Excuse me while I freshen up and put my coat in the car."

While Barrie was outside at his car, Fred came in and introduced his wife to us. I thanked them for coming and asked Fred if anybody else was coming.

"Your guess is as good as mine," said Fred. "I know that everybody got their invitations and talked about it."

After Barrie came back in I announced that the screening would start in about ten minutes, and there was food in the alcove and they should help themselves to it.

While everybody dished up food, Evan and I took pictures documenting the event. Meanwhile, Susan had dished up a plate of food for me.

It was now 2:00 PM and it was time to start the film. After more than a year of non-stop work I had come to the summit of my uphill climb. The time had come to take the last step and show Joan's family, and the interviewees what I had created, and then move on to the next phase. I felt that the film was good, but that it still needed work.

I welcomed everybody for coming and introduced the Carsons. For the next 93 minutes we watched the film. For the most part everybody sat engrossed. I didn't notice signs of boredom such as fidgeting, yawning or checking watches, which as far as I was concerned was a good sign. Although, immediately following the reenactment scenes Barrie got up and went into the restroom briefly. At the time I didn't think much about it, assuming that he had washed his hands or something -- just having finished eating.

Shortly after the end of the movie, Barrie came up to me. "Well, you did it," he said, shaking my hand. "You made a very good film about Joan. I watch a lot of independent films and you have something that's very interesting. You're really close to having something that's better than most films out there."

"Thanks," I said, grinning. "I think it's pretty close too." "Yes, I think it's something that's marketable," Barrie said patting my shoulder.

"Well don't get your hopes up too high," I said. "I might know how to make a film, but I've never been able to sell one. So, we'll see."

"Well, I have no doubt in my mind you can sell this," said Barrie. "Think positive. It's almost there…And the young woman who played Joan was unbelievable – I had to remind myself several times that it wasn't Joan."

Barrie thanked me and said he needed to get going because he and his daughter were going to the boogie.

Before Janet left she seemed equally pleased with the film as Barrie, and invited Susan and me to get together with her husband and her sometime. "My husband and I own a boat. It would be fun to have you guys come over and go out on the boat one of these days -- have a few cocktails, something casual."

"That sounds great," Susan said, smiling. "Paul and I love boats, even more so if they're somebody else's."

Janet and the rest of us laughed. After a few more hugs, Janet and her daughter left.

The last to leave was Sam Scott. I thanked him for coming and he told me how much he had enjoyed the film. Wearing his black Stetson hat, I watched him depart, backlit forlornly like a lonesome cowboy, and then sat down. I was exhausted. It had been a long day, and long year. I felt good about the film, and so it seemed had everyone else. We sat around briefly sharing observations. Susan had noticed Fred was weeping silently at the end of the film. "He's had such a bad year," she said. "I think the movie made it that much more painful for him, seeing how the dream he and others had sustained for 30 some years was now crumbling apart."

We all agreed that Fred had been treated unfairly.

During the screening I had looked around occasionally to see whether Dave was there. As Mark had predicted, he hadn't come, which meant we would not be interviewing him, so there was no point sticking around at the resort any longer. Calling it a day, we headed for our hotels to celebrate, and to rest up for the aerial filming Fred had arranged for us with Stinky's son Adam the next day.

CRITICISM

Lost Prairie, Montana: August, 2011

The night of the Lake McGregor Resort screening I slept great, relieved to have it under my belt and glad it was seemingly so well received. In the morning, after a hearty breakfast with Mark and Evan at the same resort, we arrived at Lost Prairie around 10:30 AM to work with Adam Steinke. I had prepared an aerial shot list I wanted done, and gave it to Mark. Weeks before we left, Mark had designed and machined an aluminum mounting plate for two Contour HD cameras we had purchased. The plate was meant to attach to Adam's helmet, and provide 3D footage of in-air skydiving – a first from what we were told by Fred and everybody else we talked to.

While Mark and Evan worked with Adam, Susan and I handed out more postcards for Sunday's screening. Susan then spent a good deal of time trying to track down Mike and Linda Groarke. Somehow, I had forgotten to have them sign release forms when we interviewed them, and needed their signatures, otherwise they would have to be cut from the film.

In between our tasks we would rendezvous back at our vehicles, seeking shade from the sun, and spend time watching the skydivers. On one load of jumpers we heard a woman scream from an area just outside of the drop zone -- about one hundred feet away, "Medics! Medics! Someone hit hard...hurry, hurry!" Then we heard sirens. Medics bivouacked close to us scrambled in that direction. A little while later, Evan told us he had heard it was a 27 year old and he had died. His chutes hadn't opened. And yet the boogie continued.

Susan was outraged that nobody stopped to acknowledge the fatality, not even a moment of silence. She couldn't believe they had just kept going like nothing had happened. "They are in such denial of the danger of their sport that they can't even take time to honor a death," she journaled. "Unbelievable. I've lost all respect for this community."

Once again, there had been another death at Lost Prairie. A year ago it seemed ironic to find out there had been a fatality shortly before we arrived to make a film about Joan, making it the second skydiver to die there. We had been through this sad story before. But this time it felt different...foreboding -- almost like *the god of Roprac had summoned spirits,* and they were conspiring against Lost Prairie. At the very least, the fatality did cast a dark shadow over the following day's screening. In a way, it almost felt blasphemous for me to screen the film. Would anybody come to see it, and if they did would it offend them? Most jumpers were philosophical about skydiving fatalities though, almost always saying their friends had died doing something they loved. With that caveat in mind, I decided to screen the film on Sunday as scheduled.

Due to the sobering turn of events, along with the fact that skydiving was eventually delayed while the accident was investigated, Adam couldn't jump; we decided to call it quits and headed for our hotels. Tomorrow will be a busy day with the public screening happening at 11:00 AM. Immediately following tomorrow's viewing, Mark would need to finish getting the aerial shots with Adam.

Back at our hotel that evening, I checked my emails to see if there was any response from Barrie regarding the screening. He had left shortly afterwards without too much explanation. Meanwhile, Janet had stuck around longer talking with Susan, while Mark, Evan and I packed up the gear.

Barrie's hasty departure after the movie seemed a little peculiar to me, considering he had come all the way from San Francisco and his sister Janet and niece were still there. But family dynamics are often times a tricky thing, and he might have had something else planned after he went up to the boogie.

Of course, maybe that's just the way Barrie was. It's not that I was insulted by his lack of warmth; it was just that I had kind of expected a follow up email from him considering it had been two days since the screening. More than likely he had heard about the fatality at Lost Prairie and the fact that the guy was a paraplegic. It was all over the news. Some people were suggesting that his death was a suicide because both of his parachutes were never deployed. The deceased skydiver's mother dismissed the notion saying he was happy and wasn't depressed. Coincidentally, he was from Kingston, Washington just across Puget Sound from where Susan and I lived.

The following morning I checked my emails, and again there was still nothing from Barrie. If he had heard about the skydiver's death, it hadn't motivated him to contact me. I pushed aside my concerns about Barrie and prepared myself for the day's screening.

Later that morning, Susan and I met Mark and Evan for breakfast at McGregor Lake Resort, and then proceeded to Lost Prairie around 9:00, which gave us two hours to set things up. When we pulled in, we were surprised to see that some of the skydivers had already left, which was unusual and unsettling. Susan remained positive that the ones who were still there had stayed to watch the film.

Shortly thereafter, Mark, Evan and I set up my flat screen TV, DVD player, and stereo on a folding table near the front of the tent.

Behind it, and slightly to the left of the table was a window that shone sunlight on the TV, washing out the image. Fortunately, we had brought black plastic sheeting, and Mark and Evan used it and grip clips to black out the window. To the right was another window. We were out of black sheeting, but Tony had provided a slide projector and screen for skydivers to show their still photos. Mark used the projector screen to block the window. Now that we had resolved the stray light issues, we were in business. We had a movie theater, with about fifty folding chairs that Susan had set up.

By 10:15 we were ready for the show to begin.

After Susan had finished setting up the chairs she went out promoting the film. She came back around 10:30. "A lot of people say they are coming to the screening," she said, excitedly.

"That's good to hear," I said, adjusting the speaker placements.

"Yeah, you owe me big time. Next time, you promote your film yourself."

"Hey, I would've, but I've been busy helping Mark and Evan set things up," I said. "So, next time you can help them, and I'll do the promoting."

"That doesn't sound like a deal, you know I don't know how to set up the equipment."

"I know, that's why I had you promote the film," I replied, "and the truth is, nobody does it better than you."

"Well it would be nice to hear you appreciate my doing it more often."

"I do. I appreciate everything you do," I said, turning on the TV. "If it weren't for your help and support, I wouldn't be making this film."

"Well thanks. It would just be nice to hear it once and awhile -- that's all. Now, what do you want me to do next?" Susan said, standing there holding the remaining flyers.

"Get the surveys and pens set up please so we can hand them out when people arrive," I said, adjusting the volume on the speakers.

"Okay, are they in *Big Blue*," Susan asked. I nodded yes and she turned, heading for the big blue storage bin we called Big Blue for no other reason than it was blue.

The truth was Susan loved me, loved the film, and enjoyed talking to people. She was a natural at it and had great interpersonal skills. She could talk to anybody. It didn't matter if they were rich or poor, educated, or not, she treated everybody with respect and made them feel important. She had done a great job promoting her preschool without actually knowing she was promoting it. People loved her, and so did I. The best decision I made with the film was asking her to be the interviewer. I am so lucky she decided to do it. In addition to impressing all of the interviewees, she won the respect of Mark and Mickey. With about 50 years combined experience they were seasoned professionals, and didn't hand out compliments easily.

By 10:50 about thirty people had showed up for the movie and more were filtering in. Susan and I stood just inside the entrance greeting them and handing out surveys as they entered. Moments before I was ready to do a welcoming speech, Stinky appeared. Handing me an envelope he said, "This is from Fred's wife. She thinks you're full of shit for exploiting Joanie the way you did. I'll reserve judgement until after seeing the film."

Speechless, I folded the unopened envelope and tucked it in my right rear jeans pocket.

Feeling like I had just been punched in the gut, I went up to the front of the tent and introduced myself, and the film as best I could considering the bombshell I had just been hit with. I had rehearsed my speech but was so upset I couldn't remember it and had to consult my notes. That made it worse. My mind was numb and I fumbled with the notes trying to remember where I was. Looking for a way to end the debacle, I said, "Okay, I know some of you have jumps coming up, and can't stay all that long, so I'm sure you'd rather watch the film than having me tell you more about it. Before we get started though, we would appreciate it if you would fill out the survey we handed out, and return it to us when you leave. Thank you."

I glanced over to Mark and gave him a nod to start the DVD player. The film flickered to life, and I walked over to where Susan was standing. She smiled reassuringly at me and gave me a hug and a pat on the back. I was on the verge of tears.

Standing there for ninety-three minutes watching the film seemed interminably long. At one point, four or five people started laughing during the flashback scenes, and then got up and left. I tried to make myself invisible by inching my way out the entrance.

When the group had left, Evan glanced at me and shrugged his shoulders in disbelief. At nineteen, he was sweet and naive. Unjaded, he hadn't been around long enough to understand how rude and mean some people could be, and felt sorry for me.

Things settled down after the malcontents departed, and I glanced around at the audience. Most people seemed engrossed in the film. Several were writing comments on their surveys, especially Stinky.

When the film ended, I thanked everybody for coming and reminded them to please hand in their survey and pen to Susan, who had set up several boxes on a folding table near the exit.

Three or four people came up to me afterwards and said they had enjoyed the film and could relate to Joan. One woman in particular said she had to get going and asked if she could send her survey to me. "Yes", I said, and then handed her my business card.

Stinky was the last person to leave. "I handed in my survey," he said, shaking my hand. “You can read my comments and do with them as you please." I thanked him and exhaled deeply -- finally starting to unwind.

I walked over to where Susan, Mark and Evan were standing next to the folding table.

"So have you read the letter?" asked Susan.

"No," I said. "I'm afraid to."

"What letter?" Mark queried.

"Stinky gave him a letter from Fred's wife when he came in, and said she was offended by the film," said Susan while putting pens into a zip lock bag.

"Don't read it, Paul," Mark said. "These people know nothing about making a film. All they know how to do is criticize somebody who's doing something they can't do. They're jealous. I've seen it a thousand times in LA. There are two kinds of people there, the ones that get things done and the ones who complain about them."

"It's a really good film, Paul. I liked it," Evan added. "You should be proud of it."

"Yeah, it's good. You don't need to read it. Here give it to me," Susan said, pulling the envelope out of my rear jean's pocket. "I'll hang on to it."

"Read it at your Academy Award, Paul, just to piss them off," Mark smirked.

Everybody laughed including me. But doubt had been cast and would hang over us the rest of the trip like the thunderstorms we had experienced early that morning.

Susan tried to put it in perspective: "Fred's wife isn't upset about the way you portrayed Joan in the film, she's mad that Fred's life is crumbling apart, and you are a convenient target."

"Yeah, I knew their utopia wouldn't last," Mark added. "They need somebody to blame, and you're it. It's always the outsider's fault."

I appreciated their support but the damage had been done. My confidence was shaken to the core.

"What a messed up community this has become," Susan said. "I think they've all lived way too close to one another for way too many years, and need to broaden their horizons and perspectives. It's toxic here and I don't ever want to come back."

That afternoon, Susan and I pulled out of Lost Prairie heading for home leaving Mark and Evan to finish up the aerial photography with Adam and then to spend another night there. As it turned out, they left several hours after us because Lost Prairie cleared out. As a result, we only got a small portion of the aerial footage we wanted and I ended up having to use mostly stock footage.

ANALYZING

Redmond, WA: August and September, 2011

It took Susan and me two days to get home from the screenings in Lost Prairie. We heard on the radio there was a sixty mile back up east of Cle Elum to Snoqualmie Pass, and decided to divert north to Chelan where we spent the night there in a condo we own. We were so lucky to have it. It was our getaway during the rainy months and had been our sanctuary during our property dispute with our neighbors.

A day later when we got home to Redmond, I went through the surveys with Susan, and tried to make sense of the tumultuous and painful weekend. I was relieved to be home, where I could finally unwind from the up and down emotional ride I had been on.

I had been totally blindsided by the criticism I received at Sunday's screening. I didn't realize the extent of the condemnation until about a week after we had gotten home.

Shortly before we left Lost Prairie, we heard that Barrie and Janet had gotten together with many of the interviewees the evening of the private screening. We learned that the Lost Prairie folks at *the get together* were angry by the way Joan was characterized in the film. I felt betrayed they had bad mouthed the film to Barrie and Janet even though most of them hadn't seen it.

When we were filming in Medford, all of the skydivers said they couldn't wait to see the film and were going to try to be there in Lost Prairie for its debut. Not one of them came. Perhaps the reason they didn't come was because Mike Klinke had said something bad about it. Having gotten his days mixed up, he had come a day early for his interview. When we let him in the school, we were filming the reenactment scenes where Joan talked about her sexual conquests and he stayed to watch them. It's possible he passed the information along to the Osprey's and it prejudiced them, and then word spread to the Beagle interviewees. Other than that possible explanation, I didn't fully understand why hardly any of the people we had invited showed up for the screenings, and Barrie's silence was consuming me.

On Aug 6, 2011, a week after we got home, I sent an email to Barrie thanking him and Janet for coming to the screening, and that I was disappointed by the low turnout at Friday's screening when they were there.

A day later I received a reply from Barrie. He was critical of the film. In particular he and all his family members who were at the screening, along with everybody he talked to, felt that the reenactment scenes, where Joan talks openly about her sexual exploits, were either irrelevant or insulting to Joan and her story -- depending on who he talked to.

He went on to say that nobody in Lost Prairie and Medford recognized that behavior in Joan. Everybody he talked to in the film felt it was irrelevant and didn't form a meaningful factor in her life, and was jarring with the overall tone of the film. He recommended that I make my dream, a premonition of Joan's death, the focus of the film.

In closing, Barrie said he appreciated me making the film, and felt I was close from an editing standpoint of having a very compelling film about Joan.

I was devastated by Barrie's email, the criticism I had received in Lost Prairie, and several negative emails that were sent to me. I seriously considered giving up on the project altogether. I didn't need this frustration or aggravation. Over the years I'd had a belly full of it working in corporations, and then had gone through the property dispute and lawsuit with our neighbors. During the course of this, a lot of my hair had fallen out and what hair I had left had turned gray. I was done with it. This was definitely a low point for me. I had just retired and was supposed to be enjoying life.

But the part that hurt most was that I had never set out to defame Joan or to exploit her sexuality. I had merely tried to paint a portrait of her that was accurate, and as I had remembered. I had the upmost respect and fond memories of her and merely was trying to document her story and my experiences with her in an unfiltered and honest manner, and to unlock the mystery of a dream that had haunted me for almost forty years.

If it hadn't been for that dream, and wondering whether it was possibly a premonition, I wouldn't have spent three to four thousand hours of my time, and at least fifty thousand dollars pursuing Joan's story.

Quite honestly, I knew nothing of Joan's accomplishments before embarking on this odyssey, and was surprised to learn that so many people had remembered her.

Most of us live our lives and are forgotten. We go to high school, college, get married, have kids, work at companies, get old, and then die. And we leave a ripple on the pond of time for a very brief moment.

Thirty years after we die, that ripple has ebbed, and we are forgotten forever, nothing more than a name on a tombstone or Ancestry.com. That wasn't the case with Joan; she didn't go to college, didn't get married, didn't raise a family, worked odd jobs and then died well short of her normal life expectancy. Yet thirty years after her death, people still remembered her, celebrated her, and defended her.

Maybe their memories were accurate, or maybe they were just the things of folklore. To them she was a cult hero, bigger than life. She was revered like a goddess.

Perhaps their memories of Joan had become rituals to protect Dave, from a long forgotten dark secret they were hiding that I had stumbled across.

I was dismayed by Barrie's and Janet's sudden shift in attitude towards the film. At the screening they both seemed pleased with it, and all along I had sent them links to the flashback scenes, and they never objected to them. So why the sudden shift now?

The way Mark, Evan and Susan saw it, the outrage at Lost Prairie was totally over the top. They were convinced that the Osprey's had either "circled the wagons" and were doing everything they could to discredit me in order to protect Dave, or they were so upset with the current infighting that I had become their scapegoat. Rule number one – don't attack an insular group's icon. Unwittingly, I had done this, and for that I was sorry.

Barrie, in particular, didn't want to hear about any of Joan's faults or anything that tarnished his memories of the skydivers he'd met in Kalispell. Janet, on the other hand, was much more open minded, but ultimately deferred to what Barrie wanted.

Consequently, I stopped sharing information with Barrie about Joan's relationship with Dave, and about what may have happened the day she died. I was disappointed that he didn't trust me; all I wanted to do was to tell the truth, no matter what it was. I wanted justice for Joan, and to honor her spirit in a way that would make the Carson family proud.

After mulling over Barrie's response to my email for several weeks, deciding what I was going to do with the project and what I was going to say to him, I replied.

Before I give you an update on Beagle Boogie Babe and respond to your last email, let me first express my feelings:

Filmmaking is my passion. I'm not in it for the money or the fame. In the eighties I attended film school and have spent the better part of 30 years learning the art and honing the craft of filmmaking. When it ceases to be fun, I will quit.

The events at Lost Prairie almost made me want to quit. I was really hurt by some of the names I was called and stunned by the fact that most of the interviewees did not bother to come to see the film, but then badmouthed it.

But now that the dust has settled, I've been able to focus on why I should continue and that's because I don't believe Joan would want me to quit. Some might disagree, but I did not make the film for them, I made it to answer a personal question about Joan and to tell her story; a story that she kept bottled up inside of her all these years. I merely opened the bottle and Joan's story flowed out. Actually, it gushed out...it's really amazing how that happened, but that's what happened. I feel privileged and honored to have met Joan and to be a part of this process and her story; there is something really magical about Beagle Boogie Babe. I will always treasure it as a gift from Joan and am glad to finally have been able to answer the question that nagged me for so many years.

Anyway, I want to assure you that I did not take your comments personally, as I feel that you sincerely want Beagle Boogie Babe to be successful and as her brother want a film that honors her...so do I...below are some of the responses I've had from people in the film business about BBB along with some of the steps I am taking to evaluate the film.

The owner of Clatter and Din (post production house) watched BBB and said, "Joan Lives". I think this really sums up what the film is all about. Even though she died 30 years ago, she lives on in "Beagle Boogie Babe"...That's a pretty remarkable thing when you think about the fact that all of us are going to die someday, but hardly any of us will ever have a movie made about our lives.

Mickey McMullen our production sound recorder came up to me while we were filming in Lost Prairie and said, "I think you've got something really special here." Mickey liked the project so much that in order to work on the film, he took a cut in pay from his usual $750/day to $200/day.

The reaction from all of the other people who have thus far seen it in Seattle has been very positive and they were dismayed that some people in Kalispell didn't like it. Before we showed it in Kalispell, Brendan Hogan our Post Production Sound Engineer said, "I think the Kalispell community is really going to embrace it and the skydivers there are going to love it."

Speaking of Kalispell, we handed out a survey at the screening on the 31st and yes, we did get some negative feedback, but received a number of highly positive responses on the flashback scenes as well. We noticed that some people left during the screening, but people were coming and going all the time, so we assumed they were skydivers going for a jump. That being said, I do remember one couple left shortly after Fred Sand popped in and spoke with them. The most important thing is that we are being objective about this and will be formulating a perspective that makes sense from a filmmaking standpoint.

You might be interested to know that "Beagle Boogie Babe" received an average score of 3.7 out of 5, and 80% of the respondents at the Sunday July 31 screening said they would recommend it to a friend. These are incredible scores for any film.

We plan to have a test screening tomorrow afternoon in a theater in front of an audience that is unfamiliar with the project and us. I will share those results with you along with those we received at Lost Prairie soon.

Lastly, regarding the assertion by the Kalispell group that my experiences with Joan were only important to me, I do believe that the experiences I had with Joan were meaningful to her too. In fact, both times when Joan was convalescing at your folks' place she invited me to several parties. Spike would call me and say that he and Joan were going to a party and that she really wanted to see me. At the last party, she gave me her phone number and asked me to give her a call, which I never made. I believe this was an indication that our experiences together were as meaningful and relevant to her as they were to me.

I appreciate the support you and your family have given me thus far and look forward to continuing that relationship into the future.

The day after I sent the email to Barrie, I held a public test screening at Northwest Film Forum in Seattle of the same version of the film we screened in Lost Prairie to get a second and unbiased opinion of it. I ran an ad on Craig's List advertising the test screening as a free event. After the screening we handed out the same survey we had used in Lost Prairie. Upon comparing the results to those we had gotten in Lost Prairie, I sent Barrie an email:

Just thought I would pass along the results from last weekend's screening in Seattle and at Lost Prairie on July 27th, along with the changes I will be making to improve Beagle Boogie Babe.

I think you will be pleased to know that 82% of the respondents in Seattle said they would recommend BBB to a friend, and that overall the film got a rating of 3.7 out of 5.0. These scores are great and are consistent with what we saw at Lost Prairie.

Attached is a spreadsheet which shows the breakdown and average scores for each of the questions we asked in our survey along with an overall average score from each screening. As you will see, the flashback scenes had the lowest scores.

My goal has always been to make Beagle Boogie Babe the best film possible. Below are the changes I will be making. My decision is based on your personal recommendation and the results of the surveys.

1.) FLASHBACKS - All of the flashback scenes, with the exception of the last one (where I tell Joan about my dream) will be eliminated and replaced with narration and a visual montage of sights and stills.

2.) FILM IS TOO LONG - Will cut 5 -10 minutes from interviews (Medford, Barrie/Janet and Linda).

3.) PACE OF FILM - Eliminating most of the Flashbacks and cutting 5 -10 minutes from the scenes mentioned above in item 2 will improve the pacing.

4.) NAME TITLES - Will eliminate repetitive name identifiers of interviewees.

In order to accomplish these changes, BBB will need some additional, editing, narration, music, sound mix and color correction work. I am already well over budget so I won't be shooting any new acted scenes.

I have been working on a rough sketch of the flashback changes and will send you a link soon so you can see it.

Deciding to cut most of the flashback scenes was difficult because I was emotionally attached to them. But they got the lowest score (2.1 out of 5.0) of all of the scenes. Maybe they got such low scores because, as Barrie had said, they weren't vital to the vast majority of Joan's story. Or perhaps it was because they didn't look good. Ideally, the flashback scenes would have been shot in a house and restaurant resembling the Berkeley house Joan had rented, and the restaurant where she had worked. Instead we shot them in Susan's preschool.

As a result the flashback scenes looked staged. The backgrounds and sets looked fake and not of the era. We tried to hide this by having the backgrounds in shadows. Rather than hiding things, it came off looking like poor lighting. It was my decision to shoot the scenes at the school and light them this way, so I have nobody to blame for this but myself.

My thinking was, by using the school as the set, it meant we could shoot the flashback scenes and interviews with Janet and Klinke the same weekend. Thus I would save time and money on equipment rentals and Mickey's wages. If we would have shot the flashback scenes on location, it would have taken an extra weekend and cost more. In addition to paying for another weekend of rental fees and wages for Mickey, I would have had to rent a house and restaurant for several days.

Maybe it's just as well that I didn't spend more money than I did on the flashback scenes because if they didn't fit with the film then spending more on them wouldn't have made a difference. I suppose I'll never know for sure, but my analytical side was telling my emotional being that they didn't fit.

Five days later Barrie emailed me back sounding much more positive about the film. He appreciated the update, and by the sounds of it liked the changes I proposed. Confident that I was creating an outstanding documentary, he asked to be kept updated on the progress of the film and any release dates, or screenings.

Later that same day, I emailed Barrie back with a Link to a sketch of the new flashback scenes that removed all of the scenes referring to sex.

Barrie never responded to my email, In fact I never heard from him again with the exception of a "No" reply to an Evite invitation I had sent him inviting him to a private screening of the film on Saturday October, 22, 2011 at Northwest Film Forum in Seattle.

Mark, Mickey, Evan, Susan, Joseph, and Child's band members came to the screening along with about fifty family members and friends. Joan's sister Janet and her husband attended the screening too. Afterwards, many of us went to a nearby bar to celebrate the film and Joan. Janet came and seemed pleased with the changes I had made and seemed to think that Barrie would approve too. That was good, because I had removed all but one flashback scene and replaced them with narration over B-Roll of San Francisco.

In September, a month prior to the October screening, Susan and I had gone to San Francisco to shoot B-Roll. While we were there, I thought it would be a great idea to get some shots of the old drop zone at Pope Valley so we took a day trip up there.

When we got to Pope Valley, it suddenly occurred to me that I had been there 37 years earlier, picking up a stolen truck for Spike in 1974.

That realization suddenly brought back a flood of memories of the experience, so much so that I blogged about it when we got home.

During the making of Beagle Boogie Babe there have been several coincidences. One of which happened while filming an old abandoned skydiving center in Pope Valley, California, where Joan Carson used to jump in the early 70's. It suddenly dawned on me that I had been there 37 years earlier retrieving a stolen truck for a friend's truck rental business in Seattle. Pope Valley is a hole in the wall place and off the beaten track so there is absolutely no other reason I would have ever been there -- unless I had been a skydiver back then...But there I was, filming the very repair shop where I had picked up the truck so many years ago. Coincidentally, the friend who had sent me to pick up the truck was the same guy who had set into motion the experiences I had with Joan about 8 months earlier in San Francisco.

RECOGNITION

North America and Europe: 2011 through 2014

Between November 2011 and April 2013 I submitted *Beagle Boogie Babe* to about fifty film festivals receiving rejection letters from all of them with the exception of Canada International Film Festival in Vancouver. The film won an award in "Excellence in Documentary Filmmaking". It also won an award at Bridge Fest in Vancouver.

The feedback I got from film festivals was that the movie was heartwarming and a great story, but was too long.

During the summer of 2013 I re-cut the film, shortening it from 85 minutes to 73 minutes by completely cutting the remaining reenactment scene, replacing the narration describing my experience with Joan in San Francisco with a brief text summary, and cutting non-essential side stories from interviews.

I rebranded the film, changing the name from "Beagle Boogie Babe" to "Ride the Sky". I did this because I felt it was easier to remember and wanted to remove any bias against the film. Film festivals communicate with one another and share data bases so I wanted to give the film a fresh start. All of this seemed to work because in January 2014 I received an email notifying me that "Ride the Sky" was an official selection at Flathead Lake International Film Festival (FLIC) in Polson, Montana. I was thrilled. It would make its theatrical debut in Osprey country.

Polson is located about 20 miles south of Kalispell. It also had been home to my best friend in high school, Todd, who came to the screening. He learned of the film through his daughter who still lived in Polson. I had written a press release and four local newspapers ran feature articles on the film. She had read about it in one of the local newspapers, and recalling my name from old childhood stories about me, told her dad about it.

I hadn't seen Todd in forty-one years. In addition to going to high school with him, we had lived together with Spike in Eugene, Oregon during the summer of 1969, working at the satellite office there for Northwest Truck Leasing that Spike ran.

When *Ride the Sky* screened in Montana, Todd was living in Missoula about 90 miles south of Polson. It was great seeing him again and reminiscing about the past. Seeing him also left an empty hole in my heart. We had been such good friends, and had gone our separate ways for various reasons. It wasn't that we had fought, because we really hadn't. Mostly, I think he moved to Montana because he needed to get away from his parents.

It also struck me that Todd had been instrumental in introducing me to Spike, who in turn had really put into motion my experiences with Joan. In a way, it was a fitting Todd was there for the screening and to complete the circle of yet another coincidence I had encountered during the course of making the film.

Over the span of 2014 "Ride the Sky" appeared at seven more film festivals in the U.S., and had write ups in several more newspapers. All of the articles appeared online.

FOUND

Redmond, WA: 2014

I often wondered what had happened to Joan's daughter – she was sort of the final piece of the puzzle. I wondered whether she was searching for her mother. If so, I wondered whether she would somehow hear about the film and contact me. The thought did cross my mind from time to time, but then I remembered what Janet had said about it being a *closed adoption*, and I put the thought out of my mind.

In October 2014, "Ride the Sky" was an Official Selection at Ellensburg Film Festival in Eastern Washington, which is about 80 miles from Redmond. During the screening, I suddenly contemplated whether Joan's daughter might be there. The Redmond Reporter had run an article about the film screening at the festival and I wondered whether she or somebody who knew her had read about it. I scanned the audience during the Q&A session and did see a woman sitting solo and she looked to be about the age I calculated Joan's daughter would be, and had brown hair. She asked me whether I had ever heard from Joan's daughter. "No," I replied, "but I wonder about her."

As it turned out, Joan's daughter hadn't been at Ellensburg film festival, or read the article in the Redmond Reporter. But two weeks later, on November 7, 2014, ten months after "Ride the Sky" appeared at FLIC, where it garnered four newspaper articles, I got an email from a woman claiming to be Joan's daughter.

The woman said her name was Diana, and that she had been adopted in 1970. She had just received a copy of her original birth certificate that she had requested. Her mother's name was listed as Joan Margaret Carson.

While doing some research online, Diana came across death records for Joan indicating she had died in Montana. An Internet search by her soon turned up a newspaper article about "Ride the Sky". The information in the article seemed to match the information in Joan's death record and Diana's birth certificate.

Diana assured me that she was only looking for her roots and nothing more. She claimed to have loving parents, a teenage son, and an amazing life.

Hoping the matching information was just a coincidence, and that her birth mother was still alive, Diana provided me with all the information she had on Joan, such as her birthplace and date of birth, Mother's maiden name, and Joan's date and location of death. She then asked me to confirm if the Joan I had known was indeed her birth mother. Her information matched the information I had.

It goes without saying, I was astounded by the email I had just received. I was pretty convinced she was Joan's daughter. Her story seemed plausible and there was nothing to gain for her.

Immediately, I told Susan who was in the family room, interrupting the TV program she was watching.

"What?" Susan shrieked in disbelief. "You're kidding me!"

"No, I'm not," I replied, pacing anxiously.

"You better not be, Susan said, "I just sat down. What'd she say?"

"She said she thinks she's Joan's daughter," I exclaimed, excitedly.

"Here, let me read it," said Susan getting up from the couch.

Susan followed me, along with our dog, Sadie, into the dining room. I sat down, and then opened the email. "Alright, here it is," I said.

Susan leaned over my shoulder and read the message. "Oh my god," she gasped. "Oh my…this is unbelievable."

"Well, what do you think?"

"I think it's amazing," Susan said, putting a hand on my shoulder.

"Yeah, but do you think it's real?" I asked.

"You mean, do I think it's really Joan's daughter?"

"Yeah," I replied, leaning back in the chair and looking up at her.

"It sure sounds like it," Susan mused. "You need to send her an email thanking her for contacting you and let Janet and Barrie know."

I composed an email to Diana and sent it to her that evening. I was so excited by the news that I had a hard time thinking clearly.

Diana's email had totally caught me off guard. It wasn't that I hadn't considered the possibility of Joan's daughter reading an article about the film and then contacting me could happen, but thinking something could happen, and then having it actually come true are two different things. Making the film had been full of surprises and beyond my wildest imagination. Adding one more happenstance to the list didn't seem all that unusual. The film was directing itself.

Later that evening I responded to Diana's email:

I am in complete shock too as it seems likely that you are Joan's daughter.

When I began making the film (Ride the Sky) about Joan, it was a personal quest to answer questions about a dream I had where she died while skydiving.

During my journey I discovered a lot of things about Joan that I'd never known including you. I had no idea that she had a daughter and only learned of you while interviewing her brother.

Upon hearing that she had a baby, I hoped you would hear about "Ride the Sky" and reach out.

Joan's life and tragic death has haunted, captivated and inspired me. Hearing from you brings resolution to one more chapter of her amazing story.

Your mother was a trailblazing skydiver who was fearless, generous, charismatic, hardworking, and loyal.

Through my project, I have been in contact with Joan's brother and sister and will forward your email to them. I hope they contact you as I know that's what Joan would have wanted.

If you have any more questions please get in touch, or if you are interested, I would be happy to mail you a copy of the film.

Several hours later, I tried forwarding Diana's email to Barrie but received an undeliverable message telling me the address could not be found. I hadn't heard from Barrie and Janet in nearly two years and had given up emailing them when he stopped responding to my emails. If they knew about *Ride the Sky's* film festival run, it would have been through my website or Facebook page, where I blogged about upcoming screenings and posted links to articles about the film. Regardless, it still came as a surprise to me when both of Barrie's email addresses were returned as being nonfunctional.

I still had an email address for Janet's Montessori school and hoped she still worked there; she had mentioned retiring when I had screened the film in Seattle three years prior. I composed an email and sent it to Janet late that evening and forwarded Diana's original message.

A day later I got an email from Diana thanking me and for confirming what she knew in her heart to be true that her birth mother, Joan, was dead. In the course of one day she had found her and had lost her again. She had hoped to give her a hug and thank her for the life she gave her. She welcomed hearing from Barrie and Janet, and wanted to have a copy of the film so she might better understand who Joan was.

That evening I replied to Diana's email.

I can't imagine the emotional roller coaster you have been on this past week, and I'm sorry your search did not result in connecting with Joan.

I am glad you reached out to me, and I hope the film will help fill in a few gaps for you and show you what a great person Joan was.

Below is a link to the film, Ride the Sky. This is the final version which Joan's brother and sister have not yet seen. I'll let you know when it screens at another film festival. I have also included a behind the scenes clip that you can watch afterwards.

I forwarded your email to Joan's sister and hope the family contacts you.

Several days passed and I hadn't heard from Janet and was wondering if she had sold her business, and thus hadn't received my email. I had her phone number and Barrie's, but really preferred not talking with them. Too much time had gone by and their lack of support had soured my feelings about them. Not once during the past year and a half had either one of them reached out to me, or inquired about how things were going with the film. Their lack of interest gave me the impression they were done with the film and me. The reason I had stopped emailing them was because I got the feeling they no longer wanted to hear from me and about the film, and didn't want them to feel like I was harassing them.

The screening at Lost Prairie had been a very emotional experience for them, Janet explained to me when I screened the second draft of *Beagle Boogie Babe* in Seattle. It was the reason they had left the McGregor Lake Resort screening so quickly afterwards, and had not followed up with a Thank You email. Looking back on it, I think they had gotten to the point where they just wanted to put the film behind them and stopped contacting me. I can't say I blame them. I would have probably done the same thing. It would be unsettling to have someone suddenly enter your life and probe through your family's innermost dealings and secrets. Being closest to Joan, I think it was particularly difficult for Barrie.

Unable to email him, I was about ready to try calling Janet when I received a brief email from her early on the afternoon of November 11, 2014 thanking me for passing along Diana's email, and that she had forwarded it to Barrie and her older brother.

Janet's brief email is the last time I heard from her, and the only response I've ever received from the Carson's regarding Diana. Perhaps Diana would have found them anyway without going through me, or maybe she wouldn't have. But it had only been through luck that I had managed to track down Barrie. If it hadn't been for the fact that he was a classmate, and had an uncommon spelling of his first name, I don't think I would have been able to do it.

Speculation aside, the articles about "Ride the Sky" made it easy for Diana to track down her birth family. For that I am pleased and honored to have played a role.

As distant as Janet and Barrie had been, Diana sure wasn't like that. On Sunday, November 9, 2014 she sent an email thanking me for sharing "Ride the Sky" with her. The ending of the movie when Joan dies was particularly hard for her to watch, but it confirmed what she knew in her heart that she had been loved by Joan. The timing of the film was uncanny in that a new Washington State adoption law enacted in July 2014, allowed adoptees to receive a copy of their original birth certificates listing the mother's full name and the maiden name of their mother. Prior to 2014, adoptees were only able to get non-identifying information.

I was glad Diana had watched "Ride the Sky". I could only imagine how surreal it must have been to watch a movie about her birth mother who was dead. And how sad it must have been to learn how difficult it had been for Joan to part with her.

Several weeks later, I received an email from Diana saying she had talked with Janet and Barrie on the phone and had great conversations with them. Again she thanked me for helping her connect with them and for sharing the film.

Over the next year I emailed Diana and Janet several times providing information on film festival developments with "Ride the Sky", and letting them know that the film was making its Internet release. Shortly thereafter, Diana emailed me saying she had gotten together several times with Janet and her daughter, and enjoyed getting to know them. Diana attached a photo of herself.

I emailed Diana back thanking her for letting me know she had gotten together with Janet. I also thanked her for sending me the picture. It was of her sitting on the deck of The Lost Prairie Lounge, bundled up against the winter snow covering the prairie. Diana smiled proudly in the photo, albeit with a little melancholy knowing this was where her mother had died.

The end.

AUTHOR'S NOTE

April, 2020

Prior to January 22, 1973, abortions were illegal in the U.S. and very dangerous; having one was not an option for Joan. Who knows how she would have responded if she had had one. If giving up her baby to adoption bothered her as much as it did, then how would she have dealt with aborting the child she was carrying? And then there's Diana; according to her, she has had an incredible life. As painful as it was for Joan to give up her daughter, she gave life to someone who is thankful to be alive.

Call it coincidence or call it destiny, I believe that I met Joan for a reason: to someday tell her story. Why I was chosen, I have no idea. I believe somehow our souls got intertwined in a cosmic, spiritual interplay. I am not religious, but am spiritual. If anything, my experience in creating a film about Joan has affirmed my beliefs even more so, and has given me faith in an afterlife. What it is, I have no idea. However, I believe that it is eternal and we all share in it. We all have souls and are all part of this incredible mystical mystery.

As for Dave, by all accounts he and Joan had a fight shortly before her fatal jump. We were told that the fight was physical resulting in Joan getting a black eye. It seems that her injury and mental state at the time may have been a contributing factor in her death. She probably shouldn't have made that last jump, but she did.

In all fairness to Dave it was a choice Joan made. She was an adult and made the decision to jump. It cost her her life.

The Joan that Barrie and Janet and her friends talked about was stubborn and fearless. Nobody was going to tell her she shouldn't or couldn't do something. If they did, she would turn right around and do it anyway, not out of spite, but because she felt there was no reason for her to not do it.

Numerous people we talked with in Lost Prairie said that after her fight with Dave, Joan grabbed somebody else's parachute and joined a load of skydivers -- probably over the protestations of her friends.

The sky was Joan's best friend, it was where she took her problems. It was where she forgot about her problems. It was where she could be herself. It was where she was free. Skydiving had never failed her, it had helped her deal with giving up her daughter, and it would help her now. The sky was her home.

I feel badly for Dave. We all make mistakes. He could have let us interview him and gotten it off his chest, but for reasons that are only clear to him he didn't. I can't imagine the anguish and guilt he has probably carried all these years.

In the end, I learned a lot about the sport of skydiving. I learned to compromise,and be willing to make changes to my film. I learned that giving a child up for adoption can be a painful experience for all. I learned to forgive and to seek forgiveness. And I learned to listen to my spiritual side, and to believe in an afterlife.

LIST OF CHARACTERS

Astrid – My Swedish girlfriend
Steve (Armo) Armitage – Kalispell/Beagle jumper married to Dee-Bra
Barrie Carson – Joan Carson's younger brother
Janet Bequette – Joan Carson's older sister
Joan Carson – Beagle Boogie Babe #1 and a founder of Lost Prairie
Tony Hanks – Owner of Wilderness Meadow Skydiving
Dave – Osprey skydiver and boyfriend of Joan Carson
Herb (Ferbie) Farber – Beagle skydiver and Beagle Boogie Boy
Linda McGinty/Groarke – Beagle Boogie Babe #2
Mike Groarke – Canadian skydiver who married Linda McGinty
George Holberton – Owner operator of Beagle Sky Ranch in Medford
Deborah (Dee-Bra) Kalmakava Beagle Boogie Babe #3
Bill Paulin – Osprey skydiver and a founder of Lost Prairie
Scott Rogers – Beagle Sky Ranch skydiver and Beagle Boogie Boy
Fred Sand – Osprey jumper and organizer of Lost Prairie Boogie
Sam Scott – Osprey skydiver
Spike – Manager of Northwest Truck Leasing
Dick (Stinky) Steinke – Osprey skydiver, and a founder of Lost Prairie
Sharon Tousey – Kalispell homeowner who took Joan in
Richard (Zimmo) Zimmerman – Beagle Boogie Boy

ACKNOWLEDGEMENT

Because this book and the film, "Ride The Sky", are so intertwined and symbiotic it would be impossible for me to acknowledge one without recognizing the other, so here goes:

I am forever grateful to my wife Susan for all of her help on the film and this book. In addition to being the interviewer on the film and book editor, she was my biggest supporter, providing invaluable emotional support and creative feedback.

I would also like to thank Pam Hobart-Carter for reading this book and her valuable contributions concerning structure, chapter titling, and subplot.

Thank you to my amazing crew of Mark Anderson and Mickey McMullen for their excellent technical skills, and for believing in me and the project. Without your dedication the film and book would not be possible. Evan Anderson, thank you for your honesty and loyalty.

Likewise, I can not say enough about Composer Joseph Seserko's wonderful and heartfelt soundtrack, and Child's excellent rock songs. Thank you for letting me use your songs in the film.

I deeply appreciate Janet and Barrie Carson for their moving and candid conversations, and all of the other interviewees for their, humorous, heartfelt, poignant, and informative interviews. I am forever grateful to all of you.

Lastly, I'd like to thank Diana for reaching out to me, and to Joan Carson for letting me tell her story.

For more information on the film and book, please visit raincitycinema.com

ABOUT THE AUTHOR

Paul Gorman is a graduate of the University of Washington Extension School in Advanced Filmmaking and Lake Washington Technical College in Electro-Mechanical Design.

He is a partner in Rain City Cinema LLC and was founder of Brollcloud.com

He resides in Tacoma, Washington with his wife Susan and two dogs.

www.ingramcontent.com/pod-product-compliance
Lightning Source LLC
LaVergne TN
LVHW091030080826
845145LV00002B/428